SOCIETY AND SUSTAINABILITY

DEVELOPMENTS IN CORPORATE GOVERNANCE AND RESPONSIBILITY

Series Editor: David Crowther

Recent Volumes:

Volume 1:	NGOs and Social Responsibility
Volume 2:	Governance in the Business Environment
Volume 3:	Business Strategy and Sustainability
Volume 4:	Education and Corporate Social Responsibility: International Perspectives
Volume 5:	The Governance of Risk
Volume 6:	Ethics, Governance and Corporate Crime: Challenges and Consequences
Volume 7:	Corporate Social Responsibility in the Digital Age
Volume 8:	Sustainability After Rio
Volume 9:	Accountability and Social Responsibility: International Perspectives
Volume 10:	Corporate Responsibility and Stakeholding
Volume 11:	Corporate Responsibility and Corporate Governance: Concepts, Perspectives and Emerging Trends in Ibero-America
Volume 12:	Modern Organisational Governance
Volume 13:	Redefining Corporate Social Responsibility
Volume 14:	Stakeholders, Governance and Responsibility
Volume 15:	Governance and Sustainability
Volume 16:	CSR in an Age of Isolationism
Volume 17:	The Equal Pillars of Sustainability
Volume 18:	Social Entrepreneurs: Mobilisers of Social Change
Volume 19:	Socially Responsible Plastic: Is This Possible?
Volume 20:	Achieving Net Zero: Challenges and Opportunities
Volume 21:	Corporate Resilience: Risk, Sustainability and Future Crises
Volume 22:	Innovation, Social Responsibility and Sustainability
Volume 23:	Social Responsibility, Technology and AI

DEVELOPMENTS IN CORPORATE GOVERNANCE AND
RESPONSIBILITY   VOLUME 24

SOCIETY AND SUSTAINABILITY

EDITED BY

DAVID CROWTHER
Social Responsibility Research Network, UK

AND

SHAHLA SEIFI
Social Responsibility Research Network, UK

United Kingdom – North America – Japan
India – Malaysia – China

Emerald Publishing Limited
Emerald Publishing, Floor 5, Northspring, 21-23 Wellington Street, Leeds LS1 4DL

First edition 2025

Editorial matter and selection © 2025 David Crowther and Shahla Seifi.
Individual chapters © 2025 The authors.
Published under exclusive licence by Emerald Publishing Limited.

Reprints and permissions service
Contact: www.copyright.com

No part of this book may be reproduced, stored in a retrieval system, transmitted in any form or by any means electronic, mechanical, photocopying, recording or otherwise without either the prior written permission of the publisher or a licence permitting restricted copying issued in the UK by The Copyright Licensing Agency and in the USA by The Copyright Clearance Center. Any opinions expressed in the chapters are those of the authors. Whilst Emerald makes every effort to ensure the quality and accuracy of its content, Emerald makes no representation implied or otherwise, as to the chapters' suitability and application and disclaims any warranties, express or implied, to their use.

British Library Cataloguing in Publication Data
A catalogue record for this book is available from the British Library

ISBN: 978-1-83608-501-0 (Print)
ISBN: 978-1-83608-500-3 (Online)
ISBN: 978-1-83608-502-7 (Epub)

ISSN: 2043-0523 (Series)

Printed and bound by CPI Group (UK) Ltd, Croydon, CR0 4YY

INVESTOR IN PEOPLE

CONTENTS

List of Contributors   *vii*

PART 1: TOWARDS SUSTAINABILITY

Influential Factors Behind SDGs Related-Disclosure in Large Portuguese Companies: An ISO Certification Approach   *3*
Alice Loureiro, Sónia Monteiro, Verónica Ribeiro and Kátia Lemos

Social Responsibility Management System: How to Implement in a Textile Industry Company   *29*
Francisca Pires Vaz Meneses Lopes and Maria Manuela dos Santos Natário

The Cadastral System as an Engine of Municipality to Spread the Sustainable Development Goals   *53*
Armando Dias-da-Fe, Rosmel Rodriguez and Rute Abreu

PART 2: RESPECTING INDIVIDUALS

What's in a Name: Discourses on Inequalities in the UK   *75*
Miriam Green

Impediment to Walking as a Form of Active Mobility in Akure, Nigeria   *97*
Samuel Oluwaseyi Olorunfemi and Adetayo Olaniyi Adeniran

Culture and Development: The Trauma of the Trafficked Seeking Remittances   *123*
Ahmed Abidur Razzaque Khan, Garry J. Stevens, Nichole Georgeou, Dianne Bolton and Terry Landells

PART 3: COMMUNITY AND CULTURE

**Investigating Culture and Its Influence on Socio-Economic
Development in the Kingdom of Eswatini**   *155*
Aaron Siboniso Gwebu and Md Humayun Kabir

**The Effect of Community-Based Tourism and Regional
Development: A Bibliometric Study**   *185*
*Philipe Lira de Carvalho, Mariana Lima Bandeira and Airton
Cardoso Cançado*

**An Analysis of Corporate Social Responsibility in Cross-Cultural
Scenario**   *215*
*Amit Kumar Srivastava, Shailja Dixit and Akansha Abhi
Srivastava*

**The Role of Misericórdias in the Context of the Importance of
Social Solidarity Institutions for the Third Sector**   *235*
Augusto Simões and Humberto Ribeiro

LIST OF CONTRIBUTORS

Rute Abreu	Polytechnic Institute of Guarda, CICF-IPCA, CISeD-IPV, CITUR, Portugal
Adetayo Olaniyi Adeniran	Federal University of Technology Akure, Nigeria
Mariana Lima Bandeira	Universidad Andina Simón Bolívar, Ecuador
Dianne Bolton	Western Sydney University, Australia
Airton Cardoso Cançado	Federal University of Tocantins, Brazil
Philipe Lira de Carvalho	Federal University of Tocantins, Brazil
Armando Dias-da-Fe	Polytechnic Institute of Guarda, Portugal
Shailja Dixit	Amity University, India
Nichole Georgeou	Western Sydney University, Australia
Miriam Green	Independent Researcher, UK
Aaron Siboniso Gwebu	Eswatini National Treasury, Eswatini
Md Humayun Kabir	Sol Plaatje University, South Africa
Ahmed Abidur Razzaque Khan	University of Liberal Arts (ULAB), Bangladesh
Terry Landells	Bolton Landells Consulting, Australia
Kátia Lemos	Polytechnic University of Cávado and Ave, Portugal
Francisca Pires Vaz Meneses Lopes	Polytechnic Institute of Guarda, Portugal
Alice Loureiro	Polytechnic University of Cávado and Ave, Portugal
Sónia Monteiro	Polytechnic University of Cávado and Ave, Portugal
Maria Manuela dos Santos Natário	Instituto Politécnico da Guarda, CICF-IPCA, CITUR, Portugal
Samuel Oluwaseyi Olorunfemi	Federal University of Technology Akure, Nigeria
Humberto Ribeiro	University of Aveiro, Portugal
Verónica Ribeiro	Polytechnic University of Cávado and Ave, Portugal
Rosmel Rodriguez	Universidade de Coimbra, Portugal
Augusto Simões	University of Aveiro, Portugal

Akansha Abhi Srivastava	Institute of Hotel Management, India
Amit Kumar Srivastava	Invertis University, India
Garry J. Stevens	Western Sydney University, Australia

PART 1
TOWARDS SUSTAINABILITY

INFLUENTIAL FACTORS BEHIND SDGS RELATED-DISCLOSURE IN LARGE PORTUGUESE COMPANIES: AN ISO CERTIFICATION APPROACH

Alice Loureiro, Sónia Monteiro, Verónica Ribeiro and Kátia Lemos

Polytechnic University of Cávado and Ave, Portugal

ABSTRACT

In 2015, the United Nations approved the 2030 Agenda defining 17 Sustainable Development Goals (SDGs), and 169 targets. Among those, the target 12.6 encourages companies to adopt sustainable practices and to integrate sustainability information into their reporting cycle. Thus, the aim of this paper is to understand whether ISO certification is a determinant factor in SDGs reporting. Standalone non-financial reports of the largest Portuguese companies were collected from 2016 until 2020, obtaining a total of 119 reports from 41 companies: 27 (22.7%) of the reports corresponds to non-certified companies and 92 (77.3%) to certified ones. Through a content analysis of the non-financial reports, an SDG disclosure Index (SDG_IND) was developed, to measure the level of disclosure on SDG. A set of panel data based on a Tobit regression analysis was applied, in STATA software, using the total of observations during the period 2016–2020, to verify if the variable ISO certification explains the level of SDGs disclosure. Contrary to our expectation, we did not find significant differences between certified and non-certified companies concerning the SDG-related disclosure. As far as we are aware, previous research in SDG has not considered the linkage with ISO certification. This article aims to explore this gap by investigating differences between certified and non-certified companies, regarding SDG disclosure, as whether ISO certification is a determinant factor of such disclosure.

Society and Sustainability
Developments in Corporate Governance and Responsibility, Volume 24, 3–28
Copyright © 2025 Alice Loureiro, Sónia Monteiro, Verónica Ribeiro and Kátia Lemos
Published under exclusive licence by Emerald Publishing Limited
ISSN: 2043-0523/doi:10.1108/S2043-052320240000024001

Keywords: Sustainable development goals; certification; reporting; agenda 2030; ISO; disclosure index

1. INTRODUCTION

In 2015, the United Nations (UN) adopted the 2030 Agenda, containing 17 Sustainable Development Goals (SDGs), designed to be universal and to be applied to all countries. This agenda defines the priorities and requires a global action by governments, business, and civil society. The UN 2030 Agenda represents an opportunity to improve the companies' management and the relationship with stakeholders. This Agenda represents a holist framework to analyse and measure the progress of all actors towards the SDGs achievement (Diaz-Sarachaga, 2018). Thus, companies need to be able to assess their social/environmental impacts and to review their strategies towards Sustainable development. Disclosure information on sustainability/sustainable development is a key element in the companies' transparency and accountability. Therefore, reporting can play an important role by disclosing the companies' contributions and progress towards the SDGs.

Among the goals of the 2030 Agenda, the target 12.6 encourages companies to adopt sustainable practices and to integrate sustainability information into their reporting cycle. Additionally, the International Organisation for Standardisation (ISO) described each ISO standards' contributions to the SDGs.

In the scope of SDGs reporting, international empirical research is few and recent (Curtó-Pagès et al., 2021; Haywood & Boihang, 2021; Hummel & Szekely, 2022; Monteiro et al., 2022; Pizzi et al., 2022; Schramade, 2017; Tsalis et al., 2020). As far as we are aware, previous research in SDG has not considered the linkage with ISO certification. There are some Portuguese studies evaluating sustainable development (SD) and SDGs disclosure among samples of certified companies (Carvalho et al., 2018; Carvalho, Domingues, et al., 2019; Carvalho, Santos, et al., 2019; Fonseca & Carvalho, 2019). However, the empirical literature negligees the variable certification as a potential determinant factor of SDG disclosure.

Thus, this article aims to explore this gap by investigating differences between certified and non-certified companies, regarding SDG disclosure, as whether ISO certification is a determinant factor of such disclosure.

Additionally, this paper has the following specific objectives: (a) to understand how the SDGs are disclosed in t non-financial reports, grouping certified and non-certified large Portuguese companies; (b) to understand which SDGs are referenced by certified and non-certified and which are the priority SDGs considered; (c) to understand if ISO certification influences the level of SDGs disclosure.

The rest of the paper is organised as follows: Section 1 outlines the literature review; Section 2 develops the research design, namely the research hypotheses, the sample, and the research methodology; and Section 4 discusses the study's findings. Finally, it draws the main conclusions of the research and presents its limitations and suggestion for future research.

2. LITERATURE REVIEW

2.1 ISO Certification and Commitment to SDGs

The 2030 agenda defines the priorities and requires global action by governments, business, and the society. It recognises the private sector as having a pivotal role in achieving the UN goals, providing a better and sustainable world for the future generations, because it is the main detainer of world's economy, advanced technologies and of most advanced procedures and management systems.

The sustainable development concept's transition, from a macroscale (planet) to a microscale (business community), it is believed to be closely related to management systems (MS) evolution within organisations, more specifically the adoption and certifications in quality management systems (QMS), environmental management systems (EMS), occupational health and safety management systems (OHSMS), social responsibility management systems (SRMS), and integrated management systems (IMS) (Santos et al., 2018, p. XXI).

Nowadays, numerous international independent bodies are responsible for standards publication from which organisations build, maintain, and improve their MS. One of the most known and quoted is ISO, an international and independent organisation officially founded in 1947, headquarters in Genova with a membership of 167 national standards bodies. Presently, ISO has released 24,250 International standards covering almost all aspects of technology and manufacturing and have 804 technical committees and subcommittees responsible for standards development (ISO, 2022a).

From a holistic perspective, within an organisational level, the QMS is considered to approach the economic dimension of the SD. The environmental perspective is approached by the EMS, while the social dimension is approached by the OHSMS. Consequently, the integrated management systems in quality (ISO 9001), environment (ISO 14001), security (ISO 45001/BS OHSAS 18001), and social responsibility (ISO 26000/SA 8000) is considered a useful tool for sustainable development integration within businesses (Santos et al., 2018, pp. 369–370). Additionally, some authors have already recognised the contributions of the ISO 9001 (MQS), ISO 14001 (EMS), BS OHSAS 18001 (OHSMS), and ISO 26000 (SRMS) towards the sustainable development (Başaran, 2018; Borella & Borella, 2016; Gianni et al., 2017; Merlin et al., 2012; Rebelo et al., 2016; Santos Ferreira & Gerolamo, 2016). Nevertheless, others also argue that those ISO standards do not provide specific guidelines for sustainable development, only instructs in one of its dimensions. In this sense, some defend the creation of a new standard with specific guidelines for sustainable development in all its dimensions. These models proposed for sustainable development management in organisations are grounded in the ISO high-level structure (Annex SL) and in the Deming cycle, PDCA (Plan – Do – Check – Act), the cycle for continuous improvement, one of ISO standards baselines (Asif & Searcy, 2014; Asif et al., 2011).

ISO 9001:2015 introduces a quality management system as a strategic organisational decision that can improve their general performance and provide a baseline for sustainable development initiatives (ISO, 2015b, p. 7). The standard enhances customer satisfaction as also enables the organisation to provide products/services that meets the needs of its stakeholders and relevant state and regulatory requirements. The QMS relies upon seven principles: customer focus; leadership; people engagement; process approach; improvement; evidence-based decision making; and relationship management (ISO, 2015c, Chapter 2.3). Additionally, the structure of ISO 9001:2015 is governed by the PDCA cycle which includes all the clauses of the norm and allows their interconnectivity: the context of the organisation; leadership; planning; support; operation; performance evaluation; and improvement.

The ISO 14001:2015 enables organisations to manage and improve their environmental aspects related to their activity, as to fulfil compliance obligations and achieve environmental objectives (ISO, 2015a). The EMS relies in the PDCA cycle, mentioned before. The systematic management of the environmental aspects imposed by ISO 14001 contributes to sustainability, through pollution prevention, improved environmental performance and complying with applicable laws, but it can also improve organisational, operational, people, and customer results (Fonseca, 2015).

Simultaneously, companies are increasingly committed to occupational health and workers' safety due to legal regulations and external pressures. Also to reduce direct and indirect costs resulting from workplace accidents and/or occupational diseases, but mostly to promote safety and wellbeing among their employees (Başaran, 2018). ISO 45001:2018 came to substitute the previous OHSMS standard, OHSAS 18001, and presents a management system that allows the continuous improvement, assessment of the legal and other requirements and ability to attain the established objectives in occupational health and workplace safety. The normative clauses of the system are interconnected and supported by the Denim cycle (ISO, 2019).

In the social responsibility domain, ISO presented the standard ISO 26000: 2010, guiding concepts, terms and definitions related to the matter, their background, trends, characteristics, principles, practices, and the core subjects and issues of social responsibility. ISO 26000:2010 promotes commitments to communication, performance, and other relevant information and also provides guidance to identify and engage with stakeholders. This management system attends to contribute to sustainable development and encourages organisations to go beyond the basic legal obligations. However, it is not a management system standard because it does not have requirements and cannot be used for certification (ISO, 2018b). Nevertheless, there is the 'SA 8000:2014 Social Accountability 8000' standard from Social Accountability International (SAI), the world's leading social certification programme. The standard has the following requirements: child labour, forced or compulsory labour, health and safety, freedom of association and right to collective bargaining, discrimination, disciplinary practices, working hours, remuneration, and management system (SAI, 2014). Additionally, in 2019 the 'Instituto Português da Qualidade' (IPQ) published a portuguese standard 'NP 4469:2019 Sistema de Gestão da Responsabilidade Social'. The document follows the ISO high-level structure (Annex SL) and integrates the PDCA cycle, allowing the integration with other ISO management systems. Some authors, for example, Peršič and Peršič (2016), already confirmed that the implementation of social responsibility standards has a positive impact on the SD, as well as on financial indicators.

Companies certified in two or more ISO standards can integrate their MS. The ISO never published an integrated management standard. However, the previously mentioned annexe SL allowed a language, content and structure unification between the different ISO standards and permitted companies to integrate separated MS, for example, IMS in quality, environment, and safety (9001:2015, 14001:2015, and 45001:2018, respectively). IMS offer multiple advantages to companies in multiple levels (management, employees, production, environment, market, occupational health, and safety process) and, consequently, improve their SD contribution (Başaran, 2018).

According to ISO, their standards not only contribute to sustainable development but also to the SDGs. In 2018, ISO published the document 'Contributing to the UN Sustainable Development Goals with ISO standards' where, for each SDG, they provided an example of which ISO standard stands out to SDG contribution (ISO, 2018a). The information is summarised in Table 1.

Similarly, the ISO website discriminated for which SDGs the implementation of the standard contributes. ISO 9001:2015 contributes to SDG1, SDG9, SDG12, and SDG14 (ISO, 2022e). ISO 14001:2015 contributes to SDG1, SDG2, SDG3, SDG4, SDG6, SDG7, SDG8, SDG9, SDG12, SDG13, SDG14, and SDG15 (ISO, 2022b). ISO 45001:2018 contributes to SDG3, SDG5, SDG8, SDG9, SDG10, SDG11, and SDG16 (ISO, 2022d). At last, ISO 26000:2010 contributes to all the SDGs, except the SDG17 (ISO, 2022c).

2.2 SDG Reporting

In 2015, with the announcement of the SDGs, the Global Reporting Initiative (GRI), the World Business Council for Sustainable Development (WBCSD), and the UN Global Compact to create a practical guide – SDG Compass – to support companies and other organisations to align their strategies towards the SDGs and to measure and manage their contribution. SDG Compass puts sustainability at the centre of their business strategy and helps companies to identify the GRI standards that can be used to disclose their actions to reach the SDGs (SDG Compass, 2015).

Moreover, UNGC and GRI also developed two more fundamental documents: 'Business Reporting on the SDGs: An Analysis of the Goals and Targets' and 'A Practical Guide to Defining Priorities and Reporting'. These documents do not aim to create a new reporting framework, only intend to provide a structure to help organisations reveal their contribution to SDGs considered to be a priority and to provide relevant information to stakeholders. Both documents should complement each other and be part of the regular reporting cycle of organisations.

However, the standardisation and development of reporting tolls is still in development and there is a general gap in reporting characterisation and quality evaluation (Bedenik & Barišić, 2019; Pizzi et al., 2021). In fact, none of the most

Table 1. Examples of ISO Standards Specifics Contributions to Each SDG.

Sustainable Development Goal	ISO
Goal 1. No poverty	ISO 20400, Sustainable procurement ISO 37001, Anti-bribery management systems
Goal 2. Zero hunger	ISO 22000, Food safety management ISO 26000, Guidance on social responsibility ISO 20400, Sustainable procurement
Goal 3. Good health and well-being	ISO 11137, Sterilisation of healthcare products ISO 7153, Materials for surgical instruments ISO 37101, Sustainable development in communities
Goal 4. Quality education	ISO 21001, Educational organizations – Management systems for educational organizations ISO 299993, Learning services outside formal education
Goal 5. Gender equality	ISO 26000, Guidance on social responsibility
Goal 6. Clean water and sanitation	ISO 24518, Crisis management of water utilities ISO 24521, Activities relating to drinking water and wastewater services – Guidelines for the management of basic on-site domestic wastewater services
Goal 7. Affordable and clean energy	ISO 50001, Energy management systems ISO 52000, Energy performance of buildings ISO 9806, Solar thermal collectors ISO 17225 family, Solid biofuels
Goal 8. Decent work and economic growth	ISO 45001, Occupational health and safety ISO 37001, Anti-bribery management systems
Goal 9. Industry, innovation and infrastructure	ISO 4401, Collaborative business relationship management systems
Goal 10. Reduced inequalities	ISO 26001, Guidance on social responsibility
Goal 11. Sustainable cities and communities	ISO 37101, Sustainable development in communities ISO 37120, Sustainable cities and communities
Goal 12. Responsible consumption and production	ISO 20400, Sustainable procurement ISO 14020, Environmental labels and declarations ISO 15392, Sustainability in building construction
Goal 13. Climate action	ISO 14001, Environmental managements systems ISO 14064, Greenhouse gases
Goal 14. Life below water	ISO/TC 234, ISO's technical committee of fisheries and aquaculture ISO/TC 8, Ships and marine technology
Goal 15. Life on land	ISO 14055, Environmental management – Guidelines for establishing good practices for combatting land degradation and desertification
Goal 16. Peace, justice and strong institutions	ISO 37001, Anti-bribery management systems
Goal 17. Partnerships for the goals	No specific identification

Source: ISO (2018a).

popular sustainability/non-financial reporting frameworks (such as those of the Global Reporting Initiative (GRI) and the International Integrated Reporting Council (IIRC, 2021)) included specific guidance on SDGs disclosure. Thus, the linkage of SDGs to corporate reporting is still at a very embryonic stage and it is, therefore, necessary to promote their progress.

In 2016, the GRI Standards were published in response for SDG 12.6 that calls for corporate transparency mentioning the benefits of reporting sustainability actions and encouraging companies to integrate sustainability information into their reporting cycles. The Standards have a modular, flexible, and inter-related set which starts with the universal standards and can be complete by a variety of other topics in economic, environmental, or social dimensions.

Thus, in 2016, as part of the SDGs Compass, GRI published a document 'Linking the SDGs and the GRI Standards' with a list of the existing disclosures within the GRI guidelines/Standards mapped against the 17 SDGs at the target level. This document makes it easier for organisations and reporting practitioners to assess and report how they impact and contribute to the SDGs, using the GRI Standards.

According to KPMG studies, GRI is the most widely used framework for sustainability reporting in the world. And even GRI claims to be the most used standards for SD reporting on a worldwide scale (GRI, 2022; KPMG, 2022). Globally, only the GRI Standards provide a complete set of standards that addresses all 17 SDGs. Thus, in our opinion, the sustainability reporters worldwide do not need to use any other sustainability framework for their report.

Izzo, Ciaburri et al. (2020) argue that, on the one hand, the SDGs represent an opportunity for business organisations to redefine their priorities and integrate their business models, enhancing stakeholder engagement and improving the identification of future business opportunities. On the other hand, disclosure of SDG reporting practices can be used for companies to highlight the corporate practice of adopting SDGs more by form than by substance. One of the main risks of this approach is to focus only on the good parts of the company's sustainable practices, thus adopting the latter but not the spirit of the SDGs. In this scenario, the SDGs risk becoming a compliance agenda to disseminate sustainability practices, where it matters more for companies to look like than to be.

According to Heras-Saizarbitoria et al. (2022), for many stakeholders who are really concerned with environmental and social issues, the tendency of companies towards superficial engagement with SDGs – or SDG-washing – and the lack of concrete practices to engage with Agenda 2030 targets can be used as leverage to put pressure on companies to produce more consistent CSR practices in a structured and detailed way.

In this sense, Adams (2017) considers that the integrated report is a promising approach for SDGs contribution and disclosure. The author argues that initiatives such as SDG Compass do not support disseminators in deciding how to integrate SDGs into their reports under UNGC principles or GRI guidelines/standards. Moreover, the language used in the document is much closer to the integrated reporting language than to the sustainability reporting one (UNGC principles and GRI guidelines/standards). Therefore, she states that organisations should report their contribution to SDGs targets along with the six 'capitals' provided in the Integrated Report Framework.

Recently, Adams (2020) developed the report 'The Sustainable Development Goals Disclosure (SDGD) Recommendations', which offer a new approach for organisations to address sustainable development issues aligned to the <IR> Framework, the Task Force on Climate-related Financial Disclosure (TCFD), and the GRI. These recommendations are an opportunity to establish a best practice for corporate reporting on the SDG and enable more effective and standardised reporting and transparency on climate change, social and other environmental impacts. The recommendations build on a suggested approach to contributing to the SDG aligned with long-term value creation in Adams' (2017) report. The report set out a five-step process to align an organisation's approach to the SDG with integrated thinking and long-term value creation for organisations and society as set out in the <IR> Framework.

In view of the above, major challenges are placed on organisations in identifying priority SDGs for their activities and stakeholders, incorporating them into their strategy, setting goals for their success, and measuring and reporting on their progress. Whether through sustainability reports or through integrated reports, we understand that what is important is to align these reports with the structure and scope of the SDGs and, therefore, this research area should be widely explored.

As stated before, in the scope of SDGs reporting, empirical research is few and recent. Empirical studies suggest that large companies from Europe are significantly more likely to report on the SDGs than companies in other countries (KPMG Report, 2018). The Directive 2014/95/EU requires certain large European companies to report on non-financial information. The basic requirements of the directive are to provide detailed reports on the company's environmental impact, their social and employee impact and attempts to sustain equality, overall human rights, how the mitigate corruption, and the tactics used to promote diversity. Thus, the European regulation positively impacts SDG reporting (Gazzola et al., 2020; Hummel & Szekely, 2022).

In the European context, there are some studies from Italy (Gazzola et al., 2020; Izzo, Ciaburri, et al., 2020; Pizzi et al., 2021), Spain (Centeno et al., 2018; Curtó-Pagès et al., 2021; Diaz-Sarachaga, 2021), and Greece (Tsalis et al., 2020). Other studies compare the SDGs reporting practices from different European countries (Hummel & Szekely, 2022; Izzo, Ciaburri, et al., 2020; Nichita et al., 2020; Pizzi et al., 2022).

Hummel and Szekely (2022) found a substantial increase in SDG reporting quality over time but a lack of disclosure of quantitative and forward-looking information in European companies. In 2015, only 15% of the companies refer SDGs in their reports and in 2018 the rate increased to 58%. The reporting quality rises from an average level of 1.78 in 2015 to 4.84 in 2018, on a 0–11 scale. The evaluated item with the highest score refers to priority SDG. In contrast, the lowest levels and slowest increase refer to a critical assessment of the potential negative impacts that a company's activity may have on the SDGs, as well as forward-looking statements and quantitative measures and targets.

In Spain, Curtó-Pagès et al. (2021) findings reveal SDG reporting among Spanish listed companies has increased in quantity since the first year after the approval of the 2030 Agenda. General mentions of the SDGs have increased by 31% since the approval of the 2030 Agenda (from 2016 to 2019) and the latest data available shows that more than 80% of the companies were mentioning the SDGs in their reports in 2019. Additionally, there is also a growing tendency among CEOs to mention the SDGs in their letters to stakeholders. Furthermore, a positive link is established between the adoption of GRI reporting standards or being a signatory of the UN Global Compact and SDG reporting. Centeno et al. (2018)'s results indicate that 6 (17.14%) of the Spanish companies of the IBEX 35 do not mention any of the SDG included in Agenda 2030 and 2 companies (Telefónica and Iberdrola) include all of the 17 SDGs. Diaz-Sarachaga (2021) found that intangibility, omission of negative impacts, poor standardisation, diversity of criteria, and lack of comparability are the main features of corporate reporting employed by the Spanish top sustainable firms to report their involvement in the achievement of the SDGs.

Izzo, Strologo, et al. (2020) collected the first data related to Italian listed companies related to SDG disclosure and sustainability reporting. The results indicate that companies privilege sustainability reports and non-financial statements as vehicle of communication. Only five companies did not mention any SDG and the worst disclosing sectors were healthcare and finance. Most of the firms disclosed SDGs in a specific section without including them in the business strategy. Only 5% of the analysed companies included SDGs in their business model and defined specific KPIs.

Also, in Italy, Gazzola et al. (2020) investigate the relationships between the 17 SDGs and the set of non-financial information defined in both the EU Directive 2014/95/EU and the related Italian L.D. n. 254 of 30 December 2016. Italian companies have partially increased their focus on sustainability over the years but have also adapted their approach to sustainability to the prescriptions developed within the UN 2030 framework. Results show that 35% of companies have an increase in the number of SDGs pursued, while only 6% shows a reduction. The remaining companies do not show increases or decreases in the number of SDGs compared to the previous year. The most represented SDGs are gender equity, decent work, and economic growth and responsible consumption and production.

In the Portuguese context, the studies on SD reporting are still scarce, and mainly focus on listed companies (Monteiro et al., 2022) and certified companies (Carvalho et al., 2018; Carvalho, Domingues, et al., 2019; Fonseca & Carvalho, 2019).

Monteiro et al. (2022), from a sample of 46 Portuguese listed companies, conclude that, in 2017, none published integrated reports. But nine of those companies refer to the SDGs in their reports. The companies adopted the GRI framework, and some use SR to comply the Portuguese law (no 89/2017) related to non-financial information. Of the nine companies SGDs-related reporting, not all are in the same stage. On the one hand, although seven companies report linking with the SDGs, not all are in the process of implementing their sustainability strategy in line with the SDGs. Companies that are at a more advanced stage: aligning the reporting with the SDGs, considering them in their strategy, and prioritising the most important goals are EDP, ED, and CTT.

In Portugal, some studies have urged regarding certification and SDG disclosure. Fonseca and Carvalho (2019) carried out a study based on 235 Portuguese companies certified in three standards (ISO 9001, ISO 14001, and OHSAS 18001). It was possible to understand which SDGs were most mentioned among companies SR (SDG 12, 13, 9, 8, and 17), as it also concluded that the communication of SDGs is more prominent in companies with higher turnover, in members of UNGC Portugal. However, in this study it was found that only 23.8% of companies mention the SDGs in their SR. These data agree with others already accomplished demonstrating that the number of companies mentioning the SDGs in their SR is still bellow from desirable (Rosati & Faria, 2019).

Carvalho et al.'s (2018) study aimed to understand the disclosure of information on SD in Portuguese certified organisations websites. The authors concluded that organisations with greater business volume and the public limited companies (PLC) disclosure more information on SD. It also pointed out the scarce information about SD disclosed in certified companies' websites. A similar study on 540 certified Portuguese organisations (Carvalho, Domingues, et al., 2019) identified three main commitments towards SD addressing customers, human resources, and continuous improvement. It also concluded that communication is more prominent in organisations with the following characteristics: large business volume, public business sector, members of the BCSD Portugal, and regular publishers of their annual reports on the official website. Previous studies have focussed on certified Portuguese companies, but they did not analyse if ISO certification contributes to better/higher disclosures on SD.

Thus, our study provides insights into SDG reporting's linkage with ISO certification from a Portuguese perspective, grouping certified and non-certified large companies. Empirical literature on determinants factors of SDGs disclosure, identify three main categories of determinants that impact SDG reporting: firm-level, report-level, and regulation-level (Datta& Goyal, 2022). However, the variable certification has not been studied as a potential determinant factor of SDG disclosure. Thus, our study aims to fill that gap.

3. RESEARCH DESIGN

3.1 Research Hypothesis

According to literature, the implementation of an environmental management system (EMS), especially for obtaining environmental certification, is a determining factor in the disclosure of environmental information, because companies intend to disclose the results/benefits achieved with the EMS (Barros & Monteiro, 2012). Similar influence in social and other non-financial disclosures is expected from certification in quality management systems (QMS), occupational health and safety management systems (OHSMS), social responsibility management systems (SRMS), and integrated management systems (IMS).

Based on the Institutional Theory, institutional and legislative pressures are the main drivers for the adoption of environmental/sustainable management practices, which include the implementation and certification of the management systems (Jennings & Zanbergen, 1995). By other hand, the disclosure about the sustainable practices and the benefits obtained from ISO certification gives companies greater legitimacy before the society and pressure groups (Barros & Monteiro, 2012).

As stated before, some studies explored the determinant factors for sustainable development disclosure within companies certificated, simultaneously, in the three basilar ISO standards: ISO 9001, ISO 14001, and ISO 45001/OHSAS 18001 (Carvalho, Domingues, et al., 2019; Carvalho et al., 2018; Carvalho, Santos, et al., 2019; Fonseca & Carvalho, 2019). Additionally, ISO highlights the contribution of each standard for the SDGs. However, there is a remaining gap in understanding the ISO certification itself as a determinant factor for SDGs disclosure.

Based on these arguments we expect a positive relationship between the level of SDGs disclosure and the fact of companies holding any type of ISO certification. Thus, we formulated the following hypothesis:

H1: Certified companies are more likely to have a higher level of SDGs disclosure.

3.2 Sample

In the Portuguese business context, several initiatives have been made to contribute to sustainable development evolution within organisations. BCSD Portugal has a series of other initiatives gathering multiple Portuguese organisations: Charter of Business Principles for Sustainability, Act4Nature Portugal, Mobility Pact, Meet 2030, ESI Europe, SINCERE, and LIFE Volunteer Escapes. Such initiatives are part of a general effort to help and guide businesses towards SDGs. In a report compiled for the United Nations in 2019, Portugal has been ranking among the 30 most sustainable countries in the world Portugal leads the field when it comes to Goal 7 (involving the percentage of the population with access to clean energy and technology, levels of CO_2 released through the burning of fossil fuels and the amount of renewable energy used in the consumption of energy). A concerted and effective corporate action towards SD is, therefore, possible if Portuguese companies align their activities to incorporate the SDG. Despite the apparent commitment of Portuguese corporations to the SDGs, information about their documented contribution to the 2030 Agenda is still scarce.

Most of the studies in the Portuguese context focussed on listed and certified companies' SDGs-related disclosures (Carvalho, Domingues, et al., 2019; Carvalho et al., 2018; Carvalho, Santos, et al., 2019; Fonseca & Carvalho, 2019; Monteiro et al., 2022), which represent a little part of the Portuguese corporate population.

Larger companies are increasingly concerned with improving their public image and reputation before society, considering that communicating information about their sustainable performance is a good way to legitimise themselves. According to Elalfy et al. (2021), larger companies are more likely to integrate the SDGs into their reporting than smaller companies. Previous studies indicate companies' size, business volume, or dimension is a positive determinant factor for SDGs disclosure or SD-related information disclosure (Carvalho, Domingues, et al., 2019; Carvalho et al., 2018; Carvalho, Santos, et al., 2019; Pizzi et al., 2021).

In this sense, the starting sample was selected from a special edition of Exame magazine ('500 Largest & Best Portuguese companies') published in December of 2020. Additionally, as the SDGs were released in 2015, we excluded companies that do not disclose at least one non-financial report on the corporation website, between 2016 and 2020. Thus, from the 500 largest companies, only 41 companies published any type of standalone non-financial report during the period (representing 8.2% of the initial group). From the final sample were considered sustainability reports, integrated reports, corporate responsibility reports, social responsibility reports, and management reports. After consulting the websites of the 41 companies included in the sample, we observed that not all of them had a standalone non-financial report for the entire analysed period. Thus, 119 valid documents were collected.

Table 2 presents a summary characterisation of the sample. Companies were distributed among the three general sectors of activity, where the predominant was Industry representing 51.2%, proceeded by Services with 34.1% and, lastly, 14.6% represented by Commerce. Considering the stock quotation, in 41 companies, 24.4% were listed at the Euronext Lisbon stock market while 75.6% were not.

Because this study has an ISO certification approach, the sample was divided into two groups, non-certified and certificated companies in, at least, one of these referential: ISO 45001, ISO 14000, ISO 9001, OHSAS 18001, and SA8000/NP4469. The collected data was obtained from a certified company guide of 2020 (*Listagem Geral de Empresas, Serviços e Produtos Certificados*, 2020). Concerning ISO certification, the sample the sample has a total of 32 certified in at least one of the standards considered before, which corresponds to a proportion of 78%, and 9 non-certified companies (22% of the sample) (Table 3).

Table 2. Sample Characterisation.

Sector		Frequency	Percent (%)	Listed companies		Frequency	Percent (%)
	Commerce	6	14.6		No	31	75.6
	Industry	21	51.2		Yes	10	24.4
	Services	14	34.1		Total	41	100.0
	Total	41	100.0				

ALICE LOUREIRO ET AL.

Table 3. Sample Characterisation by Certification.

Certification	Frequency	Percent (%)
No	9	22.0
Yes	32	78.0
Total	41	100.0

Regarding each standard, the frequency results are in Table 4. The most represented standard was ISO 9001 (65.9%), followed by ISO 14001 (61%) and then OHSAS 18001 (39%). Only 12.2% of the companies were SA8000/NP4469 certified, while 7.3% in ISO 45001. However, it is relevant to highlight that the established deadline for the transition from OHSAS 18001 to ISO 45001 was March 2021, and the data concerning certificated companies refers to 2020.

3.3 Methodology

Concerning the methodology, we used a content analysis of non-financial reports, seeking to characterise the largest Portuguese companies concerned with SDG-related disclosures. Through 2016 to 2020, the data was collected respecting to: report type, number of pages, framework, level of declaration, external verification, and auditor nature.

Content analysis is the research method used in most of the studies to measure quantitative and/or qualitative aspects of SDGs disclosure. Some studies analyse the presence of the SDGs disclosures (independently of their scope, depth, length, or any other factor) (Curtó-Pagès et al., 2021; Fonseca & Carvalho, 2019; Haywood & Boihang, 2021; Hummel & Szekely, 2022; Izzo, Ciaburri, et al., 2020; Monteiro et al., 2022; Nichita et al., 2020) and other studies define disclosure index and/or scores which vary according to the kind of analysis (Carvalho et al., 2018; Carvalho, Santos, et al., 2019; Centeno et al., 2018; Izzo, Strologo, et al., 2020; Pizzi et al., 2021; Tsalis et al., 2020).

Table 4. Sample Characterisation by Standards Certification.

		Frequency	Percent (%)			Frequency	Percent (%)
ISO 9001	No	14	34,1	**ISO 14001**	No	16	39,0
	Yes	27	65,9		Yes	25	61,0
	Total	41	100,0		Total	41	100,0
		Frequency	Percent (%)			Frequency	Percent (%)
ISO 45001	No	38	92,7	**OHSAS 18001**	No	25	61,0
	Yes	3	7,3		Yes	16	39,0
	Total	41	100,0		Total	41	100,0
		Frequency	Percent (%)				
SA8000/ NP4469	No	36	87,8				
	Yes	5	12,2				
	Total	41	100,0				

In our study, a content analysis was accomplished through the following terms: 'Sustainable Development Goals', 'SDG', 'priority SDG', 'priority Sustainable Development Goals'. It would be enough to find a reference to the SDGs to consider that the company disclosed about SDGs. In other words, our study did not seek to assess the quantity or quality of the disclosure made.

The information intended to identify if the company mentioned SDGs in the reports, being 0 to 'no' and 1 to 'yes'. For each SDG the same dichotomous approach was accomplished to identify which SDGs were disclosed in the report and how they were disclosed: 1 – through the report and 2 – in a specific section. The same logical sequence was followed for the priority SDGs identification in the reports. The alignment of the report with the SDGs following the GRI or IIRC guidelines was examined with 0 determined for 'Neither', 1 for 'GRI', 2 for 'IIRC', and 3 for 'Both'.

In order to test our research hypothesis, we created a non-weighted disclosure index, SDG disclosure Index (SDG_IND), to measure the level of disclosure on SDG. For the construction of the index a score was assigned according to the following criteria: 1 if the company discloses information about the SDG and 0 if it does not. The total SDG_IND value is therefore the result of the division of the total score obtained by each company by the maximum number of assigned points (17), as described below in Table 5. Thus, the index varies between a minimum of 0 and a maximum of 1 (1 means that the company discloses about all the 17 goals).

A set of panel data based on a Tobit regression analysis was applied, in STATA software, using the total of observations during the period 2016–2020, to verify if the variable ISO certification explains the level of SDGs disclosure.[1] The proposed analytical model is described in the following equation:

$$\text{SDG\_IND}_{it} = \beta_0 + \beta_1 \text{CERT}_{it} + \epsilon_{it}$$

Table 5. SDG Disclosure Index Formula.

$\text{SDG\_IND}_j = \sum_{n=1}^{i} \text{SDG}_n / i$	SDG_INDj	SDG disclosure Index – Company Total j
	SDG$_n$	SDG$_n$ under analysis. Dichotomous dummy variable with value 1 if the company discloses information about the SDG and value 0 if the company does not disclose information about the SDG
	i	Maximum number of SDG (17)

---

[1]As the dependent variable proposed for this study (SDG_IND) takes values between 0 and 1m Tobit regression is the most appropriate technique, because it considers the extremities of the rating scale in a special way. It assumes that the lower limit is the minimum observed in the data (0, in our case) and the upper limit is the maximum (1, in our case). In this regard, by using the maximum likelihood method, Tobit model provides efficient, consistent estimates of coefficients, because when the likelihood function is maximized, it incorporates information from both censored and uncensored observations.

4. RESULTS

4.1 Descriptive Analysis

Our study provides insights into SDG reporting's linkage with ISO certification, grouping certified and non-certified large Portuguese companies. The number of non-financial reports for each group was collected (Table 6). From the 119 reports analysed, only 22.7% (27) of the reports corresponds to non-certified companies and 77.3% (92) to certified ones. The total data indicate a clear discrepancy between the proportion of companies/reports from non-certified and certified companies, which is a non-favouring factor for the statistical analysis.

From this point, it is relevant to stand out that the considered sample of non-financial reports collected from non-certified companies was 27, and the sample of non-financial reports collected from certified companies was 92. These were the numbers in the proceeding considerations as the two groups were always treated separately.

As described in Table 7, the non-certified companies only disclosed two types of reports: sustainability reports and integrated reports, corresponding to 51.9%

Table 6. Non-Financial Published Reports, by Year and Discrimination by Two Groups: Non-Certified and Certified Companies.

Year	Non-Financial Reports	NCC Reports	Reports (%)	CC Reports	Reports (%)
2016	14	3	21.4	11	78.6
2017	22	4	18.2	18	81.8
2018	31	7	22.6	24	77.4
2019	30	7	23.3	23	76.7
2020	22	6	27.3	16	72.7
Total	119	27	22.7	92	77.3

NCC – Non-certified companies; CC – Certified companies.

Table 7. Type of Non-Financial Published Reports, by Year and Discrimination by Two Groups: Non-Certified and Certified Companies.

Type of Report	Total Number of Reports From NCC	Reports in the Total Years (%)	Total Number of Reports From CC	Reports in the Total Years (%)
Sustainability report	14	51.9	67	72.8
Integrated report	13	48.1	11	12.0
Social responsibility report	0	0.0	5	5.4
Management report	0	0.0	6	6.5
Environmental declaration	0	0.0	3	3.3
Total	27	100.0	92	100.0

NCC – Non-certified companies; CC – Certified companies.

and 48.1% from the total sample of 27 reports. The certified companies presented a more diversified type of reports, however, the predominance of sustainability reports as the choice of publication remains (72.8%). This result is in line with Datta and Goyal (2022), who found that sustainability reports or integrated reports are the primary sources for companies to highlight their alignment to the 2030 Agenda by reporting on SDGs.

Among the groups, similarly, the most published type of report is the sustainability report. According to KPMG studies (KPMG, 2022), GRI is the most widely used framework for sustainability reporting in the world. The latest published survey explains that two-thirds of their research sample uses GRI for their sustainability reports (KPMG, 2022). Farther, the use of GRI Standards has significantly increased from only 10% for 95% between 2017 and 2020 (KPMG, 2020).

The Table 8 demonstrate the number of reports/each year that mention the SDGs and those who identify priority SDGs. In a general perspective, 79.3% of the reports in certified companies, mentioned the SDGs, against 66.7% in non-certified companies' group. In both groups there is a tendency to increase the mention of SDGs. In 2020, all the non-financial reports collected from certified companies have some mention to the SDGs. In the non-certified group, the results are inconstant over the years, and the year 2020 does not correspond to the highest rate of SDGs disclosure.

Concerning goals prioritisation contrary to expectations, non-certified companies show higher values than certified companies, except for 2016. Nevertheless, it is important to highlight that the non-certified group has few reports, which mean that this observation could not have a proper explanation power and need more future studies to support the data.

Table 8. SDGs Mention and SDGs Prioritisation on Non-Financial Reports (NFR) Published by Certified and Non-Certified Companies (2016–2020).

	Year	NFR	NFR (SDGs mention)	%	NFR (SDGs prioritisation)	%
Non-certified companies	2016	3	1	33.3	0	0.0
	2017	4	3	75.0	3	100.0
	2018	7	4	57.1	3	75.0
	2019	7	6	85.7	4	66.7
	2020	6	4	66.7	4	100.0
Total		27	18	66.7	14	77.8
Certified companies	2016	11	5	45.5	4	80.0
	2017	18	12	66.7	5	41.7
	2018	24	20	83.3	11	55.0
	2019	23	20	87.0	12	60.0
	2020	16	16	100.0	13	81.3
Total		92	73	79.3	45	61.6

As state before, for non-certified companies, in average, 66.7% mentioned SDGs and from those reports mentioning SDGs, 77.8% prioritised UN Goals. As for certified companies, 79.3% of the reports mentioned SDGs and 61.6% of those reports had priority SDGs. In certified companies, despite the decrease from 2016 to 2017 (from 80% to 41.7%), in the following years, there was a continuous increase of reports mentioning priority SDGs.

Posteriorly, the reports mentioning each SDG individually for the two groups was fulfiled and the proportion of each UN Goal was calculated with the sample of SDGs disclosing reports in the respective group: 18 for non-certified and 73 for certified. We found that within the most mentioned SDGs, there are great similarities between both groups. Concerning the less mentioned SDGs, the results are very different between the groups (Fig. 1).

For non-certified companies the most mentioned SDGs were SDGs 3 (Good health and well-being) (94.4%), 8 (Decent work and economic growth) and 12 (Responsible consumption and production) (88.9%), 4 (Quality education) and 13 (Climate action) with 83.3%. For certified companies, the most mentioned SDGs were SDG 8 (Decent work and economic growth) (76.7%), 12 (Responsible consumption and production) and 7 (Affordable and clean energy) (75.3%), SDG13 (Climate action) (72.6%) and 3 (Good health and well-being) with 71.2%.

Our results are in line with KPMG (2022) survey, who showed the 3 SDGs most popular for companies: 8, 12, and 13. These goals are among the most frequently addressed SDG in the literature, namely SDG 8, decent work and economic growth (Curtó-Pagès et al., 2021; Fonseca & Carvalho, 2019; García-Sánchez et al., 2022; Gazzola et al., 2020; Izzo, Ciaburri, et al., 2020; Nicolò et al., 2022; Subramaniam et al., 2019; Tsalis et al., 2020; Yu et al., 2020); SDG 13, climate action (Curtó- Pagès et al., 2021; Fonseca & Carvalho, 2019; Izzo, Ciaburri, et al., 2020; Nicolò et al., 2022; Subramaniam et al., 2019; Tsalis et al., 2020), and SDG 12, responsible consumption and production (Fonseca & Carvalho, 2019; Gazzola et al., 2020; Izzo, Ciaburri, et al., 2020; Nicolò et al., 2022; Subramaniam et al., 2019).

The less mentioned in non-certified group were SDGs15 (Life on land) and 1 (No poverty) with 50%, SDG6 (Clean water and sanitation), 11 (Sustainable cities and communities), and 14 (Life below water), all representing 55.6%. In certified group, the less mentioned were SDGs16 (peace, justice, and strong institutions) (32.9%), 10 (Reduced inequalities) (35.6%), 2 (Zero hunger) (41.1%), 14 (Life below water) (45.2%), and SDG11 (Sustainable cities and communities) representing 46.6%. Tsalis et al. (2020) also found that SDG16 had the lowest score.

Lastly, regarding the SDGs prioritisation (Fig. 2), for non-certified companies the most prioritised SDGs were SDGs12 (Responsible consumption and production) (55.6%), 3 (Good health and well-being), 7 (Affordable and clean energy),. and 11 (Sustainable cities and communities) (50%) and 17 (Partnerships) representing 44.4%. The less mentioned were SDGs1 (No poverty) (5.6%), 5 (Gender equality) (11.1%), SDG14 (Life below water) and 10 (Reduced inequalities) (16.7%) and 4 (Quality education), representing 22.2%.

For certified companies the most prioritised SDGs were SDGs 7 (Affordable and clean energy) (42.5%), 8 (Decent work and economic growth) (37%), 12

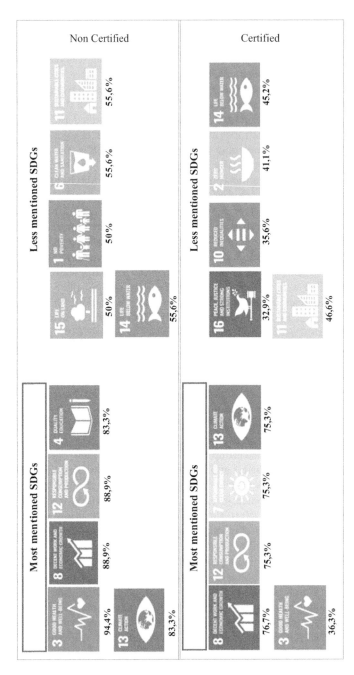

Fig. 1. SDGs Mentioned in the Non-Financial Reporting: Certified vs Non-Certified Companies.

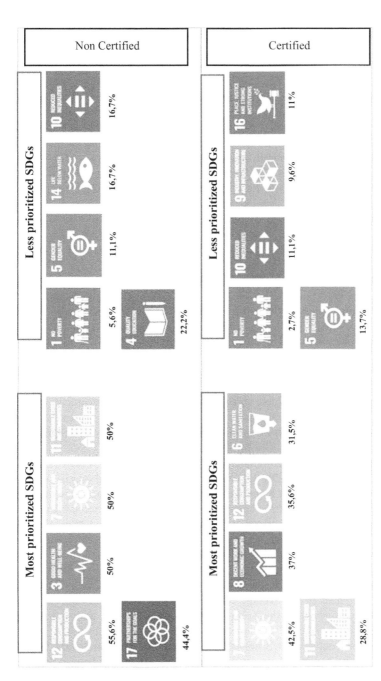

Fig. 2. SDGs Prioritised in the Non-Financial Reporting: Certified vs Non-Certified Companies.

(Responsible consumption and production) (35.6%), 6 (Clean water and sanitation) (31.5%), and 11 (Sustainable cities and communities) representing 28.8%. The less mentioned were SDGs1 (No poverty) (2.7%), 10 (Reduced Inequalities) (11.1%), and 9 (Industry, innovation and infrastructure), representing 9.6%, then SDG16 (peace, justice, and strong institutions) (11%) and 5 (Gender equality), representing 13.7%.

Thus, there are few similarities in both groups: only SDGs 12, 7, and 11 are in common. Our results agree with several previous studies on the importance of SDG 12 (Fonseca & Carvalho, 2019; Heras-Saizarbitoria et al., 2022; Izzo, Ciaburri, et al., 2020; Jimenez et al., 2021; KPMG, 2022; Nicolò et al., 2022; Subramaniam et al., 2019). In both groups, the SDG least priority is SDG 1, for combating poverty. SDG 1 is also identified in literature as one of those that receive the least attention (Curtò-Pages et al., 2021; Fonseca & Carvalho, 2019; García-Sánchez et al., 2022; Izzo, Ciaburri, et al., 2020; Nicolò et al., 2022; Subramaniam et al., 2019; Yu et al., 2020).

Fonseca and Carvalho (2019) carried out a study based on 235 Portuguese companies certified in three ISO standards. It was possible to understand which SDGs were most mentioned among companies' sustainable reports: SDG 12 (23.8%), 13 (22.1%), (21.3%), 8 (20%), and 17(19.6%). The less mentioned were: SDG1 (10.2%), 2 (11.1%), 16 (11.9%), and 11 (12.3%). Comparing the group of non-certified companies with the certified from our study and the certified from Fonseca and Carvalho's study, few similarities exist between the three groups. The only most mentioned SDG among all groups was SDG12, and the less mentioned SDG in common was SDG1. However, Fonseca and Carvalho's study sustains their work in a considerable large sample of certified companies, contrarily to our: smaller sample and not balanced between the two groups.

Comparing with the Portuguese strategy presented by the Government, which considered as national priority the goals 4, 5, 9, 10, 13, and 14, unfortunately, we can observe that our results are not aligned with the national strategy. SDG14 is among the least mentioned as a priority for companies.

To test our research hypothesis, we started to analyse the level of SDGs reporting, measured by the SDG Disclosure Index. For certified companies we observed a clear and gradual evolution between the index values presented in 2016 and those presented in 2020. The disclosure index varies between 0.2 (value obtained in 2016) and 1 (value obtained in 2020). During the period 2016 to 2020, the average value is 0.52. (Table 9). That means that, on average, the companies disclosed information about half of the 17 SDGs.

For non-certified companies there are some values' oscillations. However, during the period 2016 to 2020, the average value is 0.45. Thus, we observe no substantial differences in the average value of the index, between both groups. This result was confirmed by the Tobit regression model, which does not prove the statistical significance of the variable certification (p-value<0.05). Thus, contrary to our expectation, it is not possible to validate hypothesis $H1$. Therefore, we could not confirm that certified companies are more likely to have a higher level of SDGs disclosure.

Table 9. SDG Disclosure Index in Certified and Non-Certified Companies (2016–2020).

	Average	
Disclosure Index	Certified	Non-Certified
SDG_IND $_{2016}$	0.20	0.12
SDG_IND $_{2017}$	0.40	0.60
SDG_IND $_{2018}$	0.60	0.47
SDG_IND $_{2019}$	0.63	0.55
SDG_IND $_{2020}$	0.76	0.48
SDG_IND $_{(2016–2020)}$	0.52	0.45

This result may be because 78% of the companies included in the sample have some type of certification. It means that it is not possible to detect statistically significant differences in the SDGs reporting practices between the 2 groups of the sample. In future research, it is important to obtain a balanced sample between the groups and it would also be interesting to analyse if some individual standard referential (ISO 9001, 140001, 45001, and SA8000) have a more influent power as determinant factor for SDG disclosure or not.

5. CONCLUSIONS

The certification is a common practice for companies. The standards of the International Organisation for Standardisation (ISO) are among the most used standards all over the world. The ISO standards do not provide specific guidelines for sustainable development. However, it is recognised each standards' contributions to the SDGs. In the literature, some authors indicate that ISO 9001, 14001, 45001, and 26000 represent the three dimensions on which sustainable development is based: economic, environmental, and social dimensions.

Our study provides the first insights about SDGs disclosure–certification relationship, providing a detailed descriptive analysis of SDGs reporting practices in the largest Portuguese companies, over a 5-year period (2016–2020), comparing two groups: certified and non-certified companies.

In both groups, the most published type of non-financial report is the sustainability report. We verified similar results in the general descriptive analysis between both groups.

Certified companies present a tendency to increase SDGs disclosure and prioritisation, while in non-certified companies the results are more inconstant. We found that for non-certified companies' group, 66.7% mention SDGs and from those 77.8% prioritised the UN Goals. As for certified companies' group, 79.3% mention the SDGs and 61.6% of the reports had priority SDGs. In general, Portuguese companies are not aligned with the national strategy related to priority SDGs.

Despite some differences between the two groups, we identify SDG 8 (Decent work and economic growth), SDG 12 (Responsible consumption and production), and SDG 13 (Climate action) as the goals highlighted by companies. These goals are among the most three top SDG addressed in the literature. Concerning goals prioritisation contrary to expectations, non-certified companies show higher values than certified companies, except for 2016. Additionally, few similarities were found in both groups regarding SDGs prioritisation: only SDGs 12, 7, and 11 are in common. These goals are included in two of the 5 Pillars of 2030 Agenda, namely Prosperity (goals 7, 8, and 11) and Planet (goals 12 and 13). Carlsen and Bruggemann (2022) also found the pillar 'Planet' one of the most important indicators for a ranking of 102 countries, which highlighted the dominance of environmental concerns worldwide. Among the least mentioned and prioritised SDGs in both groups we highlighted SDG 1, bellowing to the pillar People.

The number of companies mentioning the SDGs in their reporting is still below the desirable level. However, but we observed a clear growth in the index values during period 2016–2020. During this 2016, the average value of the index is similar in both groups: SDG_index ± 0.5. Indeed, the regression model confirmed that there are no statistically significant differences between certified and non-certified companies concerning the SDG-related disclosure. Thus, contrary to our expectation, we rejected hypothesis *H1*: the variable ISO Certification do not influence the level of SDG disclosure. This result may be because we have an unbalanced sample: the group of certified companies was dominant (78%). This is one of the limitations of this study. In other future investigations, we suggest the use of a more balanced sample between the groups, to better evaluate our observations. We can also consider a more diversified sample, since our initial sample characterises only having large Portuguese companies. We could also include SME companies.

Another limitation is related to the methodology, that is the subjectivity of the content analysis. Moreover, in the content analysis we only confirm whether the SDG was disclosed, but we did not analyse the extent of its content, or the quality of the information disclosed. Thus, it would be interesting to study the depth of these disclosures.

Besides the general results demonstrate that certification is not a determinant factor, it would be interesting to evaluate if one of the ISO standards mentioned in the study has a positive relation with SDGs disclosure. Future studies could also consider the influence of other variables on SDGs disclosure, mentioned by Datta and Goyal (2022), such as firm-level characteristics (firm size, performance, sector, etc.), report characteristics (report type, framework, external verification, etc.), and regulation pressures (mandatory regulations). Our longitudinal analysis should also be combined with refined qualitative proxies representing a company's orientation towards SDGs reporting, such as in-depth interviews with top managers.

In the future, it could be also interesting to explore the on-line SDGs disclosures practices. The Internet, namely the websites, act as an important channel for the disclosure of these practices. The target 9.C of the 2030 Agenda encourages the increasing access to information and communication technology as well as the universal access to the Internet. In this sense, integrating the SDGs topic into the corporate' reporting cycle, and through an open access system, represents one big challenge. The use of the internet can increase companies' transparency and reduce information asymmetries between the stakeholders.

Despite the limitations, this study has several contributions. It extends prior empirical research on SDG reporting, by introducing a previously unexplored variable – ISO certification – as a potential determinant factor. Furthermore, it provides the initial insights into SDG reporting in Portugal, thereby contributing to a longitudinal analysis at the country level following the 2030 approval of the SDGs. These contributions enhance our understanding of the relationship between non-financial reporting and the SDGs and provide valuable insights for future research in this field.

Besides the scientific contribution, our research could have practical implications. By analysing the SDG reporting from the largest Portuguese companies, this study can help the integration of the SDGs into organisational reporting and accounting, encouraging small and medium enterprises (SMEs) to adopt the SDGs as a benchmark for their own reporting. Additionally, the findings could have relevant implications for policy formulation, particularly for regulatory bodies involved in reporting standards. The fragmented information landscape and lack of a consistent framework for measuring and reporting company contributions to the SDGs call for collaboration among international framework providers and standard-setters.

ACKNOWLEDGEMENTS

The authors acknowledge the financial support of FCT – Foundation for Science and Technology, I.P., within the scope of multi-annual funding UIDB/04043/2020.

REFERENCES

Adams, C. A. (2017). *The sustainable development goals, integrated thinking and the integrated report.* IIRC and ICAS.

Adams, C. A. (2020). *Sustainable development goals disclosure (SDGD) recommendations: Feedback on the consultation responses.* ACCA, IIRC, WBA.

Asif, M., & Searcy, C. (2014). Towards a standardised management system for corporate sustainable development. *TQM Journal, 26*(5), 411–430.

Asif, M., Searcy, C., Garvare, R., & Ahmad, N. (2011). Including sustainability in business excellence models. *Total Quality Management & Business Excellence, 22*(7), 773–786.

Barros, C., & Monteiro, S. (2012). Determinant factors of mandatory environmental reporting: The Casa of Portuguese primary metal and steel industry. *Studies in Fuzziness and Soft Computing, 286,* 123–147.

Başaran, B. (2018). Integrated management systems and sustainable development. *Intech,* 1–20.

Bedenik, N. O., & Barišić, P. (2019). Nonfinancial reporting: Theoretical and empirical evidence. In M. Sarfraz, M. Ibrahim Adbullah, A. Rauf, & S. Ghulam Meran Shah (Eds.), *Sustainable management practices.* Intechopen.

Borella, I. L., & Borella, M. R. D. C. (2016). Environmental impact and sustainable development: An analysis in the context of standards ISO 9001, ISO 14001, and OHSAS 18001. *Environmental Quality Management, 25*(3).

Carlsen, L., & Bruggemann, R. (2022). The 17 United Nations' sustainable development goals: A status by 2020. *The International Journal of Sustainable Development and World Ecology, 29,* 219–229. https://doi.org/10.1080/13504509.2021.1948456

Carvalho, F., Domingues, P., & Sampaio, P. (2019). Communication of commitment towards sustainable development of certified Portuguese organisations quality, environment and occupational health and safety. *International Journal of Quality & Reliability Management, 36*(4), 458–484.

Carvalho, F., Santos, G., & Gonçalves, J. (2018). The disclosure of information on sustainable development on the corporate website of the certified Portuguese organizations. *International Journal for Quality Research, 12*(1), 253–276.

Carvalho, F., Santos, G., & Gonçalves, J. (2019). Critical analysis of information about integrated management systems and environmental policy on the Portuguese firms' website, towards sustainable development. *Corporate Social Responsibility and Environmental Management, 27*(2), 1069–1088.

Centeno, M. E. C., Pizarro, E. G., Ramos, E. R., & Mariones, E. R. (2018). *Información no financiera divulgada por las empresas del ibex 35: análisis de la contribución a los objetivos de desarrollo sostenible de naciones unidas.* Universidad Europea de Madrid.

Curtó-Pagès, F., Ortega-Rivera, E., Castellón-Durán, M., & Jané-Llopis, E. (2021). Coming in from the cold: A longitudinal analysis of SDG reporting practices by Spanish listed companies since the approval of the 2030 agenda. *Sustainability, 13*(3), 1–27.

Datta, S., & Goyal, S. (2022). Determinants of SDG reporting by businesses: A literature analysis and Conceptual Model. *Vision, 0*(0). https://doi.org/10.1177/09722629221096047

Diaz-Sarachaga, J. M. (2021). Shortcomings in reporting contributions towards the sustainable development goals. *Corporate Social Responsibility and Environmental Management, 28*(4), 1299–1312.

Elalfy, A., Weber, O., & Geobey, S. (2021). The sustainable development goals (SDGs): A rising tide lifts all boats? Global reporting implications in a post SDGs world. *Journal of Applied Accounting Research, 22*(3), 557–575.

Fonseca, L. (2015). ISO 14001:2015: An improved tool for sustainability. *Journal of Industrial Engineering and Management, 8*(1), 35–50.

Fonseca, L., & Carvalho, F. (2019). The reporting of SDGs by quality, environmental, and occupational health and the reporting of SDGs by quality, environmental, and occupational health and safety-certified organizations. *Sustainability, 11*(20), 5797.

Gazzola, P., Pezzetti, R., Amelio, S., & Grechi, D. (2020). Non-financial information disclosure in Italian public interest companies: A sustainability reporting perspective. *Sustainability, 12*(15), 1–16.

García-Sánchez, I.-M., Amor-Esteban, V., Aibar-Guzmán, C., & Aibar-Guzmán, B. (2022). Translating the 2030 Agenda into reality through stakeholder engagement. *Sustainable Development,* 1–18. https://doi.org/10.1002/sd.2431

Gianni, M., Gotzamani, K., & Tsiotras, G. (2017). Multiple perspectives on integrated management systems and corporate sustainability performance. *Journal of Cleaner Production, 168,* 1297–1311.

GRI. (2022). *GRI - About GRI.* https://www.globalreporting.org/about-gri/

Haywood, L. K., & Boihang, M. (2021). Business and the SDGs: Examining the early disclosure of the SDGs in annual reports. *Development Southern Africa, 38*(2), 175–188.

Heras-Saizarbitoria, I., Urbieta, L., & Boiral, O. (2022). Organizations' engagement with sustainable development goals: From cherry-picking to SDG-washing? *Corporate Social Responsibility and Environmental Management, 29*(2), 316–328.

Hummel, K., & Szekely, M. (2022). Disclosure on the sustainable development goals–evidence from Europe. *Accounting in Europe, 19*(1), 152–189.

IIRC. (2021). *International <IR> Framework.* www.integratedreporting.org

ISO. (2015a). *NP EN ISO 14001:2015 Sistema de Gestão Ambiental – Requisitos e linhas de orientação para a sua utilização* (pp. 1–33). Instituto Português Da Qualidade. https://www.ipq.pt

ISO. (2015b). *NP EN ISO 9001:2015 – Sistemas de Gestão da Qualidade. Requisitos (ISO 9001:2015)* (pp. 1–40). Instituto Português Da Qualidade.

ALICE LOUREIRO ET AL.

ISO. (2015c). *Sistemas de Gestão da Qualidade – Fundamentos e vocabulário – NP/EN ISO 9000:2015* (3o Edição, pp. 1–41). Instituto Português Da Qualidade.

ISO. (2018a). *Contributing to the UN sustainable development goals with ISO standards*. https://www.iso.org/files/live/sites/isoorg/files/store/en/PUB100429.pdf

ISO. (2018b). *Discovering ISO 26000 – Guidance on social responsability* (pp. 262–266).

ISO. (2019). *NP EN ISO 45001:2019 - Sistemas de Gestão da Segurança e Saúde no trabalho. Requisitos e orientação para a sua utilização* (pp. 1–51).

ISO. (2022a). *ISO - About us*. https://www.iso.org/about-us.html

ISO. (2022b). *ISO - ISO 14001:2015 - Environmental management systems — Requirements with guidance*.

ISO. (2022c). *ISO - ISO 26000:2010 - Guidance on social responsibility*. https://www.iso.org/standard/42546.html

ISO. (2022d). *ISO - ISO 45001:2018 - Occupational health and safety management systems — Requirements with guidance for use*.

ISO. (2022e). *ISO - ISO 9001:2015 - Quality management systems — Requirements*. Instituto Português Da Qualidade. https://www.ipq.pt

Izzo, M., Ciaburri, M., & Tiscini, R. (2020). The challenge of sustainable development goal reporting: The first evidence from Italian listed companies. *Sustainability*, *12*(8), 3494.

Izzo, M., Strologo, A. D., & Graná, F. (2020). Learning from the best: New challenges and trends in IR reporters' disclosure and the role of SDGs. *Sustainability*, *12*(14), 5545.

Jennings, P. D., & Zanbergen, P. A. (1995). Ecologically sustainable organizations: An institutional approach. *Academy of Management Review*, *20*(4), 1015–1052.

Jimenez, D., Franco, I., & Smith, T. (2021). A review of corporate purpose: An approach to actioning the sustainable development goals (SDGs). *Sustainability*, *13*, 3899. https://doi.org/10.3390/su13073899

KPMG. (2020). *The time has come: The KPMG survey of sustainability reporting 2020*. https://kpmg.com/xx/en/home/insights/2020/11/the-time-has-come-survey-of-sustainability-reporting.html

KPMG. (2022). *Big shifts, small steps: The KPMG survey of sustainability reporting 2020*. https://kpmg.com/pt/pt/home/insights/2023/06/survey-of-sustainability-reporting-2022.html

KPMG Report. (2018). *How to report on the SDGs what good looks like and why it matters*. https://assets.kpmg.com/content/dam/kpmg/xx/pdf/2018/02/how-to-report-on-sdgs.pdf

Merlin, F. K., Do Valle Pereira, V. L., & Júnior, W. P. (2012). Sustainable development induction in organizations: A convergence analysis of ISO standards management tools' parameters. *Work*, *41*(Suppl. 1), 2736–2743.

Monteiro, S., Ribeiro, V., & Lemos, K. (2022). Linking corporate social responsibility reporting with the UN sustainable development goals: Evidence from the Portuguese stock market. In I. Management Association (Ed.), *Research anthology on measuring and achieving sustainable development goals* (pp. 250–268). IGI Global.

Nichita, E.-M., Nechita, E., Manea, C.-L., Manea, D., & Irimescu, A.-M. (2020). Reporting on sustainable development goals. A score-based approach with company-level evidence from Central-Eastern Europe economies. *Journal of Accounting and Management Information Systems*, *19*(3), 502–542.

Nicolò, G., Zanellato, G., Tiron-Tudor, A., & Tartaglia Polcini, P. (2022). Revealing the corporate contribution to sustainable development goals through integrated reporting: A worldwide perspective. *Social Responsibility Journal*. https://doi.org/10.1108/SRJ-09-2021-0373

Peršič, M., & Peršič, A. (2016). Standards of socially responsible management – Impact on sustainable development of the organization, the social and natural environment. *Management*, *21*(0), 207–226.

Pizzi, S., Del Baldo, M., Caputo, F., & Venturelli, A. (2022). Voluntary disclosure of sustainable development goals in mandatory non-financial reports: The moderating role of cultural dimension. *Journal of International Financial Management & Accounting*, *33*(1), 83–106.

Pizzi, S., Rosati, F., & Venturelli, A. (2021). The determinants of business contribution to the 2030 agenda : Introducing the SDG reporting score. *Business Strategy and the Environment*, *30*(1), 404–421.

Rebelo, M. F., Santos, G., & Silva, R. (2016). Integration of management systems: Towards a sustained success and development of organizations. *Journal of Cleaner Production, 127*, 96–111.

Rosati, F., & Faria, L. G. D. (2019). Business contribution to the sustainable development agenda: Organizational factors related to early adoption of SDG reporting. *Corporate Social Responsability and Environmental Management*, 1–10. https://doi.org/10.1002/csr.1705

SAI. (2014). *SAI social accountability 8000.* https://sa-intl.org/wp-content/uploads/2020/02/SA8000Standard2014.pdf

Santos, G., Almeida, L. M. M. G., Ramos, D. G. G., Carvalho, F. J. D. F., Sá, J. C. V. D., Baptista, J. S., Costa, J. T., Guedes, J. C., Freixo, J., Pereira, M. S. A., Correia, H., Oliveira, O. J. D., Barbosa, L. C. F. M., Lopes, N. A. F., Manso, V. M. V., Seabra, S., & Carnide, M. (2018). *Sistemas Integrados de Gestão – Qualidade, Ambiente e Segurança – 3a Edição* (B. Ramos (Ed.); Publindúst). Engebook.

Santos Ferreira, C., & Gerolamo, M. C. (2016). Analysis of the relationship between management system standards (ISO 9001, ISO 14001, NBR 16001 and OHSAS 18001) and corporate sustainability. *Gestão e Produção, 23*(4), 689–703.

Schramade, W. (2017). Investing in the UN sustainable development goals: Opportunities for companies and investors. *The Journal of Applied Corporate Finance, 29*(2), 87–99.

SDG Compass. (2015). *The guide for business action on the SDGs.* https://sdgcompass.org/

Subramaniam, N., Mori, R., Akbar, S., Ji, H., & Situ, H. (2019). *SDG measurement and disclosure by ASX150.* www.unglobalcompact.org.au/new/wp-content/uploads/2019/08/2019.08_SDG_Summary_Report_compressed.pdf

Tsalis, T. A., Malamateniou, K. E., Koulouriotis, D., & Nikolaou, I. E. (2020). New challenges for corporate sustainability reporting: United Nations' 2030 Agenda for sustainable development and the sustainable development goals. *Corporate Social Responsibility and Environmental Management, 27*(4), 1617–1629.

Yu, S., Sial, M., Tran, D. K., Badulescu, A., Thu, P., & Sehleanu, M. (2020). Adoption and implementation of sustainable development goals (SDGs) in China – Agenda 2030. *Sustainability, 12*(15), 6288.

SOCIAL RESPONSIBILITY MANAGEMENT SYSTEM: HOW TO IMPLEMENT IN A TEXTILE INDUSTRY COMPANY

Francisca Pires Vaz Meneses Lopes[a] and
Maria Manuela dos Santos Natário[b]

[a]*Polytechnic Institute of Guarda, Portugal*
[b]*Instituto Politécnico da Guarda, CICF-IPCA, CITUR, Portugal*

ABSTRACT

The concern with Corporate Social Responsibility has been increasing both by academics and politicians, as well as by companies and people in general, associated with the future of the next generations. Companies and organisations are increasingly aware that a differentiating factor nowadays is to be socially responsible and consequently to be certified in this area, helping them to grow and increase their notoriety and competitiveness. Companies that create and implement a Social Responsibility Management System have several advantages: increased brand recognition and consequent turnover, increased sales, improved relationship with their employees, increased competitive advantage in the market and helps the world to become better, through practices and application of current standards (IMR, 2019). Given the above it is intended in this study to identify and describe the requirements necessary for the implementation of a Social Responsibility Management System, according to the NP 4469:2019 standard, in a company in the textile industry. As a result of this proposal of SGRS in a company of workwear and personal protective equipment manufacturing, it was possible to see that the management of social responsibility can be a resource and key element to achieve success, with commitment from management and participation of all employees in decisions taken to improve the future of the company.

Society and Sustainability
Developments in Corporate Governance and Responsibility, Volume 24, 29–52
Copyright © 2025 Francisca Pires Vaz Meneses Lopes and Maria Manuela dos Santos Natário
Published under exclusive licence by Emerald Publishing Limited
ISSN: 2043-0523/doi:10.1108/S2043-052320240000024002

Keywords: Social responsibility management; work clothing and personal protective equipment manufacturing industry; CSR; PPE; NP 4469:2019

1. INTRODUCTION

A social responsibility (SR) policy necessarily implies a policy covering three pillars: social (People), environmental (Planet), and economic (Profit) (Commission of the European Communities, 2001). In this regard, the ISO 26000 standard defines SR as the set of strategic and operational policies for the achievement of sustainability at the level of organisations (IPQ, 2019). Companies that assume an ethical and socially responsible dimension tend to improve their image and gain the respect of the communities with which they interact. Social responsibility is a benefit and an added value for companies, where everyone wins (Santos, 2016).

The Corporate Social Responsibility (CSR) theme emerges in Portugal, with a systematised character in the context of the agreements established at a global level and in view of the strategies defined for the European Union. At national level, it also emerges as a way of facing challenges such as globalisation, competitiveness, the knowledge society and to overcome the backwardness of other countries (Fontes, 2011).

According to Duarte et al. (2010), cited by Lopes and António (2016), the concept of socially responsible enterprise is not assimilated in the same way by all Portuguese. There are three different views: one considers that the company should carry out its activity in an efficient and ethical manner; another that it should actively strive for the well-being of society; and another that it should adopt human resources policies that show respect for employees and their families.

An obstacle to the development of Social Responsibility and the practical application of actions in companies and in particular in small- and medium-sized enterprises (SMEs) are economic resources as well as lack of information, shortage of time, and human resources. This situation means that companies do not invest in the long term in this area, which is considered by many business leaders not to be a priority. This fact shows that SMEs are the face of who is in their leadership, because only from the understanding, attitudes, and values of the owners and managers, the positioning of the company in the field of RS is defined. The most important thing for the adoption of these practices is the awareness of the managers. This typology of companies (SMEs) is based on personal relationships, where employees have greater prominence, since these companies do not feel external pressures to implement these initiatives, they only do so to maintain recognition close to the local population (Santos, 2016).

In Portugal, a milestone in the operationalisation of Social Responsibility was the creation of the Portuguese Social Responsibility Management System Standard, NP 4469-1: 2008 (now NP 4469:2019), which specifies the requirements for a CSR management system, being applicable to organisations of different sectors and sizes (Leite & Rebelo, 2010).

In Europe, the major driving force behind CSR is the European Commission (EC), whose most important initiative is the publication of the Green Paper

'Promoting a European Framework for Corporate Social Responsibility', which is the voluntary basis and warns of the need for companies to contribute to promoting a fairer society and a cleaner environment (Commission of the European Communities, 2001).

In this regard, the European Economic and Social Committee (EESC) adopted opinion 335/2002 of 20 March 2002, which aims to complement legislative and contractual dogma, relying on social and environmental quality as a good in itself and on the integration of CSR as an essential function of the life and action of companies and as an economic and decisive asset (Fonseca, 2014).

In the Green Paper (Commission of the European Communities, 2001), two dimensions of SR are distinguished: internal and external. The internal dimension is emphasised by practices related to employees – focus on human capital, Human Resources Management, health, safety, change management – and environmental practices – activities related to Natural Resources Management and Environmental Impact. In the external dimension, the involvement of all stakeholders is emphasised, with emphasis on the theme of environmental concerns and respect for human rights.

In view of the above, this study aims to identify and describe the necessary requirements for the implementation of a Social Responsibility Management System (SGRS), according to the NP 4469: 2019 standard, in a company in the textile industry.

The paper is structured in four sections. After the introduction, section two provides a theoretical contextualisation of the thematic approach. The third section presents the empirical study with emphasis on the essential aspects in the operationalisation and implementation of a Social Responsibility Management System (SGRS) in the company under study. Finally, the final considerations are presented.

2. CONTEXTUALISATION

Organisations are today integrated in a highly competitive market, where the determinants of consumer choice go beyond price and quality. In this context, certifications are an added value, as they allow consumers to assess the degree of performance at other levels (Fontes, 2011).

Organisations that have implemented a Social Responsibility Management System are better prepared to meet the expectations and requirements of their stakeholders, whether they are customers, suppliers, consumers, regulators, or society, as it provides an innovative, competitive, and internationally recognised management approach. In the area of Social Responsibility there are several standards such as the Portuguese Standard 4469:2019, the International Organisation for Standardisation (ISO) 2600b 0, and the Social Accountability (SA) 8000 standard.

2.1 Social Responsibility Standards

The main objective of the ISO Social Responsibility standards is to ensure that companies are committed to reducing environmental impacts and social inequalities through certifications, which propose guides for company practices. The guides help to determine the actions directed towards internal and external audiences, ensuring that these are geared towards the defence of moral well-being, maintenance of values and preservation of natural resources, with a view to promoting socially sustainable performance (ISO's and social responsibility standards, 2020).

- The NP 4469:2019 Standard – Social Responsibility Management System (Requirements and Guidelines for its Use), is a national standard of requirements, certifiable according to Oliveira et al. (2015).

> This Portuguese Standard contains requirements for a social responsibility management system, which enable an organisation to develop and implement coherent policies, objectives and actions, taking into account legal, regulatory and other requirements to which the organisation subscribes. It applies to those aspects of social responsibility that the organisation identifies as those it can control and those it can influence. (IPQ, 2019, p. 9)

The main objective of this standard is to guide and support companies – of all sizes and types of activity – towards a more socially responsible performance, defining the requirements for a social responsibility management system and providing a framework and model for the pillars of Sustainable Development.

NP 4469:2019 is based on the PDCA cycle (Plan – Do – Check – Act). According to this cycle, firstly planning is done where problems, obstacles, and goals are identified, followed by the plan to solve and achieve them. Second is execution, this is where it is necessary to execute the established planning, where the activities and tasks to be put into practice are defined. Penultimately, it is necessary to verify the results obtained from the actions. In the fourth and last phase, after analysing the results with what was planned, that is, after identifying the deviations, the organisation must act on it, in order to correct them (Pacheco et al., 2012).

- The ISO 26000:2010 Standard is a Social Responsibility Guidance Standard, i.e. a standard of guidelines, but not intended for certification. It can be applied to any type of organisation. This International Standard was developed in 2010 by a process involving experts from over 90 countries and 40 international organisations involved in different aspects of social responsibility. These experts represented six distinct stakeholder groups: consumers; government; industry; workers; non-governmental organisations (NGOs); services, support, research, and others.

(International Organisation for Standardization, 2010)

This Standard indicates the seven principles of Social Responsibility to be adopted in order to facilitate the integration of SR throughout the organisation (Serrano, 2012) and which are Accountability, Transparency, Ethical behaviour, Respect for stakeholders' interests, Respect for the rule of law, Respect for international standards of behaviour, Respect for human rights. According to Serrano (2012) and Silva (2019), the character of this Standard is based on 'should', not on imposing requirements, i.e. it advises organisations. This Standard is compatible with other existing Standards or Management Systems, or those that will be created in the future, both in the area of SR and in the areas of quality, health and hygiene at work, environment, among others.

- The Social Accountability (SA) 8000 Standard was created in 1997 by Social Accountability International (SAI). It has a framework that helps organisations demonstrate their focus and dedication to treating their employees responsibly (ISOs and Social Accountability Standards, 2020). It is applicable to organisations of all types and sizes. The main function of this Standard is to declare that the company that holds it meets the basic standards set by the International Labour Organisation (ILO).

Its structure is based on the 12 ILO Conventions, the UN Declaration of Human Rights and the UN Convention on the Rights of the Child. 'This Standard is oriented towards increasing the competitive capacity of any organisation that voluntarily guarantees the ethical component of its production process and cycle, providing for compliance with national legislation and compliance with its nine requirements: Child Labour; Forced Labour; Safety and Health; Freedom of Association and Right to Collective Bargaining; Discrimination; Disciplinary Practices; Working Hours; Remuneration; Management System' (Oliveira et al., 2015, p. 168).

Certification of a Social Responsibility Management System can demonstrate an organisation's ability to develop policies and achieve SR targets, ensuring sustainable overall performance through:

- Compliance with applicable requirements;
- Implementation of control mechanisms and preventive management in the application of human rights and labour laws;
- Continuous improvement of the system's performance through the promotion of good SR practices.

(International Certification Organisation, n.d.)

It should be noted that the ISO 26000:2010 standard is an international guidance standard in terms of Social Responsibility, indicating the guidelines for the organisation to integrate social responsibility into the development of its activities, but without the purpose of certification and does not establish requirements to be met, it only makes recommendations. The NP 4469:2019 standard – Social Responsibility Management System is a Portuguese standard with certifiable requirements that demonstrates an organisation's commitment to sustainability.

The NP 4469 and ISO 26000 standards are complementary. The NP4469 standard refers to Social Responsibility, management systems and requirements, but compliance with the former does not imply compliance with all the guidelines of the ISO 26000 standard. However, adopting the former can help organisations implement the ISO 26000 guidelines. Another relevant difference is that NP 4469 is based on the PDCA cycle methodology (plan, do, check, and act). ISO 26000 does not propose a specific management system, but provides principles that can be added to existing management systems, suggesting ways of integrating social responsibility into the organisation's usual activities.

NP 4469:2019 is aligned with ISO 26000 although it is not internationally recognised, but it could be used as an example of good practice to be adopted internationally.

The international standard serves as a guideline for identifying the areas of the organisation where the inclusion of social responsibility is most relevant. It also provides guidance on how to deal with the main issues involving society and the environment (Barbosa, 2021).

2.2 Matrix Organisational Social Responsibility Guide

The Matrix Organisational Social Responsibility Guide project started from the EQUAL community initiative, which aims to promote new practices to combat discrimination and inequalities of any kind related to the labour market, in a context of transnational cooperation, and to encourage the social and professional integration of asylum seekers (Observatório Nacional, 2000) with the aim of raising awareness and promoting the implementation of Social Responsibility in Portugal.

The implementation of Social Responsibility involves the creation of a National Network for Organisational Social Responsibility (OSR), involving people and making organisations aware of the importance of OSR as an economic and social management tool, which adds value to products and improves the quality of life of workers and the community in which they operate (Matrix, 2007).

This project aims to develop a model of Organisational SR, within a national framework of sustainable development, with the intention that organisations gradually adopt principles, practices, and internal mechanisms in order to respond to the emerging needs of social cohesion and improvement of the quality of life and business competitiveness (Matrix, 2007).

The mission of this project is to implement RSO in Portugal, involving all Organisations with the aim of promoting sustainable development from the perspective of Social Responsibility. According to the General Workers' Union (n.d.), its main objectives materialise:

- the creation of a national OER model capable of responding to the European challenge;
- the development of an OER observatory for the dissemination of indicators, practices and results;
- the design of a methodological guide created with the aim of becoming a tool for organisations wishing to integrate social responsibility into their activities.

Several Portuguese Institutions and Organisations have become partners of this project, such as:

- ISQ – Institute of Welding and Quality;
- AIP – Portuguese Industrial Association;
- MARKINFAR – Portuguese Pharmaceutical Marketing Association;
- UGT – General Union of Workers;
- APG – Portuguese Association of Human Resources Managers and Technicians.

The RSO Matrix Model aims to present an integrated framework of objectives. It integrates a set of guiding principles, which organisations should seek to ensure and respect for the application of a Social Responsibility Management System. These principles have been distributed among the following 10 groups: Ethics and Transparency; Fundamental Human Rights; Good Governance; Stakeholder Dialogue; Value Creation; Human Resources; Diversity and Equality; Environmental Protection and Management; Local Community Development and Responsible Marketing (Matrix, 2007).

3. EMPIRICAL STUDY

The aim of this empirical study is to draw up a proposal for a Social Responsibility Management System for a company in the textile industry. The study therefore focusses on identifying and describing the necessary requirements for implementing a Social Responsibility Management System (SGMS) in a textile industry company located in the Centre of Portugal, using the RSO Matrix Project and the NP 4469:2019 standard as its guiding methodology.

In February 2008, the first version of Standard NP 4469 was published, being the first Portuguese social responsibility standard and a management tool regarding social responsibility issues. In 2019, the first revision of NP 4469-1: 2008, NP 4469:2019 was prepared (IPQ, 2019, p. 5).

Since social responsibility is currently a strong component of management, it is relevant to implement a system that allows the growth and development of the organisation, in terms of sustainability, well-being of people and society, added value and improved competitiveness (IPQ, 2019, p. 6). For implementation, the commitment of top management is essential, as well as the implementation of the general requirements of the standard, identifying the actions that must be implemented, monitored and the resources needed to achieve the objectives, so that certification can be carried out by an accredited entity (Almeida, 2014).

In the following, we will present the objectives, depending on the various aspects of Social Responsibility, that the company under study must consider in order to implement its Social Responsibility Management System. Thus, in the process of implementing a SGMS, it is first necessary to define the scope of the SGMS and frame the stakeholders. Subsequently, it is important to define the principles that guide the company in the process of defining and reviewing its strategies, policies, practices, and processes, to explain the leadership and its commitment to this process and to identify the company's policy in terms of social responsibility.

In order to plan the actions needed to achieve the social responsibility objectives, the company must plan: what will be done, considering the significant social responsibility aspects; the resources that will be needed; those responsible; the deadlines and the evaluation methodology (including indicators for monitoring progress towards the social responsibility objectives) (IPQ, 2019, p. 22). In this context, for the company under study (a company in the textile industry), objectives are proposed, actions to fulfil these objectives, the means used to develop them, as well as the indicators that can be assessed and monitored and the respective target, in the different themes defined in the RSO Matrix Methodological Guide (2007).

3.1 Scope of the Social Responsibility Management System

According to the NP 4469:2019 Standard, the organisation shall establish, implement, maintain, and continuously improve a social responsibility management system, including the necessary processes and their interactions. According to the requirement 3.38 of the NP 4469: 2019 Standard (IPQ, 2019), the Stakeholders of a company are people or organisations that can affect or be affected by decisions, activities, and/or products of the company. These can be either internal (e.g. employees) or external (e.g. suppliers, customers).

In the case of the *Textile Industry Company*, the Social Responsibility Management System is applied to the entire organisation, procedures, and processes. This is available and publicised on the company's website and on the company's premises, in the lounge area. In this context of the NP 4469: 2019 Standard, Table 1 shows the main stakeholders identified in the *Textile Industry Company*.

Table 1. Identification of the Stakeholders of the Textile Industry Company.

Stakeholders	Description
Management and director	Managing director and administrators
Employees	Employees
Family of employees	Spouses and children
Subcontractors	External organisations that perform part of the company's functions or processes (e.g. Bordados Patrício, MOSC, Rijoma)
Customers	Direct and indirect (McDonald's, Volkwagen Autoeuropa, Martifer, Brisa, Sonae, CUF Hospitals, TJA, Lactogal, GNR, PSP, Mota-Engil, SIEMENS, Saint-Gobain)
Suppliers	Cofra, Dunlop, Portwest, Marca, Valento, Biscana Organisations, 3M, Robusta, Swedes, Ansell, Faru, Manulatex, DPD, SOLO
Regulatory bodies	Portuguese Quality Institute (IPQ), CITEVE, SGS
Local authorities	Mangualde City Council
Competitors	CBI Indústria de Vestuário SA, Manutan Portugal. Etprotec, Sintimex

Source: Own elaboration.

Table 2. Classification of Company Stakeholders in the Textile Industry Company.

Stakeholders	Classification		Criteria				
	Internal	External	Linkage	Influence	Proximity	Dependence	Representation
Management and director	x			X	x	x	x
Employees	x		x		x	x	
Family of employees		x				x	
Subcontractors		x	x	X		x	
Customers		x	x			x	x
Suppliers		x	x			x	
Regulatory bodies		x				x	
Local authorities		x		X		x	
Competitors		x		X			

Source: Own elaboration.

Following the process, Table 2 presents the classification of the company's stakeholders, based on the criteria of linkage, influence, proximity, dependence, and representation, according to Standard NP 4469: 2019 (IPQ, 2019).

Based on the analysis of Table 2, it is possible to draw several conclusions about the stakeholders of the *Textile Industry Company* which are presented below.

The Management and the Director are a stakeholder classified as internal, this being one of the most important, since they are the ones who manage and make the most important decisions within the company and represent it in the most varied situations.

Employees, classified as an internal stakeholder, include all those who contribute to the company's growth and who are part of it. The classification criteria attributed to this stakeholder include the link they have with the organisation, proximity, and dependence.

Employees' families represent an external stakeholder, as they are financially dependent on the company for financial stability. The Textile Industry Company despite being a Small and Medium Enterprise employs about 100 people from the municipality of Mangualde.

Subcontractors are a stakeholder classified as external, according to the criteria of linkage, influence, and dependence. They are the ones who guarantee services of confection, cutting, and personalisation of articles in large quantities, and who allow the satisfaction of more customer requests.

Customers, both direct and indirect, are classified as one of the most important external stakeholders, according to the criteria of linkage, dependence, and representation, since they are the ones who guarantee and sustain the company's activity. In this sense, it is necessary to maintain a good relationship of proximity with each client and ensure their satisfaction and exceed their expectations.

Suppliers represent the most relevant external stakeholder in the organisation, through the criteria of linkage and dependence, as the company depends on its suppliers to meet customer needs. These are evaluated through factors such as product quality, order delivery times, and prices charged.

Regulatory bodies are another stakeholder categorised as external, based on the dependency criterion. They ensure legality and compliance, making the company fulfil all its obligations to all other stakeholders. CITEVE, the Portuguese Quality Institute (IPQ) and the Portuguese Environment Agency (APA) stand out as Regulatory Bodies.

The Local Authorities are presented as external stakeholders, through the criteria of influence and dependence, with the City Council and the Parish Councils being the main ones.

Competitors are an external stakeholder, based on the influence they have on an organisation, since it is from competition that companies tend to be competitive in the market and always want to improve both their services and products. On the contrary, it can be the competitors that cause changes in the progress of the company, so it is important to evaluate the market and the competitors themselves in order to be 'one step ahead' in the market.

3.2 Principles of Social Responsibility

The Textile Industry Company ensures that its conduct is based on respect for the principles of social responsibility, which guide the company in the process of defining and reviewing its strategies, policies, practices, and processes:

- Compliance with applicable laws and regulations;
- Ethical conduct in the development of its activities, in accordance with the principles of good behaviour;
- Respect for workers and their rights, employment is a free school, there is no forced or slave labour, freedom of association, non-discrimination, inhuman and harsh treatment is not allowed, working hours are in accordance with the legislation in force. The company fully subscribes to the principles of the universal declaration of human rights. Any violation of these principles should be immediately reported to the management, or reported through the whistle-blowing channel, which will ensure protected reporting on a channel: denuncias@empresadaindústriatêxtil. Textile Industry Company, S.A. assumes high standards of integrity and transparency, ensuring compliance with the legislation in force on Whistleblowing (such as harassment), safeguarding the protection of the whistleblower;
- Transparency, the company has to share information with its stakeholders, identified in the previous chapter;
- Stakeholders' right to be heard and the company's duty to react;
- Adoption of the precautionary principle;
- Prevention of pollution at source. The Textile Industry Company aligns its practices with the Sustainable Development Goals on:

- Quality Health;
- Drinking Water and Sanitation;
- Renewable and Affordable Energy;
- Industry, Innovation, and Infrastructure;
- Reduction of Inequalities;
- Sustainable Production and Consumption;
- Protection of terrestrial life.

The company's infrastructures have A+ Energy Certification, with production for self-consumption through solar energy and using photovoltaic panels. Water utilisation is carried out using home automation and a drip irrigation system. The use of a central weather station allows for the maximisation of thermal and energy efficiency. On the one hand, the use of double glazing and aluminium frames with thermal cut, as well as the existence of panels with a thickness well above average, allow the sustainable and efficient use of the entire building. On the other hand, the building's envelope, which is made of 'Portuguese pavement' instead of bituminous (aka tar), allows for greater thermal neutrality (in cold and hot) and thus greater efficiency in the air conditioning system (Textile Industry Company, 2023).

3.3 Leadership and Commitment

The Top Management according to *requirement 5.1* of Standard NP 4469:2019 must demonstrate leadership and commitment to the social responsibility management system, i.e. the Board of Directors and the Managing Director of the Textile Industry Company must ensure that the social responsibility policy and objectives are established; ensure the availability of resources necessary for the system; establish the means of communication, so that the social responsibility policy is understood and applied in the organisation, emphasising the importance of its effectiveness; guide and support people to contribute to the effectiveness of the social responsibility management system; promote continuous improvement (which according to *requirement 3.32* of Standard NP 4469:2019, consists of a recurring activity to improve performance), carrying out revisions to the system and ensuring ethical and transparent conduct in the activities developed and to be developed.

3.4 Social Responsibility Policy

The Social Responsibility Policy according to the NP 4469:2019 Standard consists of the intentions and orientation of the organisation, with regard to social responsibility, as formally expressed by its Top Management.

In the Textile Industry Company, the Social Responsibility Policy, defined by the top management (Administration and General Director), consists of becoming an innovative company, contributing to national and international development in scientific and technological terms, scrupulously respecting the environment and assuming a strategy of social responsibility towards society in general and, more specifically, towards its shareholders, employees, customers, and suppliers (stakeholders). In order to fulfil these aspects, the company also undertakes to respect and comply with the principles of social responsibility. This policy is available and publicised to all stakeholders on the company's website: www.hrgroup.pt and at the company's premises, in the lounge area.

3.5 Planning

According to the NP 4469:2019 Standard (IPQ, 2019, p. 21) the company should determine the social responsibility aspects of its decisions and activities that it can control and those that it can influence. There are seven key themes that the company should take into account, in which the aspects of social responsibility fit: Organisational governance; Human rights; Labour practices; Environment; Fair operating practices; Consumer issues; Community involvement and development.

In this context, for the Textile Industry Company the various aspects of social responsibility adapted from the RSO Matrix methodological guide, to be framed in the company for the implementation of the Organisational Social Responsibility Plan (Matrix, 2007) are: Ethics and Transparency; Fundamental Human Rights; Good Governance; Stakeholder Dialogue; Value Creation; Human Resources; Diversity and Equality; Environmental Protection and Management; Development of Local Communities; Responsible Marketing.

The social responsibility model considered in the RSO Matrix project adopts an approach that aims to implement and continuously improve the effectiveness and efficiency of the Social Responsibility Management System, through a participatory style that involves all stakeholders in the decisions made (Matrix, 2007).

In the following, objectives will be presented, according to the various aspects of Social Responsibility, which the company should consider for its Social Responsibility Management System. In order to plan the actions necessary to achieve the social responsibility objectives, the company must plan: what will be done, taking into account the significant aspects of social responsibility; the resources that will be needed; those responsible; the deadlines and the evaluation methodology (including indicators for monitoring the progress of social responsibility objectives) (IPQ, 2019, p. 22).

Table 3 proposes objectives, actions to fulfil these objectives, the means used to develop them, as well as the indicators to be evaluated and monitored and the respective target, in the *Ethics and Transparency theme*.

From the analysis of Table 3 it appears that the objectives, actions to fulfil these objectives, the means used to develop them, as well as the indicators to be evaluated and monitored and the respective target, in the *Ethics and Transparency* theme are: the fight against bribery and corruption, through practices such as a Whistleblowing Channel, a Corruption Risk Prevention Plan and a Compliance Officer; informing employees in a timely manner of possible changes that may exist in the company, by holding a general meeting, whenever necessary, since changes without prior notice cause stress and anxiety; Evaluation of the

FRANCISCA PIRES VAZ MENESES LOPES AND MARIA MANUELA DOS SANTOS NATÁRIO 41

Table 3. Aspects of Social Responsibility in Terms of *Ethics and Transparency.*

Objective	Action	Programme	Indicator	Target
Combating bribery and corruption	Practices to combat cases of bribery and corruption	Identification of cases of bribery and corruption	Number of cases of bribery and corruption every 3 years	0 cases
Inform employees in good time of any changes that may occur	Holding a general information meeting, for a possible change or decision	Provision of information to employees prior to the move, in the form of a statement prepared by management	Number of staff attending the general meeting as required	90 employees
Assessment of the organisation in relation to ethical parameters	Conducting an ethics audit	Development of an internal ethics audit	No. of audits carried out over 2 years	1 audit

Source: Own elaboration.

Table 4. Aspects of Social Responsibility at the Level of *Fundamental Human Rights.*

Objective	Action	Programme	Indicator	Target
Ensure equal opportunities for individuals with limited capabilities	Creation of a recruitment programme for individuals with disabilities	Integration of people with disabilities and reduced abilities in the company	Number of hires every 3 years	2 hires
Identify situations of violation of employees' human rights	Inform employees about possible situations that may go against their rights, through an information session	Creation of a document that enables employees to identify a possible violation of their human rights	Number of reports of human rights violations, every 2 years	0 reports of human rights violations
Promoting gender equality	Hiring that promotes gender equality	Promote equitable hiring of both men and women	Ratio of men to women, by year	50% women and 50% men

Source: Own elaboration.

Organisation in relation to ethical parameters, through an ethical audit, carried out every 2 years, which today, is a factor highly valued by certain clients.

Table 4 proposes objectives, actions to fulfil these objectives, the means used to develop them, as well as the indicators to be evaluated and monitored and the respective target, in the *Fundamental Human Rights* theme.

From Table 4, it can be seen that the main aspects of social responsibility at the level of *Fundamental Human Rights* are: ensuring equal opportunities for individuals with limited capacities, through recruitment programmes for people with some type of disability, since these people are excluded from society; identifying situations of violation of the Human Rights of employees, informing them about their rights as a human being and situations that may arise from their

Table 5. Aspects of Social Responsibility at the Level of *Good Governance.*

Objective	Action	Programme	Indicator	Target
Accountability of senior management in ensuring compliance with defined requirements, standards/documents, and policies	Identification of a senior management person responsible for social responsibility	Meeting with all department heads for the election of the social responsibility officer	Number of meetings required to verify compliance with defined requirements, standards and policies, per year	1 meeting
Promote leadership skills	Leadership training for key sector and department managers	Dissemination of the training action through internal company email	No. of training hours, every 2 years	60 hours
Manage the economic and social impact in relation to highly dependent suppliers	Comply with established agreements, in particular with regard to payment conditions and deadlines	Verification by the finance department that agreements are being complied with	No. of supplier complaints for non-compliance with established agreements per year	15 claims

Source: Own elaboration.

violation, through an information document; promoting Gender Equality, in all sectors, starting this process at the time of hiring.

Table 5 proposes objectives, actions to fulfil these objectives, the means used to develop them, as well as the indicators to be evaluated and monitored and the respective target, in the Good Governance them.

From the analysis of Table 5, it appears that the aspects of social responsibility in the *Good Governance* theme to be contemplated are: Make top management responsible for ensuring compliance with requirements, standards/documents, and defined policies, through a meeting with all department heads for the election of a person responsible for the Social Responsibility area; promote Leadership capacity, through a training action; manage the economic and social impact in relation to highly dependent suppliers, through compliance with the established agreements, namely in relation to payment conditions and deadlines, a situation that should be controlled by the Finance department.

In Table 6 are proposed objectives, actions to meet these objectives, the means used to develop them, as well as the indicators to be able to be evaluated and monitored and the respective target, in the theme *Dialogue with Stakeholders.*

Table 6 shows that in the *Dialogue with Stakeholders* theme, the main aspects to be considered are proximity to Stakeholders, through the creation of an Open Day to the company's facilities and the production process; enhancing the relationship with Stakeholders, with the holding of an annual event, to promote the creation of new partnerships/projects; evaluate the opinion of Customers, sending satisfaction surveys via email.

Table 7 proposes objectives, actions to fulfil these objectives, the means used to develop them, as well as the indicators to be evaluated and monitored and the respective target, in the *Value Creation* theme.

Table 6. Aspects of Social Responsibility at the Level of *Dialogue With Stakeholders.*

Objective	Action	Programme	Indicator	Target
Proximity to stakeholders	Creation of an open day for all stakeholders to visit the facilities and the production process	Publicise an open day visit plan via email	No. of people visiting the factory	80 persons
Emphasising the relationship with stakeholders	Holding an in-company event with relevant stakeholders that promotes relationship building and potential new partnerships	Publicising the event by sending an email to stakeholders	Number of new projects/ partnerships created every 5 years	10 new projects/ partnerships
To evaluate the opinion of customers regarding the textile industry company	Carrying out customer surveys	Sending customer surveys via email	No. of surveys answered	1980 surveys answered

Source: Own elaboration.

Table 7. Aspects of Social Responsibility at the Level of *Value Creation.*

Objective	Action	Programme	Indicator	Target
Creation of a holiday camp	Provision of a space with conditions for employees to take their children to the facilities of the textile industry company during the summer holidays	Provide information to make it known that there is a holiday camp for employees' children, through flyers	No. of children enrolled in the summer camp during the summer	15 children
Promote Solidarity campaigns	Creation of campaigns to raise money for social organisations	Dissemination of the campaign with posters placed throughout the municipality of Mangualde	No. of associations that benefited from the campaigns during 1 year	3 associations
Select and evaluate suppliers based on social responsibility practices	Identify criteria for the selection and evaluation policy and carry out the evaluation	Sending the supplier evaluation via email	No. of approved suppliers according to the criteria	350 suppliers

Source: Own elaboration.

The analysis of Table 7 shows that the main aspects to be developed in the Value Creation theme are the creation of a holiday camp for employees' children, who during school holidays do not have a place open all season to leave their children; promote Solidarity campaigns to raise monetary funds for social associations, using posters for their dissemination; select and evaluate suppliers based on Social Responsibility practice requirements, identifying criteria such as having a Code of Conduct, ensuring respect for *Human Rights.*

44   *Social Responsibility Management System*

Table 8. Aspects of Social Responsibility at the Level of *Human Resources.*

Objective	Action	Programme	Indicator	Target
Reconciling family, professional, and personal life	EFR certification – family responsible entity	Carrying out a certification audit	No. of audits every 2 years	1 audit
Health promotion for employees	Demonstrate the importance of mental health in productivity	Carrying out psychology consultations for all employees	No. of psychology consultations per year	96 consultations – 12 consultations/ employee
Effective career management	Provide realisable conditions and expectations for career progression	Publicise objectives for career progression (motivates the employee)	No. of employees who have moved up the career ladder every 5 years	15 employees

Source: Own elaboration.

Table 8 proposes objectives, actions to fulfil these objectives, the means used to develop them, as well as the indicators to be evaluated and monitored and the respective target, in the *Human Resources* theme.

Table 8 shows that at the level of Social Responsibility in the *Human Resources* theme, it is proposed: the reconciliation of family, professional, and personal life, through the Family Responsible Entity (EFR) certification (according to Standard NP 4552: 2016 Management system for reconciling professional, family, and personal life), with the aim of responding to the current socio-labour context marked by flexibility, competitiveness and commitment (Apcer, s. d); promotion of employees' mental health, through psychology consultations; effective career management, in order to provide them with the conditions and expectations to achieve their goals; promotion of employees' mental health, through psychology consultations; effective career management, in order to provide realisable conditions and expectations to employees, disclosing to them the objectives to be achieved.

Table 9 proposes objectives, actions to fulfil these objectives, the means used to develop them, as well as the indicators to be evaluated and monitored and the respective target, in the *Diversity and Equality* theme.

The analysis of Table 9 shows that the following are proposed under the *Diversity and Equality* theme: integrating people in situations of social exclusion, through the creation of agreements with Social Insertion Institutions; promoting Cultural Diversity, with the creation of a cultural event for all employees, with the aim of integrating those from other cultures and countries; promoting integration programmes for young workers between 18 and 29 years of age.

In Table 10 are proposed objectives, actions to fulfil these objectives, the means used to develop them, as well as the indicators to be evaluated and

FRANCISCA PIRES VAZ MENESES LOPES AND MARIA MANUELA DOS SANTOS NATÁRIO   45

Table 9. Aspects of Social Responsibility in Terms of *Diversity and Equality.*

Objective	Action	Programme	Indicator	Target
Integrating people in situations of social exclusion	Agreement with social insertion institutions	In the recruitment procedure, emphasise the policy of integrating people in situations of social exclusion	No. of people hired every 3 years	1 person
Promoting cultural diversity	Creating a cultural event that seeks to integrate other cultures and countries	Publicising the event by placing posters in the company and on corporate TV	No. of employees attending the event	100 employees
Promote youth integration programmes	Creation of a programme to hire young workers between the ages of 18 and 29	Dissemination of the employment programme for young people, in different areas in the company, through the institute for employment and vocational training (IEFP)	No. of hires every 3 years, or as needed	1 hire

Source: Own elaboration.

Table 10. Aspects of Social Responsibility at the Level of *Environmental Protection and Management.*

Objective	Action	Programme	Indicator	Target
Sensitisation on proper environmental management	Information sessions to raise awareness of waste that may exist in the company	Several sessions were held on a wide range of topics related to environmental impacts caused by waste	No. of information and clarification sessions held, per year	1 session
Utilisation of surplus fabrics	Utilise surplus fabrics to make items	Creation of a line of items made with 'leftovers', such as t-shirts, applying discounts	No. of tonnes of fabrics reused per year	15 tonnes
Reforestation of Serra da Estrela	Reforestation of Serra da Estrela	Publicising and promoting tree planting day through posters in the company and on corporate TV	No. of trees planted per year	50 trees

Source: Own elaboration.

monitored and the respective target, in the *Environmental Protection and Management* theme.

Taking into account Table 10, it can be seen that it is proposed in the *Environmental Protection and Management* theme: raising awareness about the correct environmental management, through information and clarification sessions on any waste that may exist in the company and how to reduce it; use of surplus fabric, with the creation of a line of articles made with 'leftover' fabrics, applying discounts on it; reforestation of Serra da Estrela, with a day dedicated to planting trees for the company's employees, encouraged by the delivery of a t-shirt and lunch offer.

Table 11. Aspects of Social Responsibility at the Level of *Local Community Development.*

Objective	Action	Programme	Indicator	Target
Supporting local institutions	Creation of solidarity day for institutions that help the community (homes, schools, associations, volunteer firefighters)	Development of a solidarity day, which encourages employees to help their own community by contributing as much food as they can	No. of institutions helped, per year	2 institutions
Increasing proximity to local communities	Participation in events of the municipality of Mangualde	Exhibitor of the textile industry company in the main events of the municipality of Mangualde	No. of participations in events per year	3 participations
Promotion and establishment of partnerships with local authorities	Partnerships with local organisations to provide services to employees and their families	Discounts on services such as gyms, crèches, supermarkets	No. of partnerships every 3 years	3 partnerships

Source: Own elaboration.

In Table 11 are proposed objectives, actions to fulfil these objectives, the means used to develop them, as well as the indicators to be able to be evaluated and monitored and the respective target, in the theme *Development of Local Communities.*

The analysis of Table 11 shows that the following objectives are proposed in the theme *Development of Local Communities*: support Local Institutions, with the creation of Solidarity Day, so that employees can contribute to local institutions with food goods; increase proximity to Local Communities, with participation in events of the Municipality of Mangualde; increase the promotion and establishment of partnerships with Local Entities, such as gyms, daycare centres, supermarkets, granting discounts that benefit both the company and the entity.

Table 12 proposes objectives, actions to fulfil these objectives, the means used to develop them, as well as the indicators to be evaluated and monitored and the respective target, in the Responsible Marketing theme.

The following objectives stand out in Table 12 in the *Responsible Marketing* theme: to avoid perpetuating stereotypes regarding the communication actions that are carried out; to raise awareness of environmental causes, by creating strategies that promote sales, as well as sensitising customers to environmental causes, through products; to communicate social causes, by donating a part of the final profits from the sale of a product for a period of time.

3.6 Support

According to *requirement 7.* of Standard NP 4469:2019 (IPQ, 2019, p. 22), composed of *resources* (requirement 7.1), *competences* (requirement 7.2),

Table 12. Aspects of Social Responsibility at the Level of *Responsible Marketing*.

Objective	Action	Programme	Indicator	Target
Avoid perpetuating stereotypes regarding the communication actions that are made	Development of communication actions avoiding the creation of stereotypes	Development of responsible communication actions, avoiding the perception of some judgement	No. of complaints about communication actions, every 2 years	0 complaints
Raising awareness of environmental causes	Incorporate information promoting environmental education in the advertising of articles	Creating strategies that promote sales, as well as raising customer awareness of environmental causes through products	No. of integrated environmental information per product (depending on the typology of the article concerned)	1 information
Communicating social causes	Communicate social and environmental causes by donating a portion of the final profits from the sale of a product. For a period of time	Publicising the campaign via email, which allows customers to understand that by purchasing certain products they are contributing to social and/or environmental causes	No. of campaigns carried out per year and per product	3 campaigns

Source: Own elaboration.

awareness (requirement 7.3) and *communication* (requirement 7.4), and *documented information* (requirement 7.5), the Textile Industry Company should:

- Determine and provide the necessary resources to establish, implement, maintain, and improve Social Responsibility performance;
- Appoint a responsible person, with the necessary skills and experience, for the area of Social Responsibility;
- Carry out the survey and records of training needs, in order to define an annual Training Plan, so that the functions performed by all employees are in accordance with the aspects of Social Responsibility;
- Raise awareness among employees of the policy and aspects of social responsibility determined above and their contribution to the Social Responsibility Management System through an annual general meeting;
- Communicate to all stakeholders the values and principles of the organisation and the Social Responsibility Management System through its Code of Conduct;
- Include the documented information required by Standard NP 4469:2019 and the information considered necessary for the effectiveness of your System, identify it, update it, and review its relevance and availability.

As *documented information* of the Social Responsibility Management System, the following documents should be part of it:

- Management Manual;
- General Code of Conduct;
- Supplier Code of Conduct;
- Code of Conduct for Subcontractors;
- Fundamental Human Rights;
- Social Responsibility Policy;
- Training Plan;
- Records of Monitoring of Social Responsibility Objectives;
- Employee Satisfaction Assessment;
- Evaluation of Customer Satisfaction, carried out through the Survey.

3.7 Operationalisation

The NP 4469:2019 Standard has as *requirement 8, the Operationalisation, and this is composed by*:

- *Requirement 8.1, Operational Planning and Control*, states that the company shall plan, implement, and control the processes necessary to fulfil the requirements of the social responsibility management system and implement the actions set out in *Chapter 4.6*.

(IPQ, 2019, p. 25)

In order to fulfil this requirement, the Textile Industry Company must establish its own criteria regarding the aspects of social responsibility (including its articles and services that the company uses) and at the same time communicate them, those that are applicable, to suppliers and subcontractors, so that all stakeholders are aware of the criteria.

Regarding the criteria defined by the company, it becomes necessary to control them, so that there are no deviations from the social responsibility policy, and hence the need to have different meetings that meet the defined social responsibility objectives and legal requirements in order to ensure that all operations are carried out in the same direction, through documented information to have confidence that the processes were carried out as established.

- *Requirement 8.2, Emergency Preparedness and Response*, states that the company shall establish, implement, and maintain a procedure or procedures to identify emergency situations and potential accidents that may have an impact on social responsibility, as well as to respond to these situations (IPQ, 2019, p. 25). To fulfil this requirement the Textile Industry Company must establish procedures for example in case of fire, implement it and test it periodically.

3.8 Performance Evaluation

Requirement 9. is about *Performance Assessment*, which encompasses requirements 9.1 *Monitoring, measurement, review and evaluation; 9.2 Internal Audit and 9.3 Management Review*, in which they state that organisations shall monitor, measure, analyse, and evaluate their performance in social responsibility; they shall conduct internal audits at planned intervals to provide information (about compliance and effectiveness) on the Social Responsibility Management System; Top Management shall review the Social Responsibility Management System, at planned intervals, to ensure its continued relevance, adequacy, and effectiveness (IPQ, 2019, p. 26).

In order to meet these requirements, the Textile Company must monitor the Social Responsibility Management System by following up on the objectives defined in Chapter 4.6 and on deviations from the set targets, which is achieved in turn through stakeholder satisfaction (e.g. by conducting surveys), compliance obligations (through a procedure, where legal compliance obligations are checked), operational controls, monitoring, measurement, analysis, and evaluation methods and when to monitor and evaluate the results.

Concerning the performance of *internal audits*, which aim to verify that the criteria of the standard are being met and that the company's own requirements are being implemented and met through the procedures. The Textile Industry Company must first define the frequency of the audits, for example, annually. Subsequently, the auditor is elected, who must be impartial to the area to be audited, the audit plan is carried out, which includes the scope, the criteria, the place where it will be done and the days and time when it will be developed. After the audit report has been prepared, the results must be communicated to the Board and the Director General and kept as evidence and documented information.

The *Management Review* should be carried out through a periodic, annual meeting, where the elements of the Administration, department heads and the person responsible for the Social Responsibility Management System are present. At this meeting, information on the performance of the System is presented, such as non-conformities, corrective actions, if any, compliance with legal obligations, audit results, and other data or indicators identified as relevant. Also included in this requirement are the Management Review Outputs, which shall include decisions related to opportunities for continuous improvement and any needs for changes to the Social Responsibility Management System. As evidence of these meetings, minutes should be taken with the headings of all those present.

3.9 Improvement

According to requirement *10. Improvement*, the company should determine opportunities for improvement and implement actions necessary to improve its performance in social responsibility (IPQ, 2019, p. 28). In this requirement are inserted the requirements *10.1 Non-conformities* and *corrective action and the requirement 10.2 Continuous Improvement*.

Faced with non-conformities, in view of the Social Responsibility policy and the requirements of the standard, the Textile Industry Company must react to it, taking immediate measures to control and correct, reduce the adverse impacts on social responsibility, and deal with the consequences. So that a non-conformity does not occur or is not repeated, it is necessary to evaluate actions to eliminate the causes of non-conformities, giving rise to corrective actions by virtue of continuous improvement. In this sense, the company must continuously improve the relevance, adequacy and effectiveness of the Social Responsibility Management System, always showing evidence of all actions.

4. FINAL CONSIDERATIONS

The main aim of this study was to present a Social Responsibility Management System for a company in the textile industry based on the NP 4469:2019 Standard and the RSO Matrix Project, enabling an understanding of how these practices can contribute to sustainable development and the company's recognition at national and international level. This proposal will also enable the company to implement more and better social responsibility practices in the future and the possibility of becoming certified in this area.

A Social Responsibility Management System requires the creation of an adequate policy aimed at the satisfaction of all stakeholders, ranging from the company's employees to the Local Community and the Environment, since this area has become increasingly important in a company, and in certain situations a requirement before customers.

The proposal of a Responsibility Management System for the Textile Industry Company involves implementing guiding principles in terms of Ethics and Transparency; Fundamental Human Rights; Good Governance; Dialogue with Stakeholders; Value Creation; Human Resources; Diversity and Equality; Environmental Protection and Management; Development of Local Communities and Responsible Marketing, which are monitored and measured through the actions and goals that have been proposed.

In addition, the requirements of Standard NP 4469:2019, which served as a guiding basis for the preparation of the proposal, were listed and it was mentioned what the company must do to comply with them in order to ensure the compliance of the Social Responsibility Management System. NP 4469:2019 is aligned with ISO 26000 although it is not internationally recognised, but it could be used as an example of good practice to be adopted internationally.

This case study contributes both to supporting the design of a Social Responsibility Management System for Portuguese companies, with the possibility of certification, but also in international terms it will support the guidelines for international companies to integrate social responsibility into the development of their activities in accordance with the ISO 26 000 standard. It will also help companies define policies and strategies to increase the inclusion of social responsibility in different areas and sectors.

The limitations encountered during the realisation of this proposal focus on the difficulty in outlining objectives according to the themes of the RSO Matrix methodological guide, in line with the possible needs of the company under analysis.

As a suggestion for future research, it is proposed to find out whether the same social responsibility management system is applied in other business areas, as well as to draw up a diagnostic report on social responsibility practices in various companies in the region.

REFERENCES

Almeida, R. (2014). *Social responsibility management system: A case study of the beverage industry.* Master's thesis. Polytechnic Institute of Guarda.

Barbosa, D. F. V. (2021). *Avaliação da maturidade do Sistema de Gestão Integrado e proposta de implementação de um Sistema de Gestão de Responsabilidade Social.* Master dissertation. ISCAC.

Commission of the European Communities. (2001). *Green paper.* COM (2001) 366 final. https://www.europarl.europa.eu/meetdocs/committees/empl/20020416/doc05a_pt.pdfconsultado. Accessed on May 29, 2022.

Fonseca, M. (2014). *Social responsibility in Portuguese companies.* Master's dissertation, Instituto Superior de Gestão de Lisboa. Common Repository. https://comum.rcaap.pt/bitstream/10400.26/9437/1/Ma%20Ceu%20Fonseca%20-%20tese.pdf. Accessed on July 17, 2022.

Fontes, A. C. M. (2011). *Corporate social responsibility: Reality or Utopia.* Master's Dissertation, Higher Institute of Accounting and Administration, University of Aveiro. Institutional Repository of the University of Aveiro. https://ria.ua.pt/handle/10773/8465. Accessed on May 3, 2022.

International Certification Organisation. (n.d.). *Social responsibility certification.* https://www.eic.pt/certificacao/sistemas-de-gestao/responsabilidade-social/. Accessed on August 22, 2022.

International Organisation for Standardization. (2010). *ISO 26000: Guidelines on social responsibility.* ISO.

ISOs and social responsibility standards. (2020). *Esolidar social impact.* https://impactosocial.esolidar.com/pt-pt/2020/01/30/isos-e-normas-de-responsabilidade-social-2/. Accessed on August 17, 2022.

Leite, C., & Rebelo, T. (2010), Exploring, characterising and promoting corporate social responsibility in Portugal. In *National symposium on research in psychology* (pp. 2209–2225). University of Minho. https://www.researchgate.net/publication/267562683_Explorando_Caracterizando_e_Promovendo_a_Responsabilidade_Social_das_Empresas_em_Portugal. Accessed on July 6, 2022.

Lopes, M. M. C., & António, N. S. (2016). Corporate social responsibility in Portugal: From myth to reality. *International Business and Economics Review*, 7, 110–138. https://recil.ensinolusofona.pt/handle/10437/8026. Accessed on June 29, 2022.

Matrix, P. R. (2007). *Methodological guide for the implementation of an organisational social responsibility plan.* RSO Matrix.

National Observatory. (2000). *EQUAL initiative.* National Observatory – Fight against poverty. https://on.eapn.pt/acontecimento/iniciativa-equal/. Accessed on September 23, 2022.

Oliveira, M., Ferreira, M. R., & Lima, V. (2015). Corporate social responsibility: Concept, management tools and standards. *Revista Brasileira de Administração Científica, 6*(2), 161–172. http://www.sustenere.co/index.php/rbadm/article/view/SPC2179-684X.2015.002.0011/622. Accessed on June 29, 2022.

Pacheco, A. P. R., Salles, B. W., Garcia, M. A., & Possamai, O. (2012). *The PDCA cycle in knowledge management: A systemic approach.* PPGEGC-Federal University of Santa Catarina-Postgraduate Programme in Engineering and Knowledge Management-apostille, 2. http://isssbrasil.usp.br/artigos/ana.pdf. Accessed on August 17, 2022.

Portuguese Institute for Quality (IPQ). (2019). *NP 4469: 2019 social responsibility management system – Requirements and guidelines for its use*. IPQ.

Santos, T. C. (2016). *Social responsibility in the context of SMEs: Positioning and engagement regarding practices – The example of the Erofio group*. Master's dissertation, University Institute of Lisbon. Repository University Institute of Lisbon. https://repositorio.iscte-iul.pt/handle/10071/13020. Accessed on June 30, 2022.

Serrano, M. M. (2012). Social responsibility and the ISO 26000 standard. *Revista de Formación Gerencial, 11*(1), 102–119. https://dialnet.unirioja.es/servlet/articulo?codigo=3934793. Accessed on August 18, 2022.

Silva, D. (2019). The 7 principles of social responsibility for your business in Brazil. https://pt.linkedin.com/pulse/os-7-princ%C3%ADpios-da-responsabilidade-social-para-o-seu-daniel-silva. Accessed on August 19, 2022.

Textile Industry Company. (2023). *Code of conduct. Internal company document*. https://www.hr-proteccao.pt/image/catalog/quem-somos/codigo_de_conduta_hr_group.pdf. Acessed on July 17, 2024.

THE CADASTRAL SYSTEM AS AN ENGINE OF MUNICIPALITY TO SPREAD THE SUSTAINABLE DEVELOPMENT GOALS

Armando Dias-da-Fe[a], Rosmel Rodriguez[b] and Rute Abreu[c]

[a]*Polytechnic Institute of Guarda, Portugal*
[b]*Universidade de Coimbra, Portugal*
[c]*Polytechnic Institute of Guarda, CICF-IPCA, CISeD-IPV, CITUR, Portugal*

ABSTRACT

The decentralisation of administrative power has been accepted as a more efficient system of managing their population in their own territories. Broadly speaking, almost all governmental and non-governmental organisations are converging on the need to transfer increasingly autonomous, endogenous, and autotrophic powers or functions to localities. Although locations are closer to people and problems, they have fewer resources, whether financial, human, or technological, which makes it difficult to obtain data and consequently make decisions. Several reasons allow the decision to be taken under political principles or others that are more difficult to legitimise. Cadastral purposes have historically been related to tax policy or taxes levied on real estate. In recent studies, it has been published that the cadastre is not only useful for taxation and real estate taxation but may also be useful for interventions that government authorities define for urban and rural development. In this paper, we address the relationships between these topics, namely, the municipalisation of some functions of the State, the implementation of the Sustainable Development Goals (SGDs) and the bases for correct decision-making based on useful information obtained by cadastral strategies. The methodology uses Gastil's theoretical model applied to cadastral system, Latour's Actor-Network Theory, and the concepts of citizen participation and open

---

Society and Sustainability
Developments in Corporate Governance and Responsibility, Volume 24, 53–72
Copyright © 2025 Armando Dias-da-Fe, Rosmel Rodriguez and Rute Abreu
Published under exclusive licence by Emerald Publishing Limited
ISSN: 2043-0523/doi:10.1108/S2043-052320240000024003

government to validate the cadastre as an interesting component for the implementation of collective initiatives aligned with the SDG. The results show that public policies need to be legitimised in the eyes of citizens and that in their eyes it is not enough just to improve the quality of their results, it is necessary to legitimise them from their conception, planning, and implementation.

Keywords: Decision making; register; counties; sustainable development goals (SDGs); Gastil model

1. INTRODUCTION

In the realm of Sustainable Development, the United Nations has championed the SDGs initiative and advocates for their application at the local level, underscoring a clear municipal focus (Siragusa et al., 2020, p. 9). It is essential to implement cadastral systems that organise municipal censuses to gather the requisite data. This data would then serve as an information source for new public policies at the municipal level, thus establishing a participatory deliberation space involving local authorities in both cadastral organisation and support for the SDGs' application within the municipal territory. Efficient management of the territory, available resources, and the needs of the population can be deemed significant steps towards achieving a more sustainable development, both locally and globally. As stated by Krigsholm et al. (2018), 'Stakeholder views should be consulted in order to better understand the role that land administration can play in supporting sustainable development'.

Currently, two primary aspects are addressed regarding registration. The first emphasises the use of equipment and emerging technologies, while the second scrutinises the theoretical framework of constructing the registry. Regarding new technologies, governments have been investing in the mechanisation and automation of the state for several decades. However, in recent years, this process has intensified and evolved into the digitalisation of the state. This phase goes beyond merely enhancing old processes and crafts systems with the potential to augment the public administration's capability, provide better and more services to taxpayers, and expand the state's control measures.

Termed electronic governance, this revolution can be analysed from various knowledge fields, as it stems from technological, social, and political advancements. It can foster novel communication and interaction methods, which potentially allow for more fluid information flow between individuals and entities (Dias-da-Fé et al., 2016).

In the second aspect, the participation and perspective of information use by different stakeholders have been studied. The value of cadastral systems in legitimising decisions hinges upon the information they provide. Given that public policies need to be legitimised in the eyes of citizens – and that merely improving their outcomes isn't sufficient – they must be validated from their conception, planning, and implementation.

Legitimacy theory has its roots in political science, mainly focussing on analysing the legitimacy of political organisations (Selznick, 1951). Legitimacy is a social construct that seeks alignment between an entity's values and its stakeholders' beliefs. Daft (1999, p. 347) defines it as 'the perception that an organization's actions are desirable, proper, and appropriate within a system of norms, values, and beliefs'.

This paper delves into the connections between several themes: the municipalisation of certain state functions, the implementation of the SDG, and the foundation for sound decision-making grounded in valuable information derived from the extensive possibilities presented by state digitalisation and the evolution of more comprehensive cadastral policies. Consequently, the research objective is to analyse the relationships between political decision-making decentralisation, cadastral information, and the implementation of the SDG.

We adopt stakeholder theory, institutional and legitimacy theory, as well as John Gastil's theoretical model applied to cadastral services. Furthermore, Latour's Actor-Network Theory and concepts of citizen participation and open governance are integrated to validate the registry as a compelling component for the execution of collective initiatives aligned with the SDGs in South America.

Diverse needs can be observed within different state spheres. For example, the informational needs of the central power differ from those of municipalities or even among various state agencies. In response, decentralising administrative power has been championed as a more efficient method of managing the population and available resources within their territories. Broadly speaking, nearly all governmental and non-governmental organisations are converging on the necessity to transfer more autonomous, endogenous, and autotrophic powers or functions to localities. Part of this shift is due to localities' enhanced capability to interact with various local actors, given their closer proximity to the people.

Although local governments are closer to the populace and their issues, they typically have fewer resources – financial, human, or technological. This scarcity hampers their ability to gather data, which in turn affects decision-making. Several reasons might cause decisions to be based on political principles or other grounds that are harder to justify. Furthermore, while decentralisation has been the path followed by most state reform programmes across Latin America for decades, urban and rural planning have evolved in markedly different directions. As a result, rural poverty remains a pressing concern (FAO, 2018, p. 80).

To address this concern, the establishment of cadastral policies at the municipal level and the creation of databases at the local level, which can be shared and accessed collaboratively, could enhance decision-making. This approach has the potential to rectify the perspective from which public policies on decentralisation and local development are determined (United Nations, 2020).

2. CONCEPTUAL FRAMEWORK

The use of registry information by various stakeholders is rooted in stakeholder theory. Each stakeholder should have the opportunity to articulate their information requirements. Stakeholder theory has become a pivotal conceptualisation in analyses of social impact and public incidence. It allows for the assessment of three fundamental variables:

(1) Number of involved participants,
(2) Institutional interconnectedness related to a specific phenomenon,
(3) The influence and impact capacity of these groups on the unfolding of events, processes, and products.

Altamirano Salazar (2018) determines the prominence (salience) of a social group based on the outcomes or objectives of a specific organisation or event. This significance will be determined by the organisation based on power conflicts or incentives that may enhance the organisation's positioning. This stakeholder taxonomy can be aligned within the framework of the SDG, focussing on social groups that can harness latent opportunities to create influence, foster accountability for agreements, develop sustainable support mechanisms, and reinforce the definitive nature of respective actions and procedures. Considering this, cadastral studies adopt a situational focus on the interests, needs, and expectations of actors to align organisational criteria with sustainable parameters that resonate with the Agenda 2023 and the SDG.

2.1 Institutional Theory and Legitimacy Theory

Understanding that state actions should be based on the need for legitimacy. Institutional theory, a thought stream focussing on the study of organisations and how they adapt to their environment, is pertinent when considering the SDG. It provides insights into how organisations can contribute to achieving these goals and how the goals can shape organisational operations. Key aspects of institutional theory in the context of the SDG include:

- Adaptation to the Environment: Institutional theory posits that organisations adapt to their surroundings to maintain legitimacy and ensure survival. In the SDGs' context, this might mean organisations adopting more sustainable practices to uphold their societal legitimacy.
- Influence of Norms and Values: Institutional theory also emphasises the role of societal norms and values in shaping organisational behaviour. With regards to the SDGs, this might mean organisations leaning into sustainable practices as they become more socially valued and accepted.
- Stakeholder Pressure: The theory suggests that organisations face pressures from their stakeholders, including clients, suppliers, employees, and society at large. In the realm of the SDGs, this could translate to organisations integrating more sustainable practices to meet stakeholder demands.

Institutional theory can provide valuable insights into how organisations can contribute to achieving the SDG and how these goals can influence organisational operations. This theory underscores the significance of environmental adaptation, societal norms and values, and stakeholder pressures in shaping organisational behaviour.

Conversely, legitimacy theory centres on societal perceptions of an organisation's legitimacy and how it can be sustained. Within the context of the SDGs, legitimacy theory offers a framework to understand how organisations can support these goals and how the goals can, in turn, affect organisational activities. Key facets of legitimacy theory in relation to the SDG include:

- Societal Perception: Legitimacy theory posits that societal perceptions about an organisation's legitimacy can impact its operations. In the SDGs' setting, this might suggest that organisations should adopt more sustainable practices to uphold their societal legitimacy.
- Information Disclosure: Legitimacy theory also emphasises the vital role of transparent information sharing by organisations to sustain their legitimacy. Regarding the SDGs, this might mean organisations publicly sharing data about their sustainable practices to retain societal trust.
- Social Responsibility: Legitimacy theory suggests organisations have a societal duty to preserve their legitimacy. In the context of the SDGs, this could indicate that organisations should embrace more sustainable measures to fulfil this duty and maintain societal credibility.

In both the dynamics of legitimacy and adaptability of social groups in response to organisations, the value of record-keeping facilitates accurate and efficient positioning. This enables a clearer understanding of capacities, focusses, and strategies that can verify the impact of processes concerning environmental sustainability.

2.2 John Gastil and the Theory on the Quality of Informational Records

Understanding the significance of maintaining quality and reliable records for public decision-making. Gastil is a scholar who has notably contributed to the study of deliberative democracy, a form of democracy that accentuates the vital role of citizen participation and deliberation in public decision-making. The quality of records emerging from Gastil's research might be pertinent to the framework of the SDG in the following ways (Gastil, 2021):

- Citizen Participation: The SDGs highlight the necessity of citizen involvement for achieving sustainable development. Gastil's research records could provide insights on facilitating and enhancing citizen participation through deliberative processes.
- Policy Formulation: The SDGs mandate the crafting of effective, inclusive, and sustainable policies. Gastil's research records could offer evidence-based recommendations for policy-making those respects and incorporates citizen perspectives and preferences.
- Transparency and Accountability: The SDs demand transparency and accountability in decision-making processes. Records from Gastil's research could shed light on designing deliberative processes that ensure both.
- Capacity Building: The SDGs emphasise capacity building at all tiers to realise sustainable development. Records from Gastil's research might offer guidance on how to enhance the capability of citizens, policymakers, and other

stakeholders to partake in deliberative processes and contribute to sustainable development.

Gastil's research quality can be deemed significant to the SDG by providing insights into citizen participation, policy formulation, transparency and accountability, and capacity-building.

2.3 Actor-Network Theory (ANT)

A rationale for studying completely distinct elements such as records, implicated technology, conceptual facets, and both local/national powers (both public and private) at the same level by examining their interrelations in the networks they form. The Actor-Network Theory (ANT) is a theoretical framework that underscores the significance of relationships and networks between actors, both human and non-human, in shaping social phenomena. Within the context of the Sustainable Development Goals (SDGs), ANT can be relevant in the following manners:

- Networks for Implementation: ANT accentuates the role of actor networks in implementing social phenomena. In the SDGs' context, this suggests that attaining the goals requires collaboration and coordination among various actors, including governments, civil society organisations, the private sector, and more. Article (1) stresses the centrality of actor networks for SDGs' realisation.
- Socio-Ecological Resilience: ANT advocates that all actors within social and ecological systems are intertwined in multiscale and diverse networks. In relation to the SDGs, this implies that achieving sustainable development demands an acknowledgement of social and ecological systems and their interrelations. Article (2) delves into how ANT can shed light on studying socioecological resilience.
- Sustainable Innovation: ANT can be leveraged to understand, trace, and succeed in a sustainable innovation development process. As per the SDGs, achieving sustainable development hinges on the creation and adoption of sustainable innovations. Article (3) posits that analysing relational and temporal dimensions significantly aids in understanding sustainable innovation.
- Complex Sustainability Issues: ANT can be wielded as a tool to navigate the intricacies of sustainability challenges. In the context of the SDGs, this suggests that sustainable development consideration should encapsulate the complexities of the entailed problems. Article (4) explores the application of ANT in unravelling sustainability topics within an Engineering and Society course.
- Stakeholder Participation: ANT can elucidate stakeholder involvement in energy transitions. Pertaining to the SDGs, this indicates that sustainable development hinges on stakeholder engagement in transitioning towards sustainable energy systems. Article (5) assesses the potential of ANT in understanding stakeholder engagement in energy transitions.

In the SDG framework, ANT stands out by emphasising the importance of actor networks, socio-ecological resilience, sustainable innovation, addressing complex sustainability issues, and engaging stakeholders.

3. DISCUSSION ON CAPILLARITY OF PUBLIC POWER AND STRENGTH OF CENTRALISED POWER

It states that the sustainable development of countries requires the existence of modern and updated cadastral systems that allow access to information about the territory in a much easier, safer, and more reliable way, in other words, that enable the use of cadastral information to suit the needs information from the entire society and each group of stakeholders. 'As day by day becomes aware, society grows in the importance of this information as a condition for social and economic development' (Torres Lopéz, 2016, p. 3).

The concept of a cadastral system pertains to the enumeration and typification of properties or lands intended to classify a population based on various variables (Amado, 2016, p. 4). Municipalities utilise this system for tax calculation purposes and as a contribution to the national statistical census carried out at least every decade. Beyond the foundational concept of cadastral systems or their organisational models, the implementation of the SDG within municipalities and localities will not achieve the anticipated results without coordinated institutions to manage cadastral information.

It is believed that cadastral information streamlines the implementation of the SDGs in municipalities and localities. To an extent, municipal cadastral policies could rectify the approach with which public policies of decentralisation and local development have been implemented (United Nations, 2020). Cadastral information allows municipalities and towns to better understand their territories. Only after achieving an acceptable level of cadastral organisation can one measure indicators in the implementation of the SDGs, be they advancements or setbacks. Whether in cities with millions of inhabitants or rural areas with only dozens, it is assumed that cadastral and cartographic knowledge is the initial step towards the municipalities' and localities' SGD.

In developing the cadastral system, available technological resources must be considered. Progress in this field can be observed through new methods employed to provide information and services by governments directly to citizens. This encompasses the capture and processing of personal or financial details, the creation of databases consolidating information from various sources, and many other evident or non-evident methods cutting across the hierarchical structure. These resources are not always accessible to local governments due to cost constraints and the requisite intellectual capital.

From a theoretical standpoint, current cadastral systems should be governed by HABITAT III (United Nations, 2017), a document from the New Urban Agenda containing 175 articles related to the Quito Declaration on Sustainable Cities and Human Settlements for All and the Quito Implementation Plan for the New Urban Agenda. The broad adoption of the intent to 'municipalise' the SDG has been widely observed. Moreover, almost all governmental and non-governmental organisations concur on the need to grant more autonomous, endogenous, and autotrophic powers or functions to municipalities (Grin, 2019, p. 82).

Even though decentralisation has been the route most state reform programmes in Latin America have taken for decades, urban and rural planning exhibits a significantly negative balance. As a result, rural poverty remains a pressing issue for governments in the region (FAO, 2018, p. 80). From the strategic and administrative perspective, we analyse, it's suggested that the municipalisation of the SDGs has been approached inversely; state reform programmes delegated powers and functions to municipalities that are disorganised in terms of cadastral organisation, necessitating their restructuring, and providing more participation opportunities to local authorities.

Administrative decentralisation holds no meaning without the tool of the cadastral system, which implies the pertinent update for effective knowledge of streets and alleys, passages, walkways, paths, barracks, and other types of roads, and the identification of various types of economic activities, establishments, and buildings (do not only refer to housing, but there are landmark buildings such as communal chambers or others of important category such as government buildings, religious or educational buildings) are of the type of individual or collective housing (firefighters, military complex, hospitals) and the conditions in which they are found (occupied, unoccupied, under construction, temporary, non-habitable dwellings).

It is sensible to point out that the effectiveness of cadastre is generally affected by the informality of certain areas that are sporadically inhabited or are irregular and rural populations, so the collection of cadastral information in these areas represents a notable difficulty. They are irregular because they are also referred to as expanding zones and sectors. Cadastral information is how municipalities and localities can get to know each other better; only after reaching an acceptable degree of cadastral organisation is it possible to measure indicators in the implementation of the Sustainable Development Goals, whether they are advances or setbacks. This also translates into several factors, including the lack of budget to carry out a national or local (focussed) census to study the population of a municipality in a particular way, the same applies to a cadastral process.

We have noted that cadastral surveys cannot be conducted frequently using traditional methods. In this regard, several international organisations dedicated to studying phenomena related to cadastral systems have begun to recommend digital technological innovations. These innovations are favoured not only because they reduce costs, making the cadastral process more economical, but also because they allow for the collection and correlation of an immense amount of data. This is especially true for multipurpose cadastres, which gather detailed information about families living in a building, their health, social security, employment, subsidies, and other pertinent data. It is pertinent to note that many countries apply the system of administrative records as a tool for updating the census, but its important element is the register of addresses of which it must be well prepared. Cadastral organisations are increasingly facing rapid technological developments, a 'technology push' that includes the internet, (geo)-databases, modelling standards, and open Geographic Information Systems (GIS). Moreover, there's an increasing demand for new services including electronic governance, environmental protection, sustainable development, and the integration of both public and private data. This evolving context necessitates the development of flexible and technological cadastral models (Velasco, 2008, p. 14).

Geographical Information Systems present an excellent opportunity for cadastral surveys to be carried out periodically with a level of detail previously unimaginable. However, technological innovations don't always address the complexities inherent in the cadastral process all at once. From staff training, defining terminology to distinguish building types, numbering these buildings, ensuring the immediate availability of residents, personnel transportation issues, personnel supervision, to processing this wealth of information into centralised and reliable databases – especially when a cadastre is outsourced to a private company, whose output must be audited and verified – this is merely a brief snapshot.

Currently, cadastral systems should be governed by HABITAT III (United Nations, 2017). The New Urban Agenda document encompasses 175 articles related to the Quito Declaration on Sustainable Cities and Human Settlements for All and the Quito Implementation Plan for the New Urban Agenda. Of these articles, two focus on the cadastre: 104. We will promote compliance with legal requirements through robust and inclusive management frameworks and responsible institutions that address land ownership registration and governance, employing comprehensive land management and property registration systems and financial systems that are transparent and sustainable.

We will support policies and capabilities allowing sub-national and local governments to register and expand their potential revenue base, for example, through multipurpose cadastres, local taxes, service fees or charges, in line with national policies while ensuring that women, girls, children, the elderly, disabled people, indigenous peoples, local communities, and impoverished families are not disproportionately affected (United Nations, 2017, pp. 32, 39).

Another organisation focussed on contributing to the Sustainable Development Goals is the Inter-American Cadastre and Property Registry Network. This network was established in 2014 after the Effective Public Management Department of the Organization of American States convened the First Inter-American Dialogue on Cadastre and Property Registry (Inter-American Cadastre and Property Registry Network, 2016). Since then, the network has focussed on strengthening the regional cadastre agenda; to that end, they present research on the relationship between the cadastral authorities of member states and the implementation of the Sustainable Development Goals. The national cadastral and property registry authorities from the Americas, recognising the importance of these two public administration functions, agreed to establish an exchange mechanism for experiences, knowledge, and cooperation, aiming to speed up strengthening their management (II Meeting and Conference of the Inter-American Cadastre and Property Registry Network, 2016).

The United Nations and the International Federation of Surveyors, known by its French acronym FIG, defined in 1996 (see Bogor Declaration in Indonesia of the United Nations Interregional Meeting of Cadastre Experts) the cadastral perspective until 2014 proposed to 'develop a modern cadastral infrastructure, facilitate an efficient land market, protect property rights, and provide support for sustainable development' (Durán, 2007). Subsequently, cadastral institutions gained such prominence that in 2003 the Permanent Cadastre Commission in the European Union was established (EUPPC, 2002), followed by the creation of the Permanent Cadastre Commission in Ibero-America in 2006 (CPCI, 2006).

As suggested in the preceding paragraphs, the cadastre is an essential element for the implementation of the Sustainable Development Goals. In the 1980s, faced with a scarcity of lands and resources, there emerged a need to enhance land use management and planning. This centred on sustainable development, environmental considerations, as well as social equity, such as indigenous rights and women's rights. This necessitated more detailed information about land and its usage, leading to the expansion of the multi-purpose cadastre (Reyes-Bueno et al., 2008). Contrary to what the previous paragraph implies, cadastres were not prioritised by Latin American municipal authorities. Let's delve into the situation of cadastre and municipalities in this context.

3.1 Situation of Cadastral Authorities in Latin America

The implementation of the Sustainable Development Goals in any state pre-supposes a certain degree of institutional functionality. This level of functionality allows central and municipal public administration bodies to monitor and manage indicators, execute the budget, and train personnel. What mainly impacts cadastral institutions are the threats typically affecting Latin American public administration. These can be defined as an insufficient sustainability of the tasks entrusted to them. Cadastral activities produce medium- and long-term effects, necessitating that initiated projects have a minimum guarantee in essential material, human, and financial means for the activity (Miranda Hita, 2007, p. 7). Although municipal public administration has an immediate responsibility over the cadastre of municipalities, municipal governments display little interest in cadastral policies (Durán, 2007, p. 8). However, municipal governments should not be perceived as the sole stakeholders involved in the implementation of the SGD in municipalities.

Professional associations, trade unions, academic associations, and other types of civil society organisations possess the opportunity to influence decision-making and the setting of public priorities ("Spanish Ministry of Economy and Finance, and CEFET Foundation, 2007a, 2007b, 2009, 2010, 2011a, 2011b). Cadastral information still does not garner adequate interest among governmental and non-governmental actors in Latin American municipalities. This implies that cadastral information lacks sufficient coordination among Latin American cadastral institutions.

3.2 John Gastil's Theoretical Model Applied to Cadastral Services

The demographic and economic growth of cities or the formulation of the Metropolis with the proliferation of new applications and computer programmes and the growing demand of the region in terms of citizen participation and open government, make registration an interesting process for the implementation of collective initiatives aligned with the Sustainable Development Goals. The Organisation for Economic Co-operation and Development (OECD, 2023) defines open government as: 'a culture of governance based on innovative and sustainable public policies and practices that are based on principles of transparency, accountability and participation that promote democracy and inclusive growth'.

It is evident that traditional frameworks of interaction between citizens and businesses with public administrations managing information, especially with cadastres, are evolving, leading to new models of citizen participation and open governance (Durán, 2010, p. 12).

Public policies need to be legitimised in the eyes of citizens. To achieve this, citizens are not only interested in enhancing the quality of the outcomes but also in ensuring that these policies are legitimised from their inception, planning, and implementation stages.

According to Suchman (1995), legitimacy can be divided into four categories: general, pragmatic, moral, and cognitive legitimacy. A fundamental component of organisations' legitimacy strategies derives from transparency in communication with the public. The availability of data encourages societal participation, strengthens democracy, promotes innovation, improves the quality of public services and public management, and facilitates the transfer and generation of new knowledge through data source associations. Furthermore, it enhances citizen oversight of governmental accounts and encourages participation in the planning and development of public policies (de Andrade, 2016, p. 5).

The participation of local authorities in cadastral services would provide this contribution to legitimise and improve the process leading to a cadastre. Let us see below the schema with which John Gastil theorises about the participation of civil society organisations in government decisions; The public–private partnership can generate administrative efficiency in terms of decentralisation and management of local development, giving it the opportunity for private sector participation in the management of localities and opening the door to the formulation of governments of different kinds, electronic, digital, and intelligent.

As acknowledged by Gastil, his theoretical model is an incomplete circuit that requires the addition of variables, and it does not always ensure demographic inclusion, equal deliberation, or procedural transparency (Gastil, 2021, p. 85). Despite its limitations, Gastil's contribution lies in creating online opportunities, as opposed to in-person ones, which are better suited for processes that do not necessitate deliberation, namely non-deliberative information collection processes.

Online participation works best when aimed at gathering information or receiving input (such as suggestions, proposals, or ideas) from citizens. In general, online setups appear more fitting for less demanding participative processes, where the focus is on information or consultation. Their performance tends to falter when deliberation is requested (Bobbio, 2019, p. 48).

Several studies on participation, deliberation, and their effects on public policies indicate that Information and Communication Technologies (ICTs) contribute to the legitimacy of public policies rooted in participative processes (Przybylska, 2021). Local powers, expressed through professional associations, student groups, labour unions, and other forms, thus have an increasing opportunity to engage with the cadastral policy of their regions.

It's crucial to emphasise that delays in land regularisation in many countries, due to institutional frailty and the lack of training of those in charge, hinder the deliberative process in citizen participation, and erode trust in collaborative processes of cadastral management and updates by residents. In conclusion, we can identify intersections between registration processes and local powers connected to participative urban operations. At times, there's a form of oversight presented through community monitoring of political actions introduced by local governments. This active citizen oversight, referred to as Community Monitoring both in Bolivia and Ecuador, represents an active vigilance from the citizenry to prevent any abuse of power.

3.3 GIS Software: Geographic Information Systems

Geographic Information Systems (GIS) are computerised tools that enable a detailed understanding of activities taking place within a specific area (Erba, 2008, p. XXX). Cadastral censuses are logistically intricate and economically costly, suggesting that cadastre cannot be conducted very frequently, at least not employing traditional cadastral methods. The cadastre has evolved into a multi-dimensional tool, with which layers of information for various purposes can now be integrated, a concept some experts term as multi-purpose cadastre.

In most Latin American countries, cadastral systems originated structured under the orthodox physical-economic-legal scheme and are developed following this philosophy. Concurrently, the multifunctional model (be it well or poorly interpreted) is gaining traction. Meanwhile, in certain jurisdictions, cadastres have been outright deactivated or remain 'outdated', with foreseeable consequences for territorial administration (Erba, 2008, p. 16).

3.4 Implications of Urban and Rural Cadastre for Local Authorities

Historically, cadastral objectives have been linked with fiscal policies or taxes levied on properties. Recent studies have highlighted that cadastres aren't solely for taxation and real estate tax purposes but can also support interventions defined by governmental authorities for both urban and rural development. In this context, cadastral functions hold significant relevance for the Sustainable Development Goals.

We've previously touched upon the institutional foundations that justify the cadastre as a development tool, as outlined in HABITAT I (United Nations, 1976), HABITAT II (United Nations, 1996), HABITAT III (United Nations, 2017) conferences, and others by the International Federation of Surveyors, as well as regional organisations like the Inter-American Cadastre and Registration Network aligned with the Organization of American States.

These conferences discussed the necessity of local authority participation in any public policy; however, as noted earlier, the cadastral process garners less interest from local authorities and the public. The implications of the urban cadastre differ considerably from those of the rural cadastre. Factors such as the topography of the area, data scarcity, absence of paved roads or bridges, isolation of certain settlements, and lack of satellite or radio communication are all challenges, these are all typical characteristics of rural populations that cadastral processes could ignore. Public policies to bring basic services to rural areas are much more expensive than urban areas.

Rural populations should be considered regardless of their population density or their economic significance within a state. Such areas are conducive to the emergence of local authorities, which, in alignment with the Sustainable Development Goals, join the complex cadastral process as a form of participation.

It is not implied that rural populations have unique attributes while urban populations do not. Urban populations require the rise of local authorities just as rural areas do. In densely populated and economically active cities, we see vertical growth at the foot of mountains or hills, the construction of unplanned neighbourhoods. This offers insights into the challenges associated with cadastral updating tasks.

3.5 Urban Land Policy in the New Cadastral Policy

Following HABITAT III (United Nations, 2017), governments, universities, international development cooperation agencies, regional organisations, and professional associations have significantly increased research into cadastral activities in Latin America and, consequently, its funding (Erba, 2013, p. 38). Forty years after HABITAT I (United Nations, 1976), there was ample motivation to reassess how cadastral administrations have been fulfiling their purpose. A new cadastral policy approach is emerging in Latin America, based on the technological possibility of multi-purpose use of cadastres, that is, a multifunctional cadastre (Amado, 2016, p. 4).

This new approach, applied to urban land policies, allows for a better understanding of natural and urban characteristics, legal and economic traits, social features, and other elements related to the availability of public services such as postal, electrical, health, or educational services. A multi-use cadastre requires a Spatial Data Infrastructure (SDI) 'because within this infrastructure, cadastral cartography is universally accepted as the basic layer; the better our cadastre is, the more we can contribute to geographic information' (OEI, 2016, p. 5).

These spatial data infrastructures do not necessarily have to be housed within cadastral or governmental institutions; geographic information systems and spatial data infrastructures present an opportunity for citizen participation because they are interoperable platforms. Interoperability entails building strategic alliances, formal partnerships, cooperation agreements, conventions, and joint efforts to share data, information, personnel, equipment, working methods, and anything else managers find useful.

Structuring cadastral data under an SDI or a GIS in the cloud also facilitates citizen participation processes. Through these platforms, individuals can exercise their rights to contribute to service network planning and/or changes in use or density, as well as fulfil their duties as taxpayers (Erba, 2019, p. 42). Based on this new cadastral policy characterised by geotechnologies and citizen participation opportunities through interoperable uses, a trend has emerged in Latin America known as Participative Cadastre (Parra, 2018, p. 4).

The involvement of community, neighbourhood, and borough organisations offers benefits such as coordinating cadastral authority procedures, gathering more comprehensive information, training personnel for cadastral tasks, and informing residents about the process, including the day and time when the cadastre will be conducted. Furthermore, it's essential to formulate a pedagogical follow-up process to build 'communities' for the continuous dissemination of information at local registry levels. This emphasises the need for coordination among social actors in local spaces to establish deliberation areas in debates, like common metadata, which can be extended to various territories under local governments.

3.6 Cadastral Update for the Equitable Redistribution of Property Tax

The advantages of participatory registration do not consist only in the quality of the information or in the number of families on which the multipurpose registry is built, updating the registry allows you to make fiscal adjustments with which the taxes paid by taxpayers can be redistributed. Elinor Ostrom's vision of the governance of the commons, in which all actors win when they organise and protect their common good (Ostrom, 2015). The involvement of local organisations in the periodic updating of the cadastre would significantly aid in the regularisation of urban lands, properties, lots, and other related classifications. Enhancing cadastral regulations, revitalising information systems, increasing the accuracy and quality of data provided to the cadastre and registry to offer strategic information to customers and users, and acknowledging the role that employees play in the growth and development of entities, are undoubtedly measures that constitute our path towards the modernisation of the General Administration of States. This is in response to the demands of citizens who hold this right both as users of the state and as customers recognised for their contributory efforts (Velasco, 2008, p. 3).

Concerns had already been raised about the low effectiveness of municipalities in cadastral activities. In Latin America, property taxes are also minimal, and most municipal authorities in the region have fiscal powers that cannot be optimised. This hampers the process of cadastral updating and the redistribution of property tax. A study by the IDB (IDB, 2014) on the hidden potential of real estate tax demonstrates that during the 2000–2010 decade, while tax collections in OECD countries increased from 0.98% to 1.15% of GDP, in Latin America, it stagnated at an average of 0.28% for the same period.

Given that the theoretical foundations of a well-managed property tax are an equitable source of income for local governments, it's essential to conduct localised studies to identify positive results on how to leverage property in developing countries (Marulanda, 2015, p. 30). While cadastres can be directed towards various purposes, in Latin America, cadastral policies have been insufficient even for their traditional roles, such as local government's fiscal policy. Such a widespread situation in Latin American states necessitates a re-evaluation of cadastral policies, coupled with the proliferation of new opportunities for the involvement of local authorities. These authorities play a pivotal role in municipal planning and legitimise cadastral activities as a means leading to improved indicators in the implementation of the Sustainable Development Goals.

4. CONCLUSIONS

This research aimed to illustrate the intricate relationship between the state, local governments (municipalities), and their cadastral reform to facilitate the implementation of the SDG. It is grounded on the logic proposed by Latour (1994), initially referring to what he termed the principle of generalised symmetry and later the Actor-Network Theory (2007). Freire (2006, p. 49) noted that Latour argued interdependent elements should be addressed within the same framework: There is no prior world of things in themselves on the one hand, and the world of men among themselves on the other, for nature and society are both effects of heterogeneous networks. This does not mean that their networks are composed of the same elements, but that they can be described in the same way, treated under the same terms (Freire, 2006, p. 49).

According to our scientific hypothesis, Latin American states need decentralisation and for this they need management tools capable of meeting the objectives of the various stakeholders. Part of this process includes the need for cadastral organisation. Whether it is a city with millions of inhabitants or rural areas with dozens of inhabitants, it is assumed that cadastral and cartographic knowledge is the first on the way to facilitate the implementation of the Sustainable Development Goals in municipalities and localities. Cartographic updating can be carried out in an analogous way with the use of paper, maps, and plans, as well as digitally with the use of tablets and scanning programmes.

Among the perspectives advocating for and justifying the organisation of land registry to implement the Sustainable Development Goals at the municipal and local levels are the insights of Leopoldo Arnaiz Eguren. He serves as the president of the Advisory Board of the Latin American Federation of Cities, Municipalities, and Local Government Associations (FLACMA). To further comprehend this standpoint, let's delve into some historical precedents.

The Conference on Land and Poverty is an annual event organised by the World Bank since 1999. It is during this conference that the World Bank releases the findings of its research on land governance in relation to the Sustainable Development Goals. Klaus Deininger, a member of the World Bank's Development Research Group for Sustainability and Infrastructure, noted that cadastral information allows for the objective monitoring of poverty reduction policies at a level of detail previously unimaginable, now achievable through geospatial technology and satellite imagery (Deininger, 2016).

Beyond the World Bank, there are other organisations dedicated to supporting the Sustainable Development Goals through municipal management. One such organisation is the Urban Housing Practitioners Hub (UHPH), which aims to enhance housing and habitat policies in Latin America and the Caribbean. To guide their initiatives, they reference a document issued by the United Nations known as the New Urban Agenda. This agenda was approved at the United Nations Conference on Housing and Sustainable Urban Development – Habitat III – held in Quito, Ecuador in 2016 (United Nations, 2017). It's important to note that these United Nations Conferences have been convened since 1976, starting with HABITAT I in Vancouver, Canada (United Nations, 1976), followed by HABITAT II in 1996 in Istanbul, Turkey (United Nations, 1996).

This leads to a point that has all the merit of being viewed critically because the cadastral institutions in Latin America do not function optimally after 40 years have elapsed between HABITAT I (United Nations, 1976) and HABITAT III (United Nations, 2017); some authors have written that the HABITAT summits have not achieved the desired effects on human settlements because they do not suit governments or multinational corporations.

It should be noted that the urbanisation process is a process of costs and requires planning in which many municipalities establish an agenda and channel their resources according to priority social problems, ignoring the importance of urban planning. In such a way that the global model of colonial capitalist development of expansion, exclusion, expulsion, fragmentation, segregation, and gentrification continues to be reproduced (Mattioli & Elorza, 2016, p. 95).

Cadastral services play an integral role in the implementation of the SDGs. This relationship is particularly evident in goals 11 'Sustainable Cities and Communities', 16 'Peace, Justice, and Strong Institutions', and 17 'Partnerships for the Goals'. Moreover, cadastral services are not just essential for the implementation but also for the measurement and evaluation of the SDGs.

The digitisation of cadastral services is a global, irreversible trend (Kaufmann & Steudler, 1998, p. 11). This digital transformation has ushered in new formulations concerning the design of cadastral processes and the imperative to make them more inclusive and participatory. From the findings, three conclusions can be drawn:

(1) The challenges of the cadastral systems in many Latin American countries are exacerbated by a dispersion of responsibilities among institutions.

(2) This dispersion of responsibilities necessitates initiatives to enhance coordination between institutions.

(3) Recent initiatives demonstrate that effective communication can result in significant improvements in coordination.

(Durán, 2007, pp. 8–9)

Given these challenges, we propose that the cadastral organisation process should be nationalised, utilising technological innovations to allow local authorities and other societal actors to partake in the cadastral organisation of municipalities. Simultaneously, the subjective ambiguity of the 'cadastral registry', as framed by its legal relationship with municipal regulations on inhabitants' rights and duties concerning information provision, is fraught with uncertainties. Factors such as fear of tax hikes might lead to misinformation during interviews and cartographic updates.

Furthermore, the participatory processes can be undermined if citizens do not understand the benefits of the cadastral process in their communities. Thus, it's crucial to address the informational needs of local authorities, encompassing non-governmental organisations, civil society organisations, international agencies, community foundations, and other organised societal expressions, as outlined by Carole Pateman in her perspective on co-governance and deliberative democracy (Pateman, 2012, p. 14).

By promoting and intensifying the communication of objectives, the significance of the cadastral system can be legitimised, mitigating the challenges. Additionally, the participation of citizens or local authorities in coordinating cadastral policies would positively influence the outcomes of the SDG because:

- Local organisations have a deeper understanding of the areas they operate in than governmental authorities. In rural areas, their involvement would enhance cadastral policy coordination and implementation. Continuous updates and perpetual involvement of local authorities are essential. For urban areas, the involvement of local organisations offers similar benefits but with distinct challenges related to telecommunications, population density, housing numbers, and classifications.
- One major hindrance is the inadequate attention municipal authorities give to cadastral services. This indifference stems from limited awareness civil society organisations have about statistical censuses, municipal governments' roles in cadastres, and the significance attributed to the cadastre by the United Nations Conferences and other international bodies concerning the SDG. The budget allocations for statistical or cadastral services are another challenge that public administrations face. Activating citizen participation in budget discussions is vital, emphasising Gastil's theoretical model which prioritises collaborative decision-making between governments and civil society for local development.
- Technological innovations alone cannot overcome the inherent challenges of a cadastre. Cadastral authorities remain paramount in implementing any

initiative, from training to funding management to logistical supply. Technologies require optimal training and pedagogical approaches. Outcomes are futile if misused or misinterpreted. Thus, participatory cadastral initiatives, even with technology, are an avenue for enhancement but do not guarantee the successful implementation of the SDG.

ACKNOWLEDGEMENTS

This research was conducted at the Research Center on Accounting and Taxation (CICF-IPCA) and was funded by the Portuguese Foundation for Science and Technology (FCT) through national funds (UIDB/04043/2020 and UIDP/04043/2020). Also, the authors would like to thank David Crowther and anonymous reviewers for improvements.

REFERENCES

Altamirano Salazar, A. W. (2018). La contabilidad creativa en el gobierno coorporativo de las empresas. *Ciencias administrativas*, *12*, 65–72.

Amado, S. (2016). *X Simposio sobre Catastro en Iberoamérica.* http://www.catastrolatino.org/documentos/Nueva_Politica_Catastral.pdf

Bobbio, L. (2019). Designing effective public participation. *Policy and Society*, *38*(1), 41–57.

Comité Permanente sobre el Catastro en IberoAmérica. (2006). Estatutos. http://www.catastrolatino.org/documentos/estatutos_CPCI_modificados_abril2011.pdf

Daft, R. L. (1999). *Leadership: Theory and practice.* LTC.

de Andrade, C. M. (2016). Interview with the information technology coordinator (CIO) of the federal revenue of Brazil. *Revista da Rede de Peritos Cadastrais Ibero-Americanos (12).* https://issuu.com/redondexpertos_ceddet/docs/catastro_logo

Deininger, K. (2016). *Harnessing the data revolution and improving land management through geospatial technology.* World Bank. https://blogs.worldbank.org/developmenttalk/harnessing-data-revolution-and-improving-land-management-through-geospatial-technology

Dias-da-Fé, A. L., Gomes, D., & Oliveira, L. (2016). An analysis of the relationship between e-government, accounting and technological innovations: After the implementation of the e-government program in Brazil. In *Proceedings of the 9th International Conference on Theory and Practice of Electronic Governance* (pp. 408–411). https://doi.org/10.1145/2910019.2910031

Durán, I. (2007). Firma Invitada. *Revista de la Red de Expertos Iberoamericanos en Catastro, 1.* http://www.catastrolatino.org/documentos/REVISTA_1_REI.pdf

Durán, I. (2010). Promote the reuse of registration information by public administrations, companies, and citizens. *Revista de la Red de Expertos Iberoamericanos en Catastro, 7,* 9–12. http://www.catastrolatino.org/documentos/REVISTA_7_REI.pdf

Erba, D. A. (2008). *El catastro territorial en América Latina y El Caribe.* Lincoln Institute of Land Policy. https://www.lincolninst.edu/sites/default/files/pubfiles/el-catastro-territorial-america-latina-full.pdf

Erba, D. A. (2013). *Definición de políticas de suelo urbano en América Latina: Teoria y práctica.* Lincoln Institute of Land Policy. https://www.lincolninst.edu/sites/default/files/pubfiles/definicion-de-politicas-de-suelo-urbanas-full.pdf

Erba, D. A. (2019). Tax policy vs cadastral policy. New dramatization. *CIAT Tax Administration Review,* (45), 37–50. https://www.ciat.org/Biblioteca/Revista/Revista_45/Espanol/RAT-45-Erba.pdf

European Union Permanent Committee on Cadastre (EUPCC). (2002). *Constitution – Act of 14 de October.* Euroadastre. http://www.eurocadastre.org/pdf/actaingles.pdf

Food and Agriculture Organization of the United Nations (FAO). (2018). *Panorama of rural poverty in Latin America and the Caribbean 2018*. United Nations. http://www.fao.org/3/CA2275ES/ca2275es.pdf

Freire, L. L. (2006). Seguindo Bruno Latour: notas para uma antropologia simétrica. *Comum, 11*(26), 46–65. https://app.uff.br/riuff/bitstream/handle/1/12232/latour.pdf

Gastil, J. (2021). A theoretical model of how digital platforms for public consultation can leverage deliberation to boost democratic legitimacy. *Journal of Deliberative Democracy, 17*(1). https://delibdemjournal.org/article/963/galley/4838/download/

Grin, E. (2019). Gestión pública y democracia participative en los gobiernos locales: posibilidades, límites y desafíos. In F. J. Velázquez López (Ed.), *Gobernanza de las Ciudades: los ODS como guía para la acción* (pp. 55–92). Escuela CLAD. https://issuu.com/clad_org/docs/4.gobernanza_digital

Inter-American Development Bank (IDB). (2014). *Subnational governments and decentralization sector framework document – Fiscal and municipal management division*. https://decentralization.net/wp-content/uploads/2015/07/IDB_SNG_and_Decentralization_SFD.pdf

Inter-American Property Registry and Registration Network. (2016). *II annual meeting of the inter-American real estate registry and registry network*. RICRP. http://portal.oas.org/LinkClick.aspx?fileticket=qOcpK2Xm608%3D&tabid=1821

Kaufmann, J., & Steudler, D. (1998). A vision for a future cadastral system. *Scientific Research, 167*, 173. https://www.fig.net/resources/publications/figpub/cadastre2014/translation/c2014-spanish.pdf

Krigsholm, P., Riekkinen, K., & Ståhle, P. (2018). The changing uses of cadastral information: A user-driven case study. *Land, 7*(3), 83. https://www.mdpi.com/2073-445X/7/3/83

Latour, B. (1993). *We have never been modern*. Harvard University Press.

Latour, B. (2007). *Reassembling the social: An introduction to actor-network-theory*. Oup Oxford.

Marulanda, G. A. (2015). Atualização cadastral permanente em Bogotá. Uma contribuição para a tomada de decisões na cidade. *Revista de la Red de Expertos Iberoamericanos en Catastro, 11*, 29–39. https://issuu.com/redondeexpertos_ceddet/docs/catastro-revista_digital-2015-_11.p

Mattioli, D., & Elorza, A. L. (2016). *Críticas al habitat III. Perspectivas y reflexiones en torno a las ciudades*. https://revistas.unc.edu.ar/index.php/ReViyCi/article/download/16273/16123/44436

Miranda Hita, J. (2007). Interview with the general director of the Spanish registry. *Revista de la Red de Expertos Iberoamericanos en Catastro, 1*, 4–7. http://www.catastrolatino.org/documentos/REVISTA_1_REI.pdf

Organização de Estados Ibero-americanos para a Educação, a Ciência e a Cultura (OEI). (2016). *X Simpósio de Cadastro na Ibero-América*. https://oei.int/pt/escritorios/paraguai/noticia/x-simposio-sobre-catastro-en-iberoamerica

OECD (Organisation for Economic Co-operation and Development). (2023). *Open government for stronger democracies: A global assessment. OECD Publishing*. https://doi.org/10.1787/5478db5b-en

Organization of American States (OAS). (2016). *II meeting and conference of the inter-American real estate registry and registry network*. RICRP. https://www.oas.org/en/sedi/ddse/pages/cpo_desoc_cides_2reunion.asp

Ostrom, E. (2015). *Governing the commons: The evolution of institutions for collective action*. Cambridge University Press.

Parra, H. J. (2018). Registro Participativo: proceso que impulsó la regularización masiva de suelos urbanos en Venezuela. *Boletín del Colegio de Geógrafos del Perú, 4.*

Pateman, C. (2012). Participatory democracy revisited. *Perspectives on Politics, 10*(1), 7–19.

Przybylska, A. (2021). Model solutions and pragmatism in developing ICT for public consultations. *Journal of Deliberative Democracy, 17*(1), 118–133. https://delibdemjournal.org/article/980/galley/4847/download/

Reyes-Bueno, F., Miranda-Barrós, D., & e Crecente-Maseda, R. (2008). La evolucíon de los sistemas cadastrales. *Revista de la Red de Expertos Iberoamericanos en Catastro, 3*, 19–20. http://www.catastrolatino.org/documentos/REVISTA_3_REI.pdf

Selznick, P. (1951). *The organizational weapon: A study of Bolshevik strategy and tactics*. Quid Pro Books.

Siragusa, A., Vizcaino, M. P., Proietti, P., & Lavalle, C. (2020). *European handbook for SDG voluntary local reviews*. Publications Office of the European Union. https://doi.org/10.2760/257092

Spanish Ministry of Economy and Finance, and CEFET Foundation. (2007a). Revista de la Red de Expertos Iberoamericanos en Catastro. http://www.catastrolatino.org/documentos/REVISTA_1_REI.pdf

Spanish Ministry of Economy and Finance, and CEFET Foundation. (2007b). Revista de la Red de Expertos Iberoamericanos en Catastro. http://www.catastrolatino.org/documentos/REVISTA_4_REI.pdf

Spanish Ministry of Economy and Finance, and CEFET Foundation. (2009). Revista de la Red de Expertos Iberoamericanos en Catastro. http://www.catastrolatino.org/documentos/REVISTA_5_REI.pdf

Spanish Ministry of Economy and Finance, and CEFET Foundation. (2010). Revista de la Red de Expertos Iberoamericanos en Catastro. http://www.catastrolatino.org/documentos/REVISTA_6_REI.pdf

Spanish Ministry of Economy and Finance, and CEFET Foundation. (2011a). Revista de la Red de Expertos Iberoamericanos en Catastro. https://issuu.com/redondeexpertos_ceddet/docs/n_8_revista_digital_de_la_rei_en_catastro

Spanish Ministry of Economy and Finance, and CEFET Foundation. (2011b). Revista de la Red de Expertos Iberoamericanos en Catastro. https://issuu.com/redondeexpertos_ceddet/docs/n__9_revista_digital_de_la_rei_en_catastro

Suchman, M. C. (1995). Managing legitimacy: Strategic and institutional approaches. *Academy of Management Review*, *20*(3), 571–610.

Torres Lopéz, R. H. (2016). Reseña Bibliográfica. *Revista de la Red de Expertos Iberoamericanos en Catastro*. http://www.catastrolatino.org/documentos/revista_12_REI.pdf

United Nations. (1976). *Habitat I*. United Nations.

United Nations. (1996). *Habitat II*. United Nations.

United Nations. (2017). *Habitat III. The new urban agenda*. United Nations.

United Nations. (2020, October). *World cities report 2020 – Human settlements programme* (pp. 75–110). https://www.un-ilibrary.org/content/books/9789210054386c008

Velasco, A. (2008). Draft standard ISO TC 211 19 152 on the cadastral model. *Revista de la Red de Expertos Iberoamericanos en Catastro*, (3), 12–16. http://www.catastrolatino.org/documents/REVISTA_3_REI.pdf

PART 2
RESPECTING INDIVIDUALS

WHAT'S IN A NAME: DISCOURSES ON INEQUALITIES IN THE UK

Miriam Green

Independent Researcher, UK

ABSTRACT

The issues raised in this chapter are primarily those of obfuscation regarding social and economic inequality in the UK. The chapter is about the way discourse in various forms serves to disguise and justify the huge inequalities in this society; legitimising and 'naturalising' them, or in Arendt's words 'lying' about them so that they are seen as 'natural and self-evident' (Alvesson & Deetz, 2006, p. 261). Issues looked at are the institutional arrangements by which government ministers give or withhold resources to and from certain categories of its citizens. This includes the UK Treasury in relation to which economic groups the Chancellor of the Exchequer decides how much to tax or not to tax. In particular what are examined are the discourses justifying these measures and establishing certain 'truths' about how things are economically and socially; which categories are entitled to or deserving of certain kinds of resources and which are not – argued here as constituting obfuscations of the 'actual' situation. Obfuscation has been defined as the action of making something obscure, unclear, or unintelligible. This, arguably, is not far removed, from the action of being deliberately untruthful or lying. The question then arises as to how close these discourses come to lying and how serious the inequalities are.

Keywords: Inequality; obfuscation; taxation; benefits; pensions; wealth differences; dominant ideology; discourse; lying

I believe always in the necessity of being attentive *first of all* to this phenomenon of language … Not in order to isolate ourselves in language … as people in too much of a rush would like us to believe, but on the contrary, in order to try to understand what is going on precisely beyond language. (Derrida, 2003, cited in Smith, 2005) (emphasis original)

Society and Sustainability
Developments in Corporate Governance and Responsibility, Volume 24, 75–95
Copyright © 2025 Miriam Green
Published under exclusive licence by Emerald Publishing Limited
ISSN: 2043-0523/doi:10.1108/S2043-052320240000024004

The following is one suggestion as to how language is being used and what might be going on beyond the language used by a BBC news broadcaster (anonymised here) in relation to a prospective increase in pensions in the UK.[1] The following is an excerpt from my response to him:

'Dear . . ..,

On 22nd June 2022 you described the proposed pension increase as "whopping" – because of the proposed 10% rise.

I would like to make a few points about your use of the word "whopping", which implies an exceptionally large and implicitly unjustified increase:

- Comparisons with other OECD countries in terms of state pensions and benefits places the UK at number 31, below, for example, the Slovak Republic, Slovenia, Costa Rica, Turkey and Korea (Commons Library Research Briefing, 2022) . . ..[2]
- My calculations put this "whopping" increase at £963.04 for those on the higher pension, resulting in a total amount of about £10,593. So, one might argue, the 10% increase doesn't amount to that much.
- Percentages obfuscate actual monetary values. Let us take, for example, the increase of one BBC presenter's salary from £315,000 to £325,00. This is by no means the highest paid person in the BBC, and certainly far from the millions paid to some. But it is an increase constituting almost as much as the entire higher pension. Yet the percentage increase is only 3%, given the original much higher salary – more than 30 times higher than the pension. There can be no argument that this 3% increase is infinitely preferable to the "whopping" 10% pension increase. . ..
- You of course are aware of this, so the question arises as to why you should put yourself in the position possibly of helping to lay blame for existing inequalities and hardships suffered by younger people at the door of the elderly, thereby risking hostility to the old by the young. And also why you should allow yourself and your excellent programme to be party to the time-honoured traditions of politicians and others which disguise and obfuscate the obscene inequalities and widespread poverty that exist in our society, in this instance among pensioners'.

From letter to BBC presenter, 3rd July 2022.

1. INTRODUCTION

The issues raised in this letter (and chapter) are primarily those of obfuscation – obfuscation of the value of the actual amount of the increase to pensioners; obfuscation of the equity or inequity of this rise; no mention of the history or context of pension rates; the absence of any comparisons with pensions in other countries or indeed with the economic situations of others in this country, where wider inequities put pensioners, among others, at the sharp end of the wealth graph of the population in this country (Barnard, 2023). One of course could excuse the presenter on this occasion as it was just one item in a busy, high profile news programme, where there was time only for 'headlines'. A counter argument might be that an alternative headline might have been about the low ranking of UK pensions in relation to that in many other countries.

What is perhaps even more interesting is why the presenter adopted this stance. As pointed out in my letter, he, an experienced economist, would have been well aware of the actual paucity of the pension increase. So why did he permit himself this obfuscation? It is outside the parameters of this chapter to speculate as to whether an instruction came from above, or whether it is because of the general political and ideological atmosphere which ignores or derides such inequalities, a subject very much of concern here.

This chapter is about the way discourse in various forms serves to disguise and justify the inequalities in this society; legitimising and 'naturalising' them, or in Arendt's words 'lying' about them so that they are seen as 'natural and self-evident' (Alvesson & Deetz, 2006, p. 261). Issues looked at are the institutional arrangements by which government ministers give or withhold resources to and from certain categories of citizens. This includes the UK Treasury in relation to which economic groups the Chancellor of the Exchequer decides how much to tax or not to tax.[3,4] What are examined are the discourses justifying these measures and establishing certain 'truths' about how things are economically and socially; which categories are entitled to or deserving of certain kinds of resources and which are not – argued here as constituting obfuscations of the 'actual' situation. The 'actual situation' is examined in terms of how different categories of people are taxed and particularly the value of tax relief awarded to certain economic strata, an amount which is lost to the exchequer, to potential improvements in public services and the welfare system, and therefore lost to the population as a whole.

2. SOCIAL CONSTRUCTIONS OR IMPOSITIONS OF VISIONS OF THE SOCIAL WORLD

At least from as early as Marx, social theorists have pointed out how dominant classes seek to impose their vision of the world as being universally true and, what is important here, fair and therefore justified – not least so that the structures in society, which work to the advantage of these privileged groups, continue to be reproduced. Bourdieu has described the dominant group as the 'real class', which

> ...is nothing but the realized class, that is the mobilized class, a result of the *struggle of classifications,* which is a properly symbolic (and political) struggle to impose a vision of the social world, or, better, a way to construct that world ... (Bourdieu, 1998, p. 11) (emphasis original)

What strengthens the credibility and position of this 'realised class' is, as suggested in the above quotation, the achievement of unifying symbols such as the imposition of names recognised and used by all in this group (Bourdieu, 1998). And as argued by Marx and others including Bourdieu, and as demonstrated in this chapter, these names and the concepts associated with them become accepted throughout society and serve to help justify the structures and policies instituted by the government, whether they are in the interests of the majority; work against them or work against a smaller section of the population.

Almost by definition these symbolic actions tend to obfuscate the strategies of a dominant class or group. Bourdieu argues that domination is not the direct and simple action exercised through the power of the dominant class. Rather it is 'the indirect effect of a complex set of actions' (Bourdieu, 1998, p. 34). It is the aim of this chapter to unpack some of those related to discourses to do with current social and economic inequalities in the UK, as well as government strategies that would have been unthinkable to a previous government, and, arguably, are in the interests of the dominant class alone.

3. DISCOURSE AND IDEOLOGY

The concept of discourse has been used by many theorists stemming at least from continental critical philosophers from the later decades of the 20th century (Alvesson & Deetz, 2006). Discourse has been distinguished from language in its contesting the neutrality of language and other forms of communication. Discourse is essentially a political tool, and, as is argued in this chapter, serves in large measure to fulfil the objectives of powerful interests and institutions, including those of the state, rather than disclosing facts which might be ideologically or practically inconvenient.

The notion of dominant ideas (here translated as dominant discourses) being accepted and adopted by the general populace, was part of Marx' theory that the ideas of dominant classes would become the dominant ideology held by the majority of people (Alvesson & Deetz, 2006). This concept of dominant classes' ideas influencing the beliefs of the general populace has been taken up by many critical theorists, offering this as an explanation for why the majority of the populace have not only allowed, but actually supported those in dominant and potentially exploitative relationships to itself.

This idea continued to be developed by critical theorists such as Lukács (1971) who argued that sectional interests were often treated as universally beneficial to everyone, and as natural and self-evident, rather than as contestable choices. Critical writers such as Braverman (1974), Lukes (1974), Edwards (1979), Clegg and Dunkerley (1980), and Salaman (1981) were particularly interested in the fact that in democratic societies the majority voted in politicians who were likely to act principally in the interests of the most powerful economic, political, and social strata, and largely against the interests of the majority of the voting public (Alvesson & Deetz, 2006).

According to Mészáros:

> In Western capitalist societies liberal/conservative ideological discourse dominates the assessment of all values to such an extent that very often we do not have the slightest suspicion that we are made to accept, quite unquestioningly, a particular set of values to which one could oppose a well founded alternative outlook . . .. For the very act of entering the

framework of the dominant ideological discourse inevitably presents one with the pre-established 'rational' determination of: (a) how much (or how little) should be allowed to be considered contestable at all; (b) from what point of view, and (c) to which end in mind. (Mészáros, 1989, pp. 3–4)

Directed to the same aim is concealment of how things are, in this instance, the extent and pervasiveness of social and economic inequality in UK and other societies, and how current economic and social policies initiated by governments and other powerful institutions can serve to maintain and increase inequality. In 1972 Fetscher wrote that

The smaller the privileged class, the greater is its *interest in the concealment of the real social conditions* .... (Fetscher, 1972) (emphasis original)

4. ON LYING

A few years after Derrida's above quote, Spire, citing Hannah Arendt, put to Derrida the notion that politics was very much about lying:

La politique est sans doute un lieu privilégié du mensonge.[5]

He continued:

Hannah Arendt le rappelle à plusieurs reprises dans *Vérité et politique*, en insistant sur les ravages de la manipulation de masse, la réécriture de l'histoire, la fabrication d'images saissisantes étant le propre de tous les gouvernements.[6] (Spire, 2005)

Arendt certainly saw lying as endemic in politics. She stated that

.... no one, as far as I know, has ever counted truthfulness among the political virtues. Lies have always been regarded as necessary and justifiable tools not only of the politician's or the demagogue's but also of the statesman's trade. (Arendt, 2022, p. 3)

Arendt allows for some political lies to be justified in the interests, for example of the collective good, it being the most important duty of politicians to ensure that their societies continue to function. However, when one is considering constitutional democracies there are dangers, as Bromwich points out, in his introduction to Arendt's book. He argues that the 'self-understanding of the people' which supports governments is under threat from challenges of the legality of elections, and now of the judicial system, and there is a need for the careful keeping of records and correction of errors to restore political integrity and dignity (Bromwich, 2022, p. xi).

Lying is not a straightforward matter. As Derrida (2005) has pointed out, there are different types of lies; different degrees; knowing/not knowing whether one is lying; telling untruths or withholding information; deceiving others or oneself; lying for a good end – discussed, controversially, by Kant (Derrida, 2005). Kant, according to Derrida, maintained that one had to be truthful on all occasions even when lying would have meant the saving of a friend's life from, for example, criminal pursuers (Derrida confessed to being put into a state of 'désarroi' (confusion) by Kant's position (Derrida, 2005, p. 100)). The question arises as to what extent obfuscation, mentioned earlier, also counts as lying.

5. INTENTIONAL LYING

Intentionality, according to Derrida (2005), is all important. Intentionality, according to him, and to the dominant philosophical view on lying is about an intentional will directed at certain themes. Those who speak and those who listen should both be tuned into the same themes regarding what they want to say and what they want to hear. But if their representations are at fault in their being unclear or ambiguous through the use of language concerned with mere style or effect rather than with truth, substance, or meaning, this would disable people from having the criteria to distinguish lies from non-lies.

According to Derrida, because lying is concerned with language, rhetorical devices such as tropes and ambiguities which rely on the fact that one does not say exactly what one wants to say in the way one would like to say it, it is often difficult to prove that a lie has been told. One can more easily demonstrate that someone has not told the truth or that they have been guilty of deception than that they have actually lied (Derrida, 2005).

Then there is the matter of half-truths, which, according to Derrida, is hugely problematic. There is the question of lying by omission, also important in Bhaskar's analysis of the importance of a 'more holistic, totalising analysis' without absences (Bhaskar, 1998, p. xxi), particularly those to do with alterity (Bhaskar, 2008). Although the issue here is not scholarship, which was Bhaskar's concern, the same reasoning applies. Omission and absence, it will be argued, are particularly relevant to those considered 'other' – in this case the poor and the variously disadvantaged.

Less problematic in terms of whether it constitutes dishonesty is deliberate concealment. Arendt makes the interesting point that facts known to the public, can, by that same public

> ...successfully and often spontaneously, taboo their public discussion and treat them as though they were what they are not – namely secrets. (Arendt, 2022, p. 16)

This can be seen in the journalist's representation of the pension increase, keeping 'secret', one could argue, the poor pension provisions in the United Kingdom in comparison with many other countries, and thereby making the pension increase appear much more sizeable than how it would be experienced by many pensioners. Another example is the current Business and Trade secretary's exhortation for people to stop talking about the Brexit vote. According to Mahmood (2023a) she was supposed to be strongly in favour of free speech.

6. FACT AND OPINION

Arendt makes the further and hugely significant point that factual truths that are unwelcome in certain powerful quarters become treated as if they were opinions. One glaring example of this is the government's recent immigration policy which is being considered for breaches of human rights (Grogan, 2023). Although this had been unwillingly acknowledged by a previous Home Secretary, it did not stop the [then] Prime Minister and Home Secretary from decrying opponents to the policy of sending refugees to Rwanda.[7] The Home Secretary accused the Labour Party of being in favour of 'open borders and unlimited immigration' (Behr, 2023). Opponents of the Rwandan policy were tarred many times with the brush of being 'lefty' lawyers. The Prime Minister described the government as being

> ...hamstrung by what the [then] Home Secretary would doubtless and rightly call the lefty human rights lawyers and other do-gooders. (McKinney, 2022)

This was criticised by the Bar Council and Law Society, which asked that Prime Minister to 'stop attacks on legal professionals' (McKinney, 2022).

Sunak the current Prime Minister similarly blamed Starmer, the Leader of the Opposition, for being a 'lefty lawyer' during a heated Prime Minister's Question Time (PMQs) on Wednesday 8th March 2023:

> He wanted to, in his words, scrap the Rwanda deal, he voted against measures to deport foreign criminals, and he even argued against deportation flights. We know why, because on this matter - he talked about his legal background - he is just another lefty lawyer standing in our way, the prime minister said. (Fouzder, 2023)

The inhumanity of the Rwanda 'deal' let alone its legality are ignored in these statements. An emotive argument against 'lefties' is substituted to arouse public hostility against opponents of the policy without entering into questions such as its legality. Sunak was similarly criticised by the Bar Council Chair for betraying 'a startling and regrettable ignorance about the role of lawyers in society' (Fouzder, 2023).

7. DISCOURSES PROMOTING AMBIGUITY AND OBFUSCATION

The examples given below, it is argued, serve to maintain and promote existing power structures and social and economic inequalities. This is shown through the naming of different processes and outcomes similarly, 'absenting' their differences although they result in very different outcomes for people according to their wealth and power in society, and conversely, the naming of particular processes and outcomes differently although they are in effect similar. These discourses serve to legitimate, protect, and hugely better the interests and bank balances of the well-to-do, and to delegitimate, to their significant disadvantage, the interests and material conditions of the poor, the unemployed, the sick and disabled, of others on the margins of society, and, increasingly also of the better-off middle classes.

Withholding information, disguising information or creating ambiguity are perhaps the types of lying most relevant to the discussion on obfuscation regarding wealth and income inequality in the UK and probably in many other countries too. Spire (2005) makes the point that philosophers from Aristotle to Heidegger, Saint Augustine, Rousseau and Kant have argued that there is a wealth of difference between an accidental lie and a deliberate use of language which invites ambiguity and uncertainty. For the purposes of this chapter the way language is used results in different distributions of resources to different groups or classes. It has been shown for a long time that resources made available to the wealthier, and particularly to the most wealthy have been described in positive terms, while those distributed (or withheld) from the poorest and most disadvantaged have negative connotations. Conversely, the same name has been used for different regulatory measures with different outcomes for different economic and social strata in the UK. It has been used with great effect regarding the umbrella concept of 'taxation', discussed later.

8. 'WE'RE ALL IN THIS TOGETHER'

'We're all in this together' was used to justify the austerity programme initiated by Cameron who became Prime Minister in 2010 and by Osborne, his Chancellor of the Exchequer (Brady et al., 2012), a programme still in place if not in name. This slogan and concept was used to justify the 'tightening of belts', principally the tightening of public services, including the health and social services and welfare provision. The wealthier had recourse to private health care and had less need of social services and benefits. There was no regulatory imposition on the wealthier and particularly the wealthiest, in the way of higher taxation, the consequences of which are discussed later. So, rather than everyone being 'in it together', it resulted in the imposition of severe hardship on many of the most disadvantaged in British society who were dependent on benefits (discussed below) and other social services from the state and from local councils (Green, 2016).

9. NORMALISATION OF THE ABNORMAL

One type of deception which is not strictly lying, but which has enormous implications for questions of social and economic inequality is what Bromwich has described as making the 'strange somehow familiar, to normalise the abnormal' (Bromwich, 2022, p. xvi). The austerity programme has led to the normalisation of the abnormal. The situations described below, often engendered or allowed by the state, and previously regarded as unacceptable and even unthinkable, have become, as Bromwich described it, normalised. What was removed was the social security 'blanket' – the ideology and system which took hold after World War II, with the idea that along with the provision of public services for all, the poorest and most disadvantaged should be protected from the utter poverty and degradation suffered by the worst off, and should have a minimal, decent standard of living. From this was born universal education until the age of 16, the National Health Service which would be free for all citizens, and a system of benefits that would ensure that people out of work or on incomes insufficient for a minimal standard of living would have protection (The Cabinet Papers, n.d.).

Despite earlier inroads into the system, such as the reduction in provisions of social housing from the 1970s, and increased under successive governments (Beckett, 2015); and the abolition of free university education in 1998 (Anderson, 2016), far more serious threats came with the introduction of the austerity programme in 2010.[8] Huge cuts were made to public services including the National Health Service, the welfare system, higher education through the abolition of grants in 2016, the police and other public services. The imposition of austerity measures, arguably still very much current although not called 'austerity' (another obfuscation), has caused impoverishment, degradation, and death to many tens of thousands (Arrieta, 2023).

10. DIFFERENT NAMES FOR SIMILAR ACTIONS BY THE STATE

To misquote George Orwell in his famous line in *Animal Farm* 'Four legs good, two legs bad' one might say: 'subsidies' and 'grants' – 'good', 'benefits' – 'bad'.[9] These are different names for funding by the state, but with very different connotations. The funding goes to different classes of people – benefits to the poor and disadvantaged; subsidies and grants to the wealthier, and in many cases as seen below, to the extremely wealthy.

What is at issue is the huge subject of monies given to people by the state. Most publicity is generally given to what have been called 'benefits' – the support for people who are poor and disadvantaged, either because they are not in employment, because they are in poor health or because they suffer a disability – physical or mental. And increasingly, people who are in employment also qualify for some benefits because the wages they receive are inadequate for their basic needs. This is not to say that such benefits are an adequate support. There are two problems here: the adequacy of the amounts awarded to people as benefits, and for many, the size of their earnings. A third problem is the connotation that 'benefits' are given to the 'undeserving poor' – to people who are described as lazy, workshy, feckless, and scroungers.[10] On the other hand, as demonstrated below, the same obfuscation appears at the other extreme: people who are awarded 'subsidies' or 'grants' are often the wealthy, who are given these without any consideration or discussion of their salaries and other sources of income, and with no negative connotations of the awarding of these monies.

The paucity of benefit provision became clear early on in the austerity period (Green, 2016). An example which hit the headlines was the case of David Clapson, living in Essex. He was a diabetic and was dependent on benefit payments from the job centre. Because he missed two appointments at the job centre he had his benefits cut completely. This led directly to his death. He was a diabetic, and because his benefits were cancelled, so was his electricity. This resulted in his life-saving insulin no longer being useable, and he died of diabetic ketoacidosis. It was found that he had hardly any food (six tea bags, an old tin of sardines and a can of soup); hardly any credit on his mobile phone and a bank account containing £3.44. His 'punishment' was entirely unjustified even by the harsh standards introduced with the austerity programme. He had actively been seeking work, demonstrated by the pile of CVs found near his body (Gentleman, 2014).

This was not an isolated case. Within 1 year of the introduction of these regulation, it was estimated that 871,000 people had lost some or all of their benefits for periods of between 4 weeks and 3 years (Gentleman, 2014). Mistakes made also took their toll. Between 2011 and 2014 approximately 70,000 chronically ill and disabled people lost benefits totalling £340 million. This was due to an error when a new system was introduced. Five thousand of them died before they could be reimbursed (Quinn, 2020).

An even more horrific example, possibly, is the way some people in care homes were treated. According to an article in the Daily Mail, elderly and disabled people in care homes were 'put up for auction' on 'eBay-style' websites by local councils, with details of their age, and the care and medication they needed. Care companies were then asked to bid to offer them a bed. The cheapest offer was usually the one taken up. If a provider's bid was considered too high, it was given the opportunity to lower it or offer extra care services. This has been described as a cattle market for grannies and the auctioning of old people. The report then went on to highlight the already inadequate provision in care homes and the high proportion failing to meet basic standards of safety and care (Lythe & Duffin, Mail Online 8 February 2015).

In the early days of austerity, between 2012 and 2013 over 860,000 people had their benefits 'sanctioned', a term for a cut or a complete cancelation in the money they had received (Jones, 2015). This was often done, according to Jones, for trivial reasons, such as missing a signing-on day, misinterpreting a question on a form and giving a 'wrong' answer, or missing an interview about which the claimant had not been informed. It was also done by people who were in competition with one another to see which team could sanction the highest number of people, the winning team showing 'gleeful delight'. A lack of sanctioning meant 'letting the side down' (Jones, 2015, p. 243).

People died as a result of these cuts or cancellations of their benefits for the inconsequential reasons mentioned above, or because they had serious health conditions which were not seen as reasons for them not to be in full-time employment (Green, 2016; Jones, 2015). This was exacerbated by the privatisation of the welfare benefits system to companies which were inefficient, careless of people's needs, and interested primarily in making money. One firm was paid

£500 million for a five-contract, which it was forced to give up for under-performance and routinely failing to meet standards (Jones, 2015).

It has been estimated that in the 4 years between 2010/2011 and 2014/2015, decreases in the financing of health and social care led directly to an additional 57,550 deaths (Martin et al., 2023). More recent statistics regarding additional deaths have been hidden from the public. A recent Secretary of State for Work and Pensions (DWP) refused to publish reports on the deaths of claimants and on the impact of various benefit sanctions.[11] According to Tapper (2022) the DWP started internal process reviews regarding the deaths of claimants possibly linked to benefit sanctions in 2019 after one claimant, Errol Graham, had died of starvation in 2018. Between 2019 and 2022 the DWP engaged in 140 internal process reviews.

The DWP Secretary of State also refused to publish the extent of support for vulnerable people regarding particular benefits, nor statistics on people with disabilities who were deemed fit for work (Tapper, 2022). This deliberate concealment of the facts could be considered to be a form of lying. It is one of Arendt's examples: being secretive about information that should be made available to the public. What have been published are statistics on previous benefits such as Personal Independence Payments.[12] In 2022, about 327,000 people were experiencing payment delays of up to 5 months. These were not regarded as a priority (Tapper, 2022).

The normalisation of previously unthinkable behaviour and outcomes regarding the poorest and most vulnerable in society is compounded by statements denying the extent of poverty and deprivation in this society, which is considered to have the sixth largest economy in the world (Danielian, 2022).

11. WHAT I TELL YOU THREE TIMES IS TRUE[13]

11.1 Food Banks

One set of denials from at least 2014 has been to do with the reasons for people using food banks – food that is organised by many charities and given freely, without payment, to people. One explanation for the vastly increased use of food banks has been the austerity programme with its reduction or cutting of benefits (Sosenko et al., 2022). The then Coalition Government denied that usage of food banks was connected to increases in benefits sanctions (Webster, 2014).[14] This denial was disproved by the evidence submitted to an all-party parliamentary inquiry in 2014. The huge escalation of benefit sanctions had resulted in desti-tution for poor claimants who 'inevitably' became dependent on food banks. The growth in food bank usage corresponded to the increase in benefit sanctions: those subjected to benefit sanctions were a substantial proportion of food bank users and likewise a substantial proportion of those sanctioned used food banks (Webster, 2014).

11.2 Blaming the Victims

There have been strong denials about the necessity for food banks at all, or certainly for the number of people using them. These denials, despite continuing evidence to the contrary, have continued to the present. One of the most notorious denials, where blame was attributed to food bank users, was made by a Conservative MP, recently appointed Deputy Chairman of the Conservative Party, the party in government. In 2022, he claimed that people who used food banks did so because they couldn't cook properly or manage their finances, despite the counter arguments by Members of Parliament (MPs) from the Labour Party and the Scottish National Party that there was poverty on a scale that should have shamed the government (Rojas, 2022). The Labour Party MP's actual response was:

> The idea that the problem is cooking skills and not 12 years of Government decisions that are pushing people into extreme poverty is beyond belief. Out of touch doesn't even cover it. (Rojas, 2022)

Research published in 2022 confirmed these statements. The 'overwhelming majority of users of food banks were severely food insecure'. The causes shown to be statistically significant included four (out of seven) that were related to poverty caused by the welfare system: the value of 'out-of-work benefit; the roll-out of Universal Credit; benefit sanctions and the "bedroom tax" in social housing' (Sosenko et al., 2022).[15,16]

This did not stop the Deputy Chairman of the Conservative Party from reiterating this claim. In March 2023 he stated that families who ate at McDonald's and at the same time used food banks were abusing the system (Forrest, 2023). Yet if one compares McDonald's price for a hamburger (0.99p) (McDonald's, 2023) with Tesco's (65p to £2.25, with the majority of hamburgers priced at £1) (Tesco.com, 2023), it does not look like an abuse of the system at all. McDonald's prices are favourable to Tesco's, especially when one takes into account the bun and garnish, not to mention the additional energy costs that would be spent at home on storing, cooking and washing up. This official seemed to know nothing of McDonald's nor of the largest supermarket's prices for what for many was a staple food. He is in good company. A previous Prime Minister and Chancellor of the Exchequer had been caught out not knowing the price of a pint of milk (Barford, 2012; BBC News, 2018).

More recently at the Conservative Party Conference in October 2023, the same Deputy Chairman of the Conservative Party declared that it was 'nonsense' to claim that there was poverty in this country now:

> If you want something you can get it. You need to get off your arse and go and get it for yourself. (Mahmood, 2023b)

This statement was made despite the research mentioned above and the End Child Poverty Coalition's assessment that there were an extra 600,000 children plunged into poverty in 1 year because of the government's cancelation of extra support for families claiming Universal Credit (Mahmood, 2023b). The Joseph

Rowntree Foundation too had published a report in January 2023 which claimed that more than one million children had experienced destitution in 2022 – that is that they did not have adequate food, clothing, clean conditions or warmth. All in all, 13.4 million people were considered to be living in poverty in 2020–2021 – one in five of the population (Joseph Rowntree Foundation, 2023). This was a doubling in the last 5 years, owing to benefit cuts and cost of living pressures (Butler, 2023).

There is a long tradition of blaming the victims rather than the perpetrators. One notable instance was in 1992 when the then Secretary of State at the Department of Social Security, Lilley, entertained an earlier Conservative Party conference in 1992. He wanted to 'close down the something for nothing society', which he infamously outlined through an imitation of the Lord High Executioner's 'little list' song from *The Mikado* by Gilbert and Sullivan. In this imitation he accused some benefit claimants of making bogus claims, others of sponging on the state for left-wing political causes, and young women of deliberately getting pregnant in order to get housing ahead of more legitimate claimants (BBC, 2007, cited in Wikipedia).

In a recent letter to *The Guardian* it was pointed out that there have been decades where the myth has been perpetrated of wealth and success being earned through ability and hard work, and the poor having only their personal shortcomings to blame. The writer goes on to state that

> No political party ... has dared draw attention to the reality that most wealth and success stems from a mix of good fortune and the appropriation of other people's resources and labour over centuries. (Mardell, 2023)

She goes on to argue that

> The current distribution of wealth and success is a consequence of political decisions, and of a determination by those benefitting from the system to hold on to what they've got. Yes, a handful of individuals can make a quantum leap from poverty to fortune, but most are constrained by the realities of an economic system that has, for decades, seen a reduction in the share of the national wealth going to those reliant on their own labour for income. (Mardell, 2023)

12. 'WE ARE WHERE WE ARE' ...

The potential dishonesty here lies in the implication that one cannot do anything to change 'where we are'. This idea has been put forward by both Conservative and Labour politicians, notably in discussions about whether or not more money can be made available for public and services and benefits. The example that was clearly shown to be false, ridiculed and now part of English idiom, were the then Home Secretary's and Prime Minister's assertions in 2017 that there was 'no magic money tree' in response to requests for more finance for the NHS. However, Boait (2017) has pointed out that there are in fact two main money trees: commercial high street banks, which, for example, can make loans; and the central bank, the Bank of England, which can create billions through

Quantitative Easing. The problem with the money trees was that they were used selectively – mainly for financial and property markets, raising asset and stock prices, which served to make the rich richer – and not for what the public needed (Boait, 2017). The amount of money that would be available with a different taxation system would, as demonstrated below, release eye-watering sums and make an extremely large money tree, if not a forest of money trees.

13. THE SAME NAME FOR DIFFERENT ACTIONS BY THE STATE

13.1 Percentage Increases

One example of the same name having very different practical outcomes are percentage increases. Percentage increases are normally used when discussing rises in people's salaries. As shown in the letter to the BBC presenter, what this does is disguise the amount of the addition, and serves to minimise and obfuscate the actual monies involved. The highest paid salaried person in the world in 2022 was the footballer, Lionel Messi, who earned $130 million dollars from his salary and endorsements (Myson, 2022). In percentage terms, 10% of this would be $13 million; 1% adds up to $1.3 million, and a 0.1% increase in Messi's salary would add up to $130,000. To get anywhere near to the 10% pension increase of £963 mentioned earlier, the percentage increase in Messi's salary would be approximately 0.001%, amounting to $1,300 – 10,000 times less of a percentage increase. In other words, a 10% increase for Messi would be approximately 10,000 times more in value than a 10% increase for pensioners.

Yet salary increases and other money transactions are often discussed in percentage increases rather than in actual amounts – disguising the smallness of some increases, as in the case of the pensioners, and doing the opposite in the case of seemingly small percentage increases on large amounts. It can be argued that this is an example of the obfuscation of the actual scale of inequalities in this society and also of the processes involved in decisions regarding the allocation of resources.

13.2 Taxation

Taxation is probably the most important mechanism for determining and regulating the distribution of wealth and income in the UK, and, as some have argued, globally (Bhambra, 2021).[17] Taxation, as demonstrated below, has different outcomes for different economic strata and for those pursuing different types of economic activity. Yet the umbrella term 'taxation' is used. It is a subject that is often not discussed - the elephant in the room. If it is discussed, it is usually discussed in negative terms – the old 'bogey' and something to be avoided. It is considered to be so unpopular with the public, that any suggestion of progressive taxation policies could lose elections for political parties advocating them (Diamond, 2022).

Bhaskar (1993), basing his ideas on Hegel, has unpacked the concept of absence manifesting as negation, in the guises of incompleteness, inexplicitness, and inconsistency. He discusses the broader question of paradigmatic 'monovalence', which disregards other approaches and possibilities and leads to the screening of human existential questions. Absences act as 'constraints' on want and needs and on well-being more generally (Bhaskar, 1993, pp. 40, 42). One such absence is where the concepts of tax and taxation are treated as a universal, ignoring or 'absenting' the different types of taxation there are and more importantly who is best able to pay tax and the extent to which they should be taxed. Other issues absented are to do with the purposes of taxation and how fiscal policies affect different social and economic strata.

13.3 Different 'Logics' Regarding Taxation

There are different logics, emphases, and foci regarding taxation: how much the wealthiest in society should pay; the extent to which they should shoulder the obligation to support those less advantaged in society; or whether their tax contributions should simply be weighed in comparison to others'. Generally, concepts such as the richest having a responsibility to ensure that everyone in the society has the basic requirements for an adequate life in terms of food, shelter, medical care, physical protection, and a good education which would give all the chance of a decent job, career, and life chances, are not part of current political or any other mainstream discourse.

On being questioned about the extent of inequality in this country an MP justified the current tax system on the grounds that it was similar to that in other countries and that the richest 5% paid the most tax (50%). His argument for income taxes being progressive was that: the wealthiest paid the most amount of tax.

Because the tax was 'progressive' according to the MP, the wealthiest should therefore not be taxed further. Generally, the subject is avoided by the right because, as this MP argued, the tax system is a fair one and needs no alteration or scrutiny. On the left, the subject is often avoided for fear of it being used as a successful election stick to beat it with and to endanger its chances of winning elections.

Personal Communication with MP, 15th May 2023.[18]

This was one reason given for the Labour Party losing the 1992 General Election. Diamond (2022) described the budget suggested by the then leader of the Labour Party, John Smith, as 'infamous', as it was in favour of increasing child benefit and the state pension. The way it would be funded would be by raising National Insurance contributions on higher-income earners. This was used against Labour by the Conservative-supporting tabloid media who described these measures as a tax bombshell, and represented Labour as a threat to the livelihoods and aspirations of many 'Middle England' voters.[19]

90 *What's in a Name*

Diamond sees any repetition of such suggestions as highly risky for the chances of the Labour Party winning the next election, as these could be represented as constituting an existential threat to the aspirations of the new working and middle-class voters and their increasingly precarious personal prosperity (Diamond, 2022).

13.4 Effects of Current Tax System on Inequality

The personal prosperity of the new working and middle-classes that Diamond mentioned, their personal well-being in terms of an adequate health service, adequate protection through the security of a financial safety blanket, physical protection in terms of a large enough and uncorrupted police force and a decent education for their children and for them as adults, have been eroded by the austerity programme, and are in fact at risk from further erosion because of the increasing withdrawal of funding from public services and the equally serious retreat by the government from its responsibility for providing those services (Green, 2016).

If one considers tax regulations and the way the system is weighted, it does not favour the new working and middle-class voters. In 2023, Sikka showed how the tax system, instead of reducing inequalities and redistributing income and wealth, was regressive and does the reverse. It levies lower taxes on the rich and deepens inequalities (Sikka, 2023).

He had pointed out in 2022 that UK households were facing a huge decline in disposable income because of increases in energy, food, and transport bills, with wages below rates of inflation (Sikka, 2022).

In 2023, he unpacked the system of taxation which supported his contention that the tax system deepened inequalities, favouring those who profited from unearned income as against those who earned income by working:

- earned income recipients, both salaried and self-employed were taxed as follows:
  - a tax-free annual allowance of £12,570
  - 20% income tax on income between £12,571 and £50,270; 40% on income between £50,270 and £125,140; 45% on income above £125,140
  - National Insurance (NI) at the rate of 12% on income between £12,570 and £50,270, with only 2% on income above £50,271[20]
- unearned income, for example through capital gains, the stock market and commodities speculations, the sale of second homes, artwork and antiques, businesses and other investments, were taxed at lower rates:
  - the tax free allowance was less - £6,000, but ...
  - they were taxed at the lower rates of between 10% and 28%
  - there were no NI contributions, although these taxpayers also used the NHS and social care.

(Sikka, 2023)

MIRIAM GREEN

Sikka went on to compare two people with the identical gross annual income of £32,000. One was a worker on earned income; the other a speculator who had made £32,000 in capital gains. Sikka calculated that the worker would receive £25,782 after the personal allowance deduction (£12,570), income tax at 20% (£3,886), and NI at 12% (£2,332). The speculator would receive £29,400 after the capital gains allowance (£6,000), capital gains tax at 10% (£2,600). There was no NI tax for the speculator. So the worker would pay £6,218 as tax and NI; the speculator would pay tax of £2,600. The worker paid 19.4% of their wage in income tax and NI; the speculator only 8.1%. Sikka showed the additional inequality here if one took into account usage of the NHS and social care: the worker on earned income paid £3,618 more in tax and NI and had a lower take home pay; the speculator also used the NHS and social care, as a 'free ride' as they paid no NI and took home £3,618 more than the worker (Sikka, 2023).

These differences pale into insignificance when one considers the capital gains made by the very wealthy. HMRC's capital gains statistics for 2021–2022 showed that 394,000 people accrued £92.4 billion. They paid capital gains of £16.7 billion, but no NI. This is a rate of just over 18%. If they had been taxed at the same rate as earned income, an additional £17 billion would have been collected in tax. If they had had to pay NI, this would have added another £8 billion. So the rich were given a tax perk of £25 billion. The highest gains however were made by the very wealthy. Those who earned more than £5 million only paid 20% tax from investments and 28% from property gains instead of the 45% rate for those in employment (Sikka, 2023).

This is not where subsidies for the wealthy stop. There are various tax reliefs which mainly benefit the very few, and which are worth hundreds of billions that could be added to the public coffers. According to Sikka (2022) there are about 1,140 different tax reliefs worth £480.2 billion. Then there is tax relief on approved pension schemes which mainly benefits those paying 40%–45% income tax. This is worth around £42.7 billion. Those on lower incomes receive half the tax relief of those on higher incomes. Sikka estimated that if everyone were on the lower rate of tax relief, this would give the government an extra £10 billion. NI is another case where those earning between £12,571 and £50,270 pay 13.25% national insurance as compared with those earning more, who pay only 3.25% (Sikka, 2022). If one adds up these estimates, the government is giving away £557.9 billion annually to the wealthiest. This is money that could be spent on public services for everyone, including health and social care provision; with more aid to the poorest, most vulnerable and disadvantaged, enabling them to live decently and independently.

Despite the assertion by the MP mentioned above that the tax system was progressive, Sikka's conclusion is:

> The UK tax system is regressive. It penalises worker, pensioners and their families. It rewards speculators and rentiers. If favours financial speculation over the hard graft of work. It shows that our political system is disconnected from the masses. Ministers increasingly identify with the richer classes and care little about the plight of low/middle income families. (Sikka, 2022)

14. CONCLUSION

Arguably, this is dangerous stuff. The power of discourse, obfuscation, straight denials, and the different methods of lying, have for the moment made the multiple state strategies intent on maintaining and increasing these huge inequalities acceptable to and accepted by the majority of the population in the UK. This may continue; it has for many decades.

But how long such a situation is sustainable is open to question. If the general public or a substantial section of it becomes aware of these huge inequalities, their obfuscation, and the effects on their own standards of living and well-being, the system could become unsustainable and lead to political upheavals and a swing to the fascist far right, already happening in parts of Europe. Tony Judt predicted just this happening more than 25 years ago, and for these reasons (Judt, 1997).

There is much more at risk. According to Arendt, it is much more than deception about particular issues. What is at stake is the sustainability of 'common and factual reality itself'. Like Judt she foresees the consequences for trust in politics as potentially huge: the downgrading or degradation of truth being a danger for democracy and a haven for tyranny (Arendt, 2022, p. 17).

NOTES

1. British Broadcasting Corporation. This is a British public service broadcasting service.

2. The Organisation for Economic Co-operation and Development is a forum where the governments of 37 democracies with market-based economies collaborate to develop policy standards to promote sustainable economic growth.

3. The UK Treasury is the government's economic and finance department, responsible for control over public spending and the government's economic policy.

4. The Chancellor of the Exchequer is *the government's chief finance officer. Shelhe is* one of the most senior members of the Cabinet, and is responsible for raising government revenue through taxation and other means, and for public spending.

5. Politics is without doubt an arena which favours lying.

6. Hannah Arendt recalls this on several occasions in *Truth and politics*, emphasising the toll from mass manipulation, the rewriting of history and the fabrication of striking images being within the remit of all governments.

7. The Home Secretary is in charge of the Home Office, an important ministerial department of the UK government. It is responsible for immigration, security, law, and order, policing in England and Wales, and the fire and rescue service in England.

8. The most affordable housing, linked to local incomes.

9. Orwell (1945).

10. A phrase made famous in George Bernard Shaw's *Pygmalion*, 1913.

11. The Department for Work and Pensions is the UK's largest public service department and is responsible for welfare, pensions, and child maintenance policy.

12. Personal Independence Payments (PIPs) are for a long-term physical or mental health condition or disability (Gov.UK).

13. The Bellman in Lewis Carroll (1876) *The Hunting of the Snark*.

14. There was a Coalition Government between the Conservatives and the Liberal Democrats from 2010 to 2015.

15. Universal Credit is a benefit for those on low incomes with less than £16,000 in monies, savings or investments (Gov.UK).

16. The 'bedroom tax' led to a reduction in benefits for those considered to be under-occupying their social housing property, for example, having more than one

MIRIAM GREEN

bedroom for a couple (Money Helper). This was the case even if the extra bedroom was needed for example for someone with certain disabilities.

17. Bhambra has pointed out that taxation among other things was extracted from the colonies and redistributed to the metropolis, the UK, serving to support the war efforts and a welfare state.

18. Yet, this Conservative MP was not averse from considering the burden on the poorest when criticising the Labour London Mayor for regressive burdens on the poorest through his imposition of a tax on higher polluting older cars: 'The ULEZ [Ultra low emission zone] charge is a regressive tax on the lowest paid, who are the group most likely to own older vehicles subject to daily charges of £12.50 to drive on London's roads, equivalent to over £4,500 a year' (MP, 2023b).

19. The phrase 'Middle England' generally refers to middle class or lower-middle class people in England who are conservative voters traditionally. They are thought to be able to influence election results and are as many live in marginal constituencies and could be swayed by successful campaigning (Wikipedia).

20. National Insurance is similar to income tax, it helps pay for some state benefits to individuals, for example when ill, unemployed, retired, or bereaved.

REFERENCES

Alvesson, M., & Deetz, S. (2006). Critical theory and postmodernism approaches to organization studies. In S. Clegg, C. Hardy, T. B. Lawrence, & W. R. Nord (Eds.), *The Sage handbook of organization studies* (2nd ed., pp. 255–283). Sage.

Anderson, R. (2016). University fees in historical perspective. *History and Policy.* https://www.historyandpolicy.org/policy-papers/papers/university-fees-in-historical-perspective. Accessed on October 3, 2023.

Arendt, H. (2022). *On lying and politics.* Library of America.

Arrieta, T. (2023, January 1). Austerity in the United Kingdom and its legacy: Lessons from the COVID-19 pandemic. *The Economic and Labour Relations Review.* https://www.cambridge.org/core/journals/the-economic-and-labour-relations-review/article/austerity-in-the-united-kingdom-and-its-legacy-lessons-from-the-covid19-pandemic/DB72A7DC5E6009335A4C0D3E15C8AA14. Accessed on October 3, 2023.

Barford, V. (2012). Should politicians know the price of a pint of milk? *BBC News.* https://www.bbc.co.uk/news/magazine-17826509. Accessed on August 16, 2023.

Barnard, H. (2023). How do we defuse the pensioner poverty time bomb? *Joseph Rowntree Foundation.* https://www.jrf.org.uk/blog/how-do-we-defuse-pensioner-poverty-time-bomb. Accessed on September 27, 2023.

BBC. (2007, October 3). Your favourite conference clips. *BBC News Online.* https://en.wikipedia.org/wiki/Peter_Lilley. Accessed on August 16, 2023.

BBC News. (2018). https://www.bbc.co.uk/news/uk-politics-44524605. Accessed on June 18, 2018.

Beckett, A. (2015). The right to buy: The housing crisis that Thatcher built. *The Guardian.* https://www.theguardian.com/society/2015/aug/26/right-to-buy-margaret-thatcher-david-cameron-housing-crisis. Accessed on October 3, 2023.

Behr, R. (2023, March 15). 'Stop the boats': Gimmicks are all the Tories have left to offer. *The Guardian.*

Bhambra, G. (2021, February 24). *A polity divided: Empire, nation and the construction of the British welfare state.* LSE.

Bhaskar, R. (1993). *Dialectic: The pulse of freedom.* Verso.

Bhaskar, R. (1998). General introduction. In M. Archer, R. Bhaskar, A. Collier, T. Lawson, & A. Norrie (Eds.), *Critical realism: Essential readings* (pp. ix–xxiv). Routledge.

Bhaskar, R. (2008). *Dialectic: The pulse of freedom.* Routledge.

Boait, F. (2016/2017). The truth behind the "magic money tree". *Positive Money.* https://positivemoney.org/2017/06/magic-money-tree/. Accessed on October 11, 2023.

Bourdieu, P. (1998). *Practical reason: On the theory of action.* Polity Press.

Brady, B., Dugan, E., & Merrick, J. (2012, January 29). We're all in this together, says PM. Really, Mr Cameron? *The Independent*. https://www.independent.co.uk/news/uk/politics/we-re-all-in-this-together-says-pm-really-mr-cameron-6296344.html. Accessed on October 11, 2023.

Braverman, H. (1974). Labor and monopoly capital. *Monthly Review Press*.

Bromwich, D. (2022). Introduction. In H. Arendt (Ed.), *On lying and politics*. Library of America.

Butler, P. (2023, October 21). Cost of living leaves 1m UK children destitute. *The Guardian*.

Carroll, L. (1876). *The hunting of the snark*. Macmillan and Co.

Clegg, S., & Dunkerly, D. (1980). Organization, Class and control. *Routledge and Kegan Paul*.

Commons Library Research Briefing. (2022, March 11). https://commonslibrary.parliament.uk/type/research-briefing/. Accessed on October 11, 2023.

Danielian, P. (2022, August 30). A fairer measure of Britain's wealth, Letter. *The Guardian*. https://www.theguardian.com/business/2022/aug/30/a-fairer-measure-of-britains-wealth. Accessed on October 3, 2023.

Derrida, J. (2005). *Sur Parole: Instantanés philosophiques*. éditions de l'aube.

Diamond, P. (2022, April 8). It is never 'Labour's turn': Learning from 1992. *Progressive Britain*. https://www.progressivebritain.org/it-is-never-labours-turn-learning-from-1992/. Accessed on August 29, 2023.

Edwards, R., (1979). *Contested terrain: The transformation of the workplace in the twentieth century*. Basic Books.

Fetscher, I. (1972). The young and the old Marx. In S. Avineri (Ed.), *Marx' socialism*. Lieber-Atherton.

Forrest, A. (2023). MP Lee Anderson claims families 'abusing' food banks then taking kids to McDonald's. https://www.independent.co.uk/news/uk/politics/lee-anderson-food-banks-b2292708.html. Accessed on August 16, 2023.

Fouzder, M. (2023, March 8). Sunak criticised for 'startling ignorance' over 'lefty lawyer' attack. *Law Society Gazette*. https://www.lawgazette.co.uk/news/sunak-criticised-for-startling-ignorance-over-lefty-lawyer-attack/5115357.article. Accessed on August 10, 2023.

Gentleman, A. (2014). 'No one should die penniless and alone': The victims of Britains's harsh welfare sanctions. *The Guardian*. @ameliagentleman 3 August 2014 18.00 BST. https://www.theguardian.com/society/2014/aug/03/victims-britains-harsh-welfare-sanctions

Gov.UK. https://www.gov.uk/pip. Accessed on September 29, 2023.

Green, M. (2016). Neoliberalism and management scholarship: Educational implications. *Philosophy of Management, 15*(3), 183–201. https://doi.org/10.1007/s40926-016-0042-x

Grogan, J. (2023). Rwanda policy unlawful: Unpacking the Court of Appeal's decision. *UK in a Changing Europe*. https://ukandeu.ac.uk/rwanda-policy-unlawful-unpacking-the-court-of-appeals-decision/. Accessed on September 29, 2023.

Jones, O. (2015). *The establishment: And how they get away with it*. Penguin Books.

Joseph Rowntree Foundation. (2023, January 26). UK poverty 2023: The essential guide to understanding poverty in the UK. https://www.jrf.org.uk/report/uk-poverty-2023. Accessed on October 26, 2023.

Judt, T. (1997, September–October). The social question redivivus. *Foreign Affairs, 76*(5), 95–117.

Lukács, G. (1971). *History and class consciousness: Studies in Marxist Dialectics* (trans. R. Livingstone). Merlin Press.

Lukes, S. (1974). *Power: A radical view*, Macmillan.

Mahmood, B. (2023a, March 31). Kemi Badenoch says 'stop talking about Brexit vote'. *Left Foot Forward*. https://mail.google.com/mail/u/0/?tab=wm&ogbl#inbox/FMfcgzGslkqVfWRGgxvlVgrlCzFpSFMS. Accessed on August 10, 2023.

Mahmood, B. (2023b, October 4). Disgraceful Tory Deputy Chairman Lee Anderson says 'nonsense' to claim there is poverty. *Left Foot Forward*. https://leftfootforward.org/2023/10/disgraceful-tory-deputy-chairman-lee-anderson-says-nonsense-to-claim-there-is-poverty/?mc_cid=f6c4e1d083&mc_eid=de814083c2. Accessed on October 11, 2023.

Mardell, J. (2023, August 12). Letter to The Guardian.

Martin, S., Longo, F., Lomas, J., & Claxton, K. (2023). Causal impact of social care, public health and healthcare expenditure on mortality in England: Cross-sectional evidence for 2013/2014. *BMJ, 11*(10). https://bmjopen.bmj.com/content/11/10/e046417. Accessed on August 18, 2023.

McDonald's. (2023). https://burgerlad.com/mcdonalds-menu-prices-uk/. Accessed on August 16, 2023.

McKinney, C. J. (2022, June 15). 5 times the Johnson government complained about 'lefty lawyers'. *The University of Law, Legal Cheek.* https://www.legalcheek.com/2022/06/5-times-the-johnson-government-complained-about-lefty-lawyers/. Accessed on October 17, 2023.

Mészáros, I. (1989). *The power of ideology.* Harvester Wheatsheaf.

Orwell, G. (1945). *Animal farm: A fairy story.* Secker and Warburg.

Quinn, B. (2020, January 16). 5,000 people died before being repaid over benefits error. *The Guardian.* https://www.theguardian.com/society/2020/jan/16/people-died-benefits-error. Accessed on October 17, 2023.

Rojas, J.-P. (2022). Tory MP criticised for saying food bank users just need to learn how to cook. https://news.sky.com/story/tory-mp-criticised-for-saying-food-bank-users-just-need-to-learn-how-to-cook-12610728. Accessed on August 12, 2023.

Salaman, G. (1981). *Class and the corporation.* Fontana.

Shaw, G. B. (1913). *Pygmalion: A play in five acts.* Constable.

Sikka, P. (2022, April 1). The UK's tax system is regressive, rewards the wealthy and is in urgent need of reform. *Left Foot Forward: Leading the UK's progressive debate.*

Sikka, P. (2023, August 4). Britain's tax system is rigged in favour of the rich. *Left Foot Forward: Leading the UK's progressive debate.*

Smith, J. K. A. (2005). *Jacques Derrida: Live theory.* Continuum.

Sosenko, F., Bramley, G., & Bhattacharjuee, A. (2022). Understanding the post-2010 increase in food bank use in England: New quasi-experimental analysis of the role of welfare policy. *BMC Public Health, 22,* article no. 1363. https://bmcpublichealth.biomedcentral.com/articles/10.1186/s12889-022-13738-0. Accessed on August 12, 2023.

Spire, A. (2005). Du mensonge en politique. In J. Derrida (Ed.), *Sur Parole: Instantanés philosophiques* (pp. 91–114). éditions de l'aube.

Tapper, J. (2022, August 14). British minister accused of trying to hide reports on impact of Tory welfare reforms. *The Observer.* https://www.theguardian.com/society/aug/14/British-minister. Accessed on August 2, 2023.

Tesco.com. (2023). https://www.tesco.com/groceries/en-GB/shop/fresh-food/fresh-meat-and-poultry/fresh-beef/beef-burgers. Accessed on August 16, 2023.

The Cabinet Papers. (n.d.). The welfare state. *The National Archive.* https://www.nationalarchives.gov.uk/cabinetpapers/alevelstudies/welfare-state.htm. Accessed on October 3, 2023.

Webster, D. (2014). The role of benefit sanctions and disallowances in creating the need for voluntary food aid. *All Party Parliamentary Inquiry into Hunger and Food Banks in Britain.* https://cpag.org.uk/sites/default/files/uploads/CPAG-All-Party-Parl-Inq-D-Webster-evidence-rev-2-Jul-14.pdf. Accessed on August 8, 2023.

IMPEDIMENT TO WALKING AS A FORM OF ACTIVE MOBILITY IN AKURE, NIGERIA

Samuel Oluwaseyi Olorunfemi and
Adetayo Olaniyi Adeniran

Federal University of Technology Akure, Nigeria

ABSTRACT

This study examined the factors militating against walking as a form of active mobility in Akure, Nigeria. For questionnaire administration, from the 548,315 population of Akure, two hundred and seventy-four (274) household heads representing 0.05% of the entire population of Akure were sampled with the aid of a structured and self-administered questionnaire using a systematic sampling technique. The elicited data were analysed using descriptive and inferential statistics. From the analysis, the major impediments to walking were the socio-cultural belief that anybody walking was poor, followed by accessibility to motorised transport, and inadequate pedestrian facilities. These situations have significantly deterred people from seeing walking as an active form of mobility in the study area. Thus, the study recommends a strong sensitisation and awareness programme to robustly enlighten people on the need to embrace walking as a form of urban mobility. Also, the government should adequately and sustainably invest more in pedestrian facilities that will promote the culture of walking among people and/or road users in Akure, Nigeria. More importantly, for inclusiveness in urban planning, road infrastructure should be designed alongside other road elements to ensure seamless negotiations between pedestrians and vehicles without any form of conflict.

Keywords: Impediment; mobility; active mobility; walking; pedestrians; Akure; Nigeria

---

Society and Sustainability
Developments in Corporate Governance and Responsibility, Volume 24, 97–121
Copyright © 2025 Samuel Oluwaseyi Olorunfemi and Adetayo Olaniyi Adeniran
Published under exclusive licence by Emerald Publishing Limited
ISSN: 2043-0523/doi:10.1108/S2043-052320240000024005

1. INTRODUCTION

Over time, movement from one place to another has been a vital part of human activity. This is because people need to fulfil a desired purpose which can only be achieved through movement within the environment. Human needs can be met through social, political, and economic interaction. Movement in the context of walking from one location to another is one way of achieving these needs. This is why it was stated by the United Nations Environment Programme and United Nations Human Settlements Programme (2022) that we are all pedestrians because every single trip either by public or private vehicles, starts and ends with walking.

This assertion implies that walking stands as a first and end form of mobility irrespective of the type of mode of transport one is using (UNEP, 2017). In the same vein, Oyesiku (2021) stated that walking is the common mode of mobility and the basic transportation mode in both urban and rural areas and has been in existence for thousands of years. It is often undertaken within a limited range for several reasons beyond the carrying out of household activities. It is found to be healthy exercise and, for this reason, is highly recommended as a popular and effective form of transportation system, and was established well before animal carts and the first mechanised mode of transportation.

According to Busari (2019), walking is the most harmless, oldest, and dominant transport means everywhere. It is attractive to all and does not require special skills. In other words, it is a celestial gift for every living creation. Erik (2011) observed that walking has played a dominant role in urban transport systems, especially in the 20th century and has equally contributed to the physical activity echelons of the urban populations. Olojede et al. (2017) viewed walking as a form of active mobility that is self-driven, emission-free, and environmentally friendly means of mobility.

Similarly, Oyesiku (2021) opined that in overland transportation, walking has the advantage of being less expensive in created footpaths, sidewalks and walkways that are usually part of the street construction in cities and urban centres. He also narrated other reasons for making walking an important mode of land transportation including health benefits from walking, overwhelming availability, environmentally friendly posture as no pollution or heat is generated excessively and above all, a sense of cognition making pedestrians appreciate the surrounding environment. Interestingly, among the active mobility types in every aspect as reported by the International Transport Forum (2011) and Olojede et al. (2017), walking is by far cheaper than bicycling, and roller skates, among others as no financial cost whatsoever is required for its operation.

Thus, the most dominant form of active mobility is walking. This is because there is no other mode of transport that is completely independent of walking. This implies that walking connects other modes of transport. It usually takes place within neighbourhoods and particularly city centres and Centre Business Districts (CBDs) of major metropolitan cities. It has been discovered for a long time, that most academic institutions at all levels, from primary through secondary to tertiary institutions, particularly university campuses have encouraged walking as part of internal circulation and mobility (Oyesiku, 2021). It can be further explained that as transport is ubiquitous, so also is walking among all other modes.

It was noted in the report of ITF (2011) that active travel especially walking constitutes a source of great pleasure for many citizens. To a large extent, many choose to walk due to its associated health benefits as it increases muscle strength and flexibility, cardiovascular fitness, improved joint mobility, decreases stress levels, improves posture and coordination, strengthens bones, decreases body fat levels, and prevents disease among others in the developed nations (Olojede et al., 2017; State of Victoria, 2016). However, despite the unique features of walking as a form of active mobility, it lacks the necessary infrastructure that ordinarily should be adopted by people in many parts of Africa, especially in Nigeria. Walking as a form of mobility has been widely studied in developed nations, why it has received little or no attention in Africa, especially in Nigeria (Busari, 2019).

Similarly, Roberts et al. (2006) and Olojede et al. (2017) revealed that active travellers are vulnerable travellers, especially in low- and middle-income nations where most of the estimated 30,000 people who are seriously injured in road traffic crashes are found and most of the casualties are pedestrians and cyclists. Also, according to the Federal Road Safety Commission (FRSC) (2010) of Nigeria, Olorunfemi (2021) and Akanmu (2023) majority of the victims of road traffic crashes are vulnerable road users or active travellers (pedestrians). The reasons for the occurrence of such incidents are that the road or highway planning standards do not intentionally recognise pedestrians as an integral part of traffic in the planning of new transport facilities. This implies that pedestrians are marginalised in terms of road infrastructure investments that could cater for their needs.

Although, transport services help meet critical mobility needs but also create a challenging environment for walking and cycling (Busari, 2019). Thus, in a way, their existence could be viewed by reckless drivers as an 'illegal encroachment' on the designed road space (Olojede et al., 2017). Despite the above challenges to walking, the major and natural (God-given) form of mobility is walking. As such, research in this area should be encouraged to ensure a safe and seamless walking environment. Although walking in developed nations has become a focal area in research, it has not been well-studied in developing nations.

Akure is a medium-sized city in Nigeria, the challenges impeding walking in Akure as a form of active mobility are not different from what is obtainable in other big cities in Nigeria. This occurred due to the increases in motorised transport coupled with inadequate infrastructure for pedestrians to secure and prevent them from the externality imposed by motorised transport. To ameliorate this challenge, there is a need to understand the demands and needs of people walking by taking crucial action to protect and enable them to contribute unswervingly to realising many of the Sustainable Development Goals. Safe and enabling human-scale environments improve individual and community health, especially for the urban poor. It is against the aforementioned that this study seeks to examine the impediment to walking as a form of mobility in Akure, Nigeria.

2. LITERATURE REVIEW

2.1 Conceptual Review

2.1.1 Attributes of Walking

The concept of walking has been recognised since time immemorial as a gift from God; while global walking rates are declining, walking remains the most common means of transport in Africa, either in combination with other transport modes (e.g., public transport) or as the main mode itself (Jennings et al., 2017; United Nation Habitat, 2013).

Walking is an excellent mode of transportation (Cairney, 1999). It has been the principal mode of transportation for nearly all of human history. For all of the beneficial features of walking, it is, for all practical purposes, devoid of negative externalities as a form of transportation (Chang, 2008). Walking produces no noise or pollutants. It requires no specific equipment or fuel except from what the pedestrian consumes in the form of food and drink, and is primarily plant-based, solar energy. Furthermore, the simple act of walking delivers important health advantages to the walker (Burr, 2009).

Walking is economically effective, both in terms of direct expenses to walkers and in terms of infrastructure creation and upkeep. Walking may entertain tourists and energise communities that would otherwise feel dead (Avenoso & Beckmann, 2005). Walking is a component of practically all public transport travels, according to the Lagos Non-Motorized Transport Policy (2018), hence nearly all commuters walk as part of their daily excursions.

2.1.2 Walking Pattern in the Developed Countries

Walking is sometimes faster in congested cities which are characterised by increased vehicle ownership and vehicle usage for individuals (in many cities with poor transport planning and policy), slower vehicle speeds, longer travel duration, and increased vehicular queuing (many unmoving vehicles); as a result, many people consider walking for short-distant trips.

Walking is also well-accepted to be good for one's health. As a result, roadways in town centres are progressively being blocked to autos and made open only to walkers. Walking is often promoted by governments for its health advantages. Access for handicapped individuals is also granted, albeit it is heavily regulated.

Walking is the most environmentally friendly mode of transportation for short distances. It produces almost no noise or air pollution and utilises significantly fewer nonrenewable resources than any other means of motorised transportation (Schneider et al., 2022). Walking, like every other mode of transportation, takes energy to be propelled (Adeniran et al., 2023). The energy required for walking is supplied directly by the traveller, and the utilisation of that energy provides an excellent cardiovascular workout. Walking offers not only physical but also emotional and social health advantages to people of all ages and capacities.

Walking takes up a fraction of the area required for driving and parking a car (Schneider et al., 2022). Walking is also more cost-effective than driving a car or taking public transit, both in terms of direct user expenditures and investments in public infrastructure. Walking is the most socially fair means of transportation since it is cheap for almost everyone (Bruntlett & Bruntlett, 2021).

The percentages of walk mode of all journeys range from roughly 12% in the United States and New Zealand to 26% in the United Kingdom (Bieker et al., 2020; United Kingdom Department for Transport, 2020). The low rates of walking recorded for Ireland (Central Statistics Office, 2019), Canada (Statistician Commuters, 2020), and Australia (Australian Bureau of Statistics, 2018) are very definitely understated because they only represent the journey-to-work as reported by their respective national censuses. According to travel surveys that include all trip reasons, the walking mode share of business commutation trips is nearly always lower than the walk shares of other trips, such as recreation and exercise (Buehler & Pucher, 2021).

There are several probable explanations for the difference in walk mode share. For example, the low walk mode shares (all trip purposes) in the United States (12%) (USDOT, 2018, 2019) and Sweden (15%) are likely due in part to their low population densities and high car ownership rates in comparison to the other countries (Buehler & Pucher, 2021; Luoma & Sivak, 2014; Traffic Analysis, 2020). The low walk mode share (16%) in the Netherlands, Europe's most densely populated country (Netherlands Ministry of Transport, 2017), is largely related to the prevalence of cycling for short journey lengths (Kunert et al., 2002; Wardlaw, 2014). Low levels of cycling in France and the UK, on the other hand, may help explain greater levels of walking (Buehler & Pucher, 2021; SDES, 2022).

2.1.3 Walking Pattern in Africa

Porter et al. (2020), Tiwari et al. (2020), and Jennings et al. (2017) revealed that daily trips involving walking in many African cities are made up between 50% and 90%. Similarly, in a global context, UN Environment (2021) and Benton et al. (2023) estimated that about 78% of people walk for travel every day for an average of 55 min per day on foot. People in low-income countries continue to work out of necessity, oftentimes to save on the high cost of public transport, which would require between 30% and 49% of household income (Benton et al., 2023).

Despite the momentum gained in walking as a dominant means of mobility in Africa as reported by Benton et al. (2023), walking infrastructure has been noticed to be a major hindrance to the sustainability of this type of mode due to its inadequacy or non-existent (United Nation Habitat, 2013). The inadequate provision of walking infrastructure makes walking unsafe and vulnerable to people. It is also pertinent to note that distance plays a prominent role in the walking culture of people.

For example, 36% and 38% of road fatalities and road injuries, respectively, on walkers in Africa for were accounted for in 2019 (UN Environment, 2021). Out of 54 countries in Africa, only 21 countries have a proper and efficient walking which is categorised under the Non-Motorized Transport (NWT)

102   *Impediment to Walking as a Form of Active Mobility*

policies and plans (UN Environment, 2021). Among these 21 countries, Jennings et al. (2017) stated that only Uganda and South Africa have country-specific pedestrian infrastructure guidelines.

2.1.4 Variation of Waking Within Cities and Metropolitan Areas

Within cities, there is a wide range of walking levels. In general, the denser, mixed-use centre parts of cities have shorter average journey lengths and hence greater walking levels than the same cities' outlying areas. Cities have larger modal shares of walking trips than suburban parts of their metropolitan areas for comparable reasons. In New York City, for example, the modal share of walk trips in 2019 was 54% in Manhattan, 48% in the Inner Bronx, Queens, and Brooklyn, 33% in the Outer Bronx, Queens, and Brooklyn, and only 5% in Staten Island (USDOT, 2019), which has the lowest population density and the highest levels of car ownership and use (Buehler & Pucher, 2021).

In Berlin, the city core had a 33% walk modal share in 2012 (City of Berlin, 2023), declining to 27% in the city's outer districts and 18% in the suburbs. In Munich, the walk mode share was 36% in the city centre in 2012 (City of Munich, 2015), 31% in the city's outlying districts, and 21% in the suburbs (Buehler et al., 2017). In Hamburg, the walk share of trips was 33% in the city centre in 2012 (City of Hamburg, 2015), 24% on the city outskirts, and 17% in the suburbs (Bieker et al., 2020).

In 2012, the proportion of people who walked in Vienna was 33% in the city centre, 23% in the city's outskirts, and 19% in the suburbs (Buehler et al., 2017). Similarly, in 2021, the proportion of people walking in Inner London was 37%, whereas in Outer London, it was 24% (Luoma & Sivak, 2014). In 2016, the City of Paris had a walking mode share of 52%, but this reduced to 42% in the inner suburbs and 29% in the outer suburbs (City of Paris, 2016).

2.1.5 Summary of Conceptual Review

Walking in the developed countries is purposed at maintaining a healthy living and as a means to save trip time wasted in traffic delay and vehicle congestion, while walking in the developing countries is purposed at saving some money as a result of high cost of public transport.

Walking mode share is largest in cities' core areas and decreases as one moves out from the centre. Walk mode share is lower in the suburbs than in the city, and walk mode share is lower in the outer suburbs than in the inner suburbs.

2.2 Empirical Review

A walking trip is defined by James et al. (2001) as a journey covering approximately 2 km. Busari (2019) countered that some individuals walk up to five times this amount each day and that most people walk more than 2 km each day. This was supported by studies by Krizek (2003) and Hoehner et al. (2005), which found that individuals will walk up to 400 metres (0.25 miles) depending on their goals. The results of Hoehner et al. (2005), McDonald (2012), McMillan et al. (2006), Sharples and Fletcher

(2000), and Yaser et al. (2016) are likewise consistent with this. These writers did, however, claim that travelling this distance is contingent upon several factors, including infrastructure and safety. The fundamental element of the pedestrian environment is the way the transportation system is managed in terms of providing the required pedestrian amenities and geometric layout. In addition, additional factors must also be taken into account when deciding whether or not to walk for a daily excursion (Busari, 2019; Hoehner et al., 2005). According to research by Sharples and Fletcher (2000), zebra crossings should be used wherever possible when designing pedestrian facilities to encourage walking in contemporary culture. Walking distance increases with increased utilisation of urban public areas (Busari, 2019).

Additionally, the Environment Programme and the United Nations Human Settlements Programme (2022) found that a major threat to road and individual safety in Africa is the growing motorisation of the continent combined with dangerous infrastructure for walkers. Cities and metropolitan areas become less accessible and progressively more dangerous when there is no safe route for individuals to stroll. This leads to the marginalisation of vulnerable road users and people who encounter additional obstacles related to their gender. Similarly, Busari (2019) reported that travel volume has been found to positively correlate with automobile ownership, which inevitably led to traffic congestion and other environmental problems including pollution and climate change, among others. Similar to this, Busari et al. (2017) believed that having access to private vehicles has a detrimental impact on walking as a mode of transportation.

In addition to the aforementioned, Busari (2019) observed that the location of service effect for pedestrian walk trips is largely influenced by land use. Studies by Busari et al. (2012), Guy (2016), and Living Streets (2001) have shown how walk trips are influenced by pedestrian networks, urban morphology, and land use. The utilisation of interchanges (Stradling, 2002) and school travel are two more concerns that impact walk trips (Busari, 2019). Another element influencing the decision to go on a walk excursion is gender. McDonald (2012), Hsu and Jean-Daniel (2014), Guliani (2015), and McMillan et al. (2006). The findings of studies by McDonald (2012), McMillan et al. (2006), Harten and Olds (2004), and Johnson et al. (2010) found that males are more likely to walk than females.

On the other hand, studies by Wilson et al. (2010) and McDonald (2012) revealed an inverse association between age and walk distance. According to Benton et al. (2023), there is a plethora of research demonstrating the advantages of walking for people, economies, urban quality, and climate. Walking is an important means of transportation, although there isn't much research or literature on the subject in Africa, according to Loo and Siiba (2019), Porter et al. (2020), and Sagaris et al. (2022). The developed world, particularly North America, Europe, and Australia, is home to the majority of walking-related research and policy formation (Benton et al., 2023; Jennings, 2020; Sagaris et al., 2022).

Similarly, different from industrialised and many developing countries, African nations have unique challenges related to social, economic, demographic, topographical, and historical aspects of walking (Anciaes et al., 2017;

Benton et al., 2023). African nations are forced to depend on the experience and data of industrialised nations, where the emphasis is on encouraging walking, even though this emphasis may not apply to African cities (Jobanputra & Jennings, 2021). The problem facing Africa is how to maintain the percentage of people who walk throughout the continent despite low road safety, inadequate infrastructure, and a lack of other pedestrian amenities. It also involves figuring out how to remove these obstacles, which are particularly prevalent in Nigerian towns.

While few studies have been documented in underdeveloped countries, several have been undertaken in industrialised countries on walking. Busari (2019), for example, examined non-motorised trip patterns in Sub-Saharan Africa: evaluation of walk trips, focussing on Ota, Nigeria. The information required for the study was gathered by the author using the survey technique, which involved administering questionnaires. 53.2% of the respondents, according to the author, walk daily to access mode, access sub-mode, or for leisure.

In a Nigerian metropolis, Olojede et al. (2017) investigated the factors that influence walking as an active method of transportation. In Ilesa, a significant city in Osun State, Nigeria, their study looked at variables that affected people's decision to walk as an active form of transportation. The three main residential zones of the city (the high-density, medium-density, and low-density zones) were sampled by the authors using a multistage sampling technique. It was found that the respondents' decision to walk was greatly influenced by factors such as relative affordability, the absence of personal vehicles, and favourable weather. Additionally, the respondents' age and income varied depending on the residential zone.

Research on 'walking is our asset' and how to keep walking a valued form of transportation in African cities was conducted by Benton et al. in 2023. To comprehend why walking receives only minimal resource allocation and operationalisation, they investigate the political and decision-making processes in African transport agencies. The material was acquired by the writers through interviews with national and local stakeholders involved in African transportation policy and practice. The results showed that stakeholders and people who are not required to walk undervalue walking. Ineffective policies and a lack of ability and expertise to impact change are examples of obstacles to change.

Three major obstacles were identified by Acheampong et al. (2022) after doing a review of sustainable mobility in Africa. The first issue is that walking conditions throughout East and West Africa have gotten worse due to rising traffic congestion. They cited research done in Accra (Møller-Jensen et al., 2012), Nairobi (Campbell et al., 2019), Dar es Salaam (Melbye et al., 2015), and the Greater Kumasi conurbation (Acheampong & Asabere, 2022). The second issue that has been noted has to do with how far many informal settlements are from the hubs of social and economic activity.

The time and money that less fortunate citizens spend travelling often in poorer conditions to get necessities such as work and healthcare chances. The last problem focusses on increasing funding for extensive transportation networks, frequently for automobiles and other motorised transit, with minimal consideration for locals' daily requirements. Considering that most trips in African cities are taken on foot and that there is little to no pedestrian infrastructure, this is a serious mistake. Additionally, motorised vehicles and other activities, such as retailing, are occupying areas on and surrounding roadways that are meant for walking (Acheampong & Siiba, 2018).

From the above, it is indicated that none of the studies work on the impediment to walking as an active form of mobility. This stands as the research gap that the study tends to fill. To our knowledge, this study is the first attempt to empirically examine the impediments to walking in Nigeria and Akure in particular.

2.3 Theoretical Review

2.3.1 Modal Split Theory

The modal split model was developed in the 1950s in response to transportation issues plaguing many American cities, such as increased traffic demand and congestion. This sparked research and thought regarding transport as a science, leading to the formulation of modal split theory (Ungvarai, 2019). In transportation engineering, the modal split, also known as modal choice or modal share, is commonly used to assess transportation behaviour. According to Ungvarai (2019), the modal split hypothesis demonstrates 'the proportion of travellers utilising a certain mode of transport compared to the ratio of all journey modes'.

Modal split entails 'calculating the number of trips between an origin and destination that are divided into segments belonging to different modes of transportation' (Ortuzar & Willumsen, 2011). Furthermore, it forecasts how future journeys will be divided among the various forms of transportation accessible to a prospective traveller. The outcome describes trip makers' behaviour while choosing a mode of urban transportation, given that the trip maker has access to many forms of urban transportation. Buses, cars, taxis, bicycles, walking, tricycles, and trains are all ways of transportation. Several criteria, such as trip type, trip purpose, degree of service, cost of transportation, age, sex, income, distance, comfort, and availability, may impact the choice of a certain mode (Okoko, 1998).

For transportation analysis, the modal divide offers both advantages and downsides. It has the theoretical benefit of being the most developed of the four modelling processes in travel demand. This is due to a significant study into travel mode selection (Ortuzar & Willumsen, 2011). However, the model's drawback, particularly in transportation research, stems from its lack of providing insufficient information on commuter travel modes (Ungvarai, 2019). As a result, the model is entirely theoretical, relying on the validity of current theory and the intuitiveness of assumptions (Ortuzar & Willumsen, 2011).

The modal split option is based on the assumption of two-way travel. Stratified diversion curve models, as well as probabilistic models such as discriminant analysis and logit analysis, are examples of modal split models. When more than two competing means of transport are involved in the research, calibrating the diversion curve model becomes difficult. As a result, in modal split analysis, probabilistic models (discriminant analysis) and multinomial models are often used (Okoko, 1998; Ramayah et al., 2010). Multinomial logit models are types of discrete choice models that represent individual trip-maker decision responses as a function of commuter choice characteristics as well as each individual's socioeconomic circumstances (Khan, 2007).

This is a disaggregate approach that recognises that aggregate behaviour is the result of numerous individual decisions. As a result, individual choice responses are modelled as a function of the characteristics of the alternative modes available to them as well as the socioeconomic characteristics of each individual. The capacity of models to forecast the repercussions of transport policy initiatives that impact mode choice is their strength (Ortuzar & Willumsen, 2011). According to the model's utility theory, mode choice is typically a sign of worth to a person.

In other words, a decision-maker selects one of an unlimited number of mutually incompatible possibilities from an exhaustive choice set. As a result, the individual is regarded to have chosen a mode that maximises his utility based on parameters such as journey time, waiting time, access time, and transportation charges, among others (Khan, 2007).

3. METHODOLOGY

3.1 Study Area

Akure-south is situated in Nigeria's southwest region. It serves as Ondo State's capital. The states of Ekiti and Kogi to the north, Edo and Delta to the east, and Osun and Ogun to the west encircle Ondo State. In the southern portion, it borders the Atlantic Ocean internationally. The study area is located between longitudes 5°5' and 5°30' east of the Greenwich meridian and latitudes 7°4' and 7°25' north of the equator. The display of the Nigerian map with Ondo State highlighted is shown in Fig. 1.

The state of Ondo is renowned for its advancements in the finding of bitumen and its ability to produce gas and oil. There was a noticeable difference in the style and standard of living between Europeans, educated elites, and indigenous people throughout the colonial era. Every social group was chosen in various areas. It is evident how different they were in Akure. The Oke-Eda (Alagbaka) region was home to the Europeans. At Sijuwade, the educated Nigerians resided behind the Europeans (Erezene, 2016).

The population of Akure Township in 1991 according to the population census was *239,124*. The population of the city increased to *353,211* by 2006 (NPC, 2006), and according to projections utilising a 2.5 growth rate, that number is expected to reach *476,785* by 2018. With its capital city of Akure, Ondo State has a significant position in Nigerian affairs. The historical and cultural context of this job contributes to its relevance. Maps of Akure and it's road networks are presented in Figs. 2 and 3.

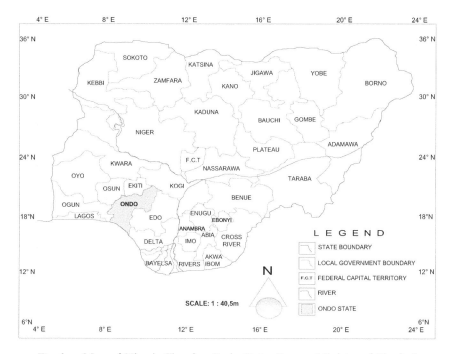

Fig. 1. Map of Nigeria Showing Ondo State. *Source:* Ministry of Physical Planning and Urban Development (2023).

3.2 Method of Data Collection

The survey technique was used in this study to elicit information that will actualise the study's aim. Personal observation and questionnaires were the primary methods of data collection. Additionally, desk research was utilised to compile pertinent literature. To determine the sample size for the study, the population figure of Akure was sourced and it was put at 744,000 (Population Stat, 2023) and this was subjected to the Taro Yamane formula:

$$n = \frac{N}{N + 1e^2} \tag{1}$$

where

n is the sample size
N is the population under study
e is the margin error term.

The population figure of Akure was equated into the above formula to arrive at 400 population sample size for the study at a margin error term of 0.05%. This implies that four hundred (400) questionnaires were administered for the study

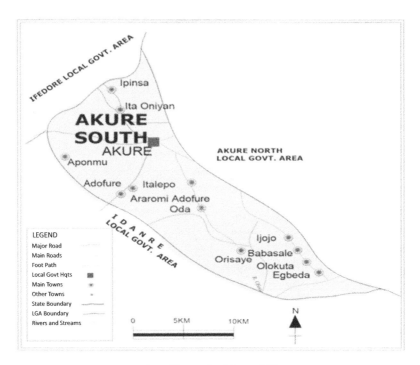

Fig. 2. Shows the Map of Akure.

using a systematic sampling method. It is important to note that out of the four hundred (400) questionnaires administered, only two hundred and seventy-four (274) were retrieved and this was adopted for the analysis of the study. Data analysis was done using Statistical Packages for Socio Science (SPSS) version 24 and data were presented using descriptive statistics which entails frequency and percentages, and inferential statistics which entails binary logistic regression.

3.3 Model Specification

The variables used to determine the major impediments to walking in Akure were measured using a dichotomous scale (0 = No and 1 = Yes) and analysed with logistic regression. The dependent variable in this study 'impediments to walking (ItW)', is of the dichotomous type in the form of 'Yes or No'. The Binary logistic regression model used is presented below.

$$P(\text{Yes ItW}) = (x) = \frac{e^{g(x)}}{1 + e^{g(x)}} \qquad (2)$$

and thus:

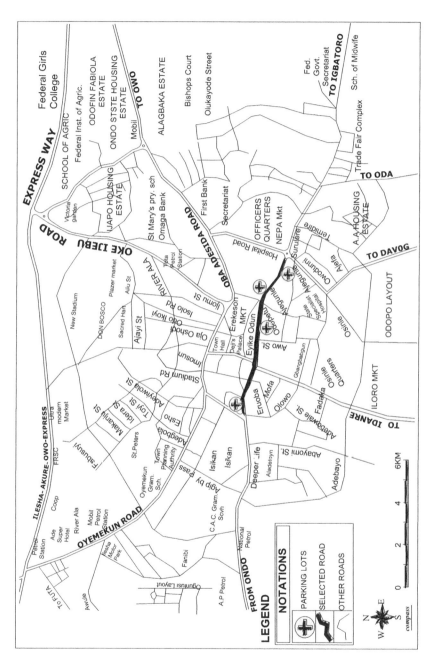

Fig. 3. The Network of Roads in Akure South City With Selected Road Corridor.

$$P(\text{No ItW}) = 1 - P(\text{no ItW}) = 1 - \pi(x) = \frac{1}{1 + e^{g(x)}} \tag{3}$$

where $g^{(x)}$ stands for the function of the independent variables:

$$g(x) = \beta_0 + \beta_{1\text{Pwc}} + \beta_{2\text{Amt}} + \beta_{3\text{Hp}} + \beta_{4\text{Ipi}} + \beta_{5\text{Scb}} + \beta_{6\text{Rss}} + \beta_{7\text{Rsct}}$$

where

Pwc represents poor weather conditions;
Amt represents access to motorised transport;
Hp represents health problems;
Ipi represents inadequate pedestrian infrastructure;
Scb represents societal or cultural belief;
Iss represents inadequate safety and society; and
Rsct represents relatively slow compared to other means of transport.

The logistic regression determines the coefficients that make the observed outcome (Yes ItW or No ItW) most likely using the maximum-likelihood technique. These variables were measured with a dichotomous scale (Yes and No response).

4. RESULTS AND DISCUSSION

4.1 Socio-Economic Characteristics of the Respondents

The socio-economic characteristics of the respondents that were sampled in the study area are shown in Table 1. The variables examined include gender, marital status, age, educational status, occupation, and monthly income. The gender of the respondents shows that 57.0% were males and 43.0% were females. This implies that the highest percentage of those who engage in walking in Akure is males. Supporting the above, Johnson et al. (2010) revealed that boys tend to walk than girls. This may be accredited to the fact that males are more active and can engage in strenuous activities or risks than their female counterparts. The age revealed that 15.3% of the respondents fell below the age of 20–30 years, 43.3% were within the age of 20–40 years, 35.0 % fell within 41–60 years, and 7.0% were 60 years and above. This shows that the majority of the respondents fall within the age bracket of 41–60 years. This age bracket falls within the active age group, perhaps this might be the reason for their involvement in walking.

The investigation into their marital status indicates that 32.0% were single, 53.0% were married, divorced accounted for 12.0% and 6.0% were found to be widowed. This suggests that a sizeable proportion of the respondents who are married engage in walking activities. One can infer that this fraction (married population) is involved in walking activities to enhance their body system by keeping fit regularly. The educational status of the respondents shows that 8.0% had no formal education, 13.0% possessed primary school education, 28.1% had

Table 1. Socio-Economic Characteristics of Respondents.

S/N	Socio-Economic Characteristics of Respondents	Frequency	Percentage
1.	*Gender*		
	Male	156	57.0
	Female	118	43.0
	Total	274	100.0
2	*Age Status*		
	Less than 20	42	15.3
	20–40	119	43.4
	41–60	95	35.0
	60 and above	18	7.0
	Total	274	100.0
3.	*Marital Status*		
	Single	87	32.0
	Married	139	53.0
	Divorce	33	12.0
	Widow	15	6.0
	Total	274	100.0
4.	*Educational Status*		
	No formal education	21	8.0
	Primary school	35	13.0
	Secondary school	77	28.1
	Tertiary education	141	52.0
	Total	274	100.0
5.	*Occupational Status*		
	Student/Apprenticeship	91	37.0
	Trading/Artisan/Professional	117	43.0
	Civil servant	53	19.3
	Retired	12	4.4
	Total	274	100.0
6.	*Monthly Income*		
	Under 50.000	88	32.1
	51,000.00–100,000.00	134	49.1
	101,000.00–150,000.00	38	14.0
	150,000.00 and above	14	5.1
	Total	274	100.00

Source: Author's Field Work (2023).

secondary education, and 52% acquired tertiary education. This shows that the majority of respondents are educated and with this, it is believed that this will improve and enhance their awareness regarding walking in the study area because education is a form of liberation and light from ignorance.

Investigation into the occupational status of the respondents revealed that 37.0% of them were students/apprentices, 43.0% were traders/artisans/professionals, 19.3% were civil servants, and retirees accounted for 4.4%. The highest earners among respondents (49.1%) are those that earn between ₦51,000.00 ($65.59) and ₦100,000.00 ($128.89) monthly. Others revealed that they earned between ₦101,000.00 ($129.89) and ₦150, 000.00 ($192.91) (14.0%), while (5.1%) of the respondents earned ₦150,000.00 ($192.91) and above and those who earned below at ₦50, 000.00 ($65.59) accounted for 32.1%. From the analysis, it is revealed that the majority of the respondents still live below average living standard as indicated by the United Nations that anybody living below $100.00 is poor and this may affect the people's standard of living and health condition (Agbola & Agunbiade, 2007; Gbadamosi & Olorunfemi, 2016; Olarenwaju, 1996).

4.2 Motivation for Walking

Authors such as Busari (2019), Olojede et al. (2017), and Okoko (2006) have revealed several reasons that motivate many people to engage in walking. The reasons that motivate many people to walk in Akure are revealed in Fig. 4. It was indicated that 30.0% of the sampled respondents claimed that the reason that motivated them to walk was that it has no financial involvement, 24.0% stated awareness of the health benefits, 20.0% opined lack of personal automobiles such as cars and motorcycles, 15.3% responded to avoid traffic congestion and others which accounted for 5.0% claimed to enjoy the breeze weather of the day when not going far and to exercise, to keep the body fit. It is found from the above, that the majority of the respondents engage in walking because it has no financial implication. This corroborates the findings of Olojede et al. (2017) where cheapness or no financial cost to the factors influence the decision to walk in Ilesha Nigeria.

4.3 Impediments to Walking

Impediments to walking as identified in Akure, Nigeria include societal belief that anybody mostly found walking is poor, access to motorised transport, inadequate

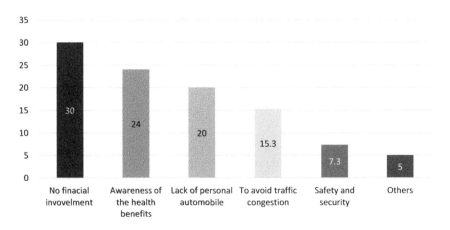

Fig. 4. Motivation for Walking. *Source:* Author's Field Work (2023).

Table 2. Model Summary Results.

Step	-2 Log-Likelihood	χ^2 (8, 0.05)	Cox & Snell R Square	Nagelkerke R Square
1	38.166[a]	12,156	0.621	0.761

Source: Author's Field Work (2023).

[a]It is essential to note that if the P value of the computed test is less than 0.05, the relationship that exists between two variables is significant, otherwise not significant.

pedestrians' infrastructure, and health problems among others. To achieve this objective, the feasibility test of the logistic regression model was carried out using the Likelihood Test as shown in Table 2. The magnitude of the contribution of the independent variables to the dependent variable in the logistic regression model below can be seen in the Nagelkerke R Square value, which revealed the R Square value of 0.761 which indicates that the independent variables can explain the dependent variable by 76.1% while the remaining 23.9% is explained by other independent variables that are not captured in the existing logistic regression model.

Table 2 also obtained the value of -2 log-likelihood $= 38.166$ and the value of χ^2 (df, α) $= 12,156$. It means that the value of $G > \chi^2$ (df, α) then reject H_0 means that there is at least 1 parameter $\beta_i \neq 0$ where 1 or more predictor variables have a significant effect on the response variable.

Partial analysis results for each independent variable in the equation are shown in Table 3. According to Table 3, it was found that the societal or cultural belief that anybody walking is poor, access to motorised transport, and inadequate pedestrians infrastructure were the major impediments to walking in Akure as shown in the following results respectively [($p = 0.001 < 0.05$: Exp value (β) $= 27.236$); ($p = 0.023 < 0.05$: Exp value (β) $= 17.251$); ($p = 0.003 < 0.05$: Exp value (β) $= 22.294$)].

From the foregoing, it is noted that major impediments to walking in the study area were the societal or cultural belief that anybody walking is poor, access to

Table 3. Results of Partial Independent Variable Analysis.

Step 1[a]	Var	β	SE	Wald	Df	Sig	Exp (β)	Exp (β)	
								Lower	Upper
	Pwc	-1.337	1.777	2.383	1	0.425	0.008	0.004	1.611
	Amt	2.143	1.157	4.231	1	0.023	17.251	1.613	157.315
	Hp	0.189	0.182	2.274	1	0.359	0.736	0.616	1.254
	Ipi	3.176	1.236	4.379	1	0.003	22.294	1.732	163.428
	Sbp	3.362	1.377	6.213	1	0.001	27.236	1.986	252.461
	Iss	-2.225	1.699	2.273	1	0.354	0.228	0.018	1.735
	Rsct	0.186	0.128	1.741	1	0.792	0.354	0.148	1.571
	Const	-12.478	6.589	4.212	1	0.028	0.000		

Source: Author's Field Work (2023).

Note: p-value $= 0.05$. The variables represented boldly are significance variables which P value is less than 0.05. Three variables were found to be significant and explained further.

motorise transport, and inadequate pedestrian infrastructure such as a walkway, crossing lane, bust stop to protect pedestrians from sun or rain among others.

4.3.1 The Societal or Cultural Belief That 'Anybody Walking Is Poor' Impedes Walking

Nigeria is a large country with diverse environmental, geographic, economic, and socio-cultural conditions. There are huge variations in both the practice and prevalence of walking and the ways it is valued by citizens. The societal or cultural belief that anybody walking is poor has hindered many who ordinarily should walk to some places within the city, have to rely on car or motorcycle for their daily mobility which invariably deepens the existing road transport externality in the city. This belief is also agreed in the findings of Olvera et al. (2013) which found that high levels of poverty make walking remain dominant in African cities. With this ideology in the mind of the citizens, they will strive to do away with walking and getting access to a motorised vehicle by all means.

4.3.2 Access to Motorise Transport Impedes Walking

Rapid urbanisation is accelerating accessibility to motorised transport. Yet without the economic development to adequately support this urban growth, the urbanisation of many cities in Africa is unplanned, unstructured, and seemingly random (Doan & Oduro, 2012). This is also applicable to the condition of many Nigerian cities including Akure. This unconstrained development creates sprawling cities that are too large to manoeuvre by foot, subsequently causing higher dependency on road-based transport (Wang & Kintrea, 2019). This prioritisation of motorised transport conflicts with the fact that walking is a more common mode than the modes to which investment is directed. There is a concern that the substantial number of people who currently rely on walking will switch to motorised modes to reduce this daily mobility burden and road traffic danger (Vanderschuren et al., 2017). This unsustainable shift towards motorisation will have long-term and devastating effects on individual and public health, the environment, and the economy at large.

4.3.3 Inadequate Pedestrian Infrastructure Impedes Walking

Although walking is the dominant mode of transport in Africa and Nigeria in particular, walking infrastructure is inadequate or non-existent (United Nation Habitat, 2013). The inadequate provision of walking infrastructure makes walking extremely dangerous. Only Uganda and South Africa in Africa have country-specific pedestrian infrastructure guidelines, even though walking makes up between 50% and 90% of daily trips in many African cities (Jennings et al., 2017).

Busari (2019) noted that walking is being challenged because it lacks the necessary facilities in most countries in Africa. Research by James et al. (2001) revealed that aggressive headlight is a cause of unsuitable walking as a form of transportation mode. Sharples and Fletcher (2000) found that lack of Zebra

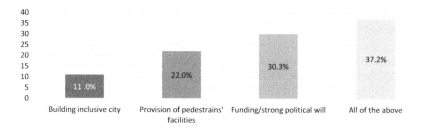

Fig. 5. Strategy for Improving Walking Culture.

crossing among the pedestrian walking facilities is a factor that discourages walking.

4.4 Strategy for Improving Walking Culture

The analysis of the strategy for improving walking in Akure is shown in Fig. 5. It was found that 30.3% of the respondents advocated for funding/strong political drive, 22.0% of them found the provision of pedestrian facilities, 11.0% of them affirmed building an inclusive city, and 37.2% identified all the variables as a major player for improving walking culture. The indication from the above shows identified variable can improve walking culture. This is because when funding is available, it will take strong political will to spend the funds on the appropriate project that will benefit the masses. To provide adequate pedestrian facilities and build an inclusive city that is for all requires adequate funding and strong political will. No wonder, it was reported by UNEP (2022) that no matter how well a walking policy is written, without funding and political will, it will be a challenge for the policy to become a reality.

5. CONCLUSION

Since time immemorial, movement from one place to another has been an integral part of human activity. The needs of the people can be met through social, political, and economic interaction. Movement in the context of walking from one location to another is one way of achieving people's needs. Despite the relevance attached to walking as a form of mobility, it is not without several limitations. Previous studies revealed that more than a quarter of the people killed in road accidents are pedestrians, and this is expected to increase steadily due to a limited if not lack of, investment in pedestrian facilities that will enhance walking as a form of mobility.

The above-mentioned inadequacies can be reversed and rapid progress made towards finding a lasting solution to road accidents, while at the same time making walking a fascinating form of mobility. This can be done through the adoption of non-automobile transportation and, in this case, movement within urban and rural areas. Manifestly, walking is the safest and most readily available means of transportation involving physical activity rather than any form of motorisation for movement between locations that requires no technical skill. It is relatively cheap and, to a large extent, accessible to all, except the physically challenged. Also, it is emission-free and environment-friendly. Despite the unique characteristics of this mode, little or no attention has been given to it in the areas of underfunding of pedestrian facilities and disadvantaged cultural beliefs that walk against the full-scale adoption of walking as a major form of active mobility in Nigeria.

The study has examined impediments to walking as a form of active mobility in Akure Nigeria. Findings show that societal or cultural belief that anybody walking is poor, access to motorised transport (such as cars, taxis, and motorcycles), and lack of walking infrastructures (such as a walkway, crossing lane, bus stop to protect pedestrians from sun or rain, rail guide to protecting pedestrian carriageway among others) were found as the major impediments to walking in Akure.

Going by the above, there is a need for strong advocacy either private or government to carry out adequate sensitisation and awareness campaigns to educate people more on the importance of walking by changing their mindset from the belief that anybody walking is poor and walking is for exercise purposes only. Apart from them realising the health benefits of walking, there is a need for an understanding of its prominent role play in the environment as it is capable of limiting noise and air pollution commonly generated through the usage of motorised transport which are detrimental to human health.

For the effectiveness of this type of campaign, both hard and soft mediums of awareness can be adopted. The soft awareness can be done with the help of socio media such as Facebook, Instagram, telegram, TikTok, WhatsApp, and media houses (Newspaper, Radio, and Television) among others. The hard awareness can take the form of physical campaigns in public places such as motor parks, churches, mosques, schools, market places, among others. Also, there is a need for private and public partnerships in building sustainable pedestrian infrastructure that is inclusive in nature to protect and secure pedestrians from the threat imposed by other road users (i.e., the motorist and motorcyclist). Policy on town or city should focus on building inclusive towns or cities that are capable of accommodating every road user irrespective of their state or condition without prejudice to any group. This will create seamless and harmonious active urban mobility operation between walking, cyclists and other modes of transport that will bring about a safe and secure environment.

6. CREDIT AUTHORSHIP CONTRIBUTION STATEMENT

The authors confirm contribution to the paper as follows: study conception and design: *Samuel O. Olorunfemi, Adetayo O. Adeniran*; data analysis, discussion, and proofreading: *Samuel O. Olorunfemi*; analysis and interpretation of results: *Samuel O. Olorunfemi, Adetayo O. Adeniran*; draft manuscript preparation: *Samuel O. Olorunfemi*. All authors reviewed the results and approved the final version of the manuscript.

ACKNOWLEDGEMENTS

We thank the Editor and Reviewers for their insightful contributions to the improvement of this article.

REFERENCES

Acheampong, R. A., & Asabere, S. B. (2022). Urban expansion and differential accessibility by car and public transport in the greater Kumasi city-region, Ghana-A geospatial modelling approach. *Journal of Transport Geography*, *98*, 15–24.

Acheampong, R. A., Lucas, K., Poku-Boansi, M., & Uzondu, C. (2022). Introduction: Transport and mobility situations of African cities. In *Transport and mobility futures in urban Africa* (Vol. 2022, pp. 1–8). Springer.

Acheampong, R. A., & Siiba, A. (2018). Examining the determinants of utility bicycling using a socio-ecological framework: An exploratory study of the tamale Metropolis in northern Ghana. *Journal of Transport Geography*, *69*, 1–10.

Adeniran, A. O., Muraina, M. J., & Ngonadi, J. C. (2023). Energy consumption for transportation in Sub-Sahara Africa. In D. Crowther & S. Seifi (Eds.), *Achieving net zero (Developments in corporate governance and responsibility)* (Vol. 20, pp. 203–231). Emerald Publishing Limited. https://doi.org/10.1108/S2043-052320230000020009

Agbola, T., & Agunbiade, E. (2007). *Urbanization, slum development and security of tenure: The challenges of meeting Millennium Development Goals (MDG) 7 in Metropolitan Lagos, Nigeria.* PRIPODE Workshop on Urban population, Development Countries. https://www.ciesin.columbia.edu/repository/pern/papers/urban_pde_agbola_agunbiade.pdf

Akanmu, A. A. (2023). *Transportation infrastructure and city livability in Lagos Metropolis, Nigeria.* Unpublished PhD Thesis. Department of Logistics and Transport Technology, Federal University of Technology Akure.

Anciaes, P. R., Nascimento, J., & Silva, S. (2017). The distribution of walkability in an African city: Praia, Cabo Verde. *Cities*, *67*, 9–20. https://doi.org/10.1016/j.cities.2017.04.008

Australian Bureau of Statistics. (2018). *2016 census of population and housing, journey to work files.* Australian Bureau of Statistics.

Avenoso, A., & Beckmann, J. (2005). *The safety of vulnerable road users in the Southern, Eastern and Central European countries (The "SEC Belt").* European Transport Safety Council.

Benton, J. S., Jennings, G., Walker, J., & Evans, J. (2023). Walking is our asset: How to retain walking as a values mode of transport in African cities. *Cities*, *137*, 104297. https://doi.org/10.1016/j.cities.2023.104297:1-9

Bieker, G., Tietge, U., Rodriguez, F., & Mock, P. (2020). *European vehicle market statistics, 2019/2020.* International Council on Clean Transportation.

Bruntlett, M., & Bruntlett, C. (2021). *Curbing traffic: The human case for fewer cars in our lives.* Island Press. ISBN 978-1-64283-165-8.

Buehler, R., & Pucher, J. (2021). The growing gap in pedestrian and cyclist fatality rates between the United States and the United Kingdom, Germany, Denmark, and The Netherlands, 1990–2018. *Transport Reviews*, *41*, 48–72.

Buehler, R., Pucher, J., Gerike, R., & Götschi, T. (2017). Reducing car dependence in the heart of Europe: Lessons from Germany, Austria, and Switzerland. *Transport Reviews*, *37*, 4–28.

Burr, T. (2009). *Improving road safety for pedestrians and cyclists in Great Britain.* House of Commons, Public Accounts Committee.

Busari, A. (2019). The non-motorized trip pattern in Sub-Saharan Africa: Assessment of walk trip. *The Open Transportation Journal*, *13*, 194–202. http://doi.org/10.2174/1874447801913010194

Busari, A. A., Owolabi, A. O., Fadugba, G. O., & Olawuyi, O. A. (2012). Mobility of the poor in Akure metropolis: Income and land use approach. *Journal of Poverty and Investment Development*, *15*, 4–9.

Busari, A., Oyedepo, J., Modupe, A., Bamigboye, G., Olowu, O., Adediran, J., & Ibikunle, F. (2017). The trip pattern of low-density residential area in semi-urban industrial cluster: Predictive modelling. *International Journal of Human Capital and Urban Management, 2*(3), 211–218.

Cairney, P. (1999). *Pedestrian safety in Australia.* United States Department of Transportation, Federal Highway Administration.

Campbell, K. B., Rising, J. A., Klopp, J. M., & Mbilo, J. M. (2019). Accessibility across transport modes and residential developments in Nairobi. *Journal of Transport Geography, 74,* 77–90.

Central Statistics Office. (2019). *Census of population 2016: Profile 6 commuting in Ireland.* Central Statistics Office.

Chang, D. (2008). *National pedestrian crash report.* National Center for Statistics and Analysis, National Highway Traffic Safety Administration.

City of Berlin. (2023). *Berlin transport in figures.* City of Berlin, Transport Planning.

City of Hamburg. (2015). *Transport planning in Hamburg.* City of Hamburg, Transport Planning.

City of Munich. (2015). *Statistics for Munich.* Statistical Office Munich.

City of Paris. (2016). *Walking in greater Paris.* IAU île-de-France.

Doan, P., & Oduro, C. Y. (2012). Patterns of population growth in Peri-Urban Accra, Ghana. *International Journal of Urban and Regional Research, 36,* 1306–1325.

Erezene, H. B. (2016). European influence in Ijo-Itsekiri relations in Nigeria. *African Research Review, 10*(1), 104. https://doi.org/10.4314/afrrev.v10i1.9

Erik, S. (2011). *Assessment of active commuting behaviour – Walking and bicycling in greater Stockholm.* Örebro University.

Federal Road Safety Commission. (2010). *Road mirror.* Research Monograph No. 2. https://frsc.gov.ng/comacemirror.pdf

Gbadamosi, K. T., & Olorunfemi, S. O. (2016). Rural road infrastructural challenges: An impediment to health care service delivery in Kabba-Bunu local government area of Kogi State, Nigeria. *Academic Journal of Interdisciplinary Studies, 5*(2), 34–43. http://doi.org/10.5901/ajis.2016.v5n2p3

Guliani, A. (2015). Gender-based differences in school travel mode choice behaviour: Examining the relationship between the neighbourhood environment and perceived traffic safety. *Journal of Transport & Health, 10,* 10–16. http://dx.doi.org/10.1016/j.jth.2015.08.008

Guy, L. (2016). Cars and socio-economics: Understanding neighbourhood variations in car characteristics from administrative data. *Journal of Registry and Science, 3*(9), 2–8.

Harten, N., & Olds, T. (2004). Patterns of active transport in 11–12-year-old Australian children. *Journal of Public Health, 28*(2), 167–172. http://dx.doi.org/10.1111/j.1467-842X.2004.tb00931.x

Hoehner, C. M., Brennan, L. K., Ramirez, M. B., Elliott, S. L., & Brownson, R. C. (2005). Perceived and objective environmental measures and physical activity among urban adults. *American Journal of Preventive Medicine, 28*(2), 105–116.

Hsu, H. P., & Jean-Daniel, S. (2014). Impacts of parental gender and attitudes on children's school travel mode and parental chauffeuring behaviour: Results for California based on the 2009 national household travel survey. *Transportation, 41*(3), 543–565. http://dx.doi.org/10.1007/s11116-013-9500-7

International Transport Forum. (2011). *Pedestrian safety, urban space and health.* Research Report. www.internationationaltransportforum.org

James, B., John, G., & McKaskill, J. (2001). Potential for increasing walking trips. In *Proceedings of Australia: Walking the 21st Century,* 20–22 February 2001, Perth, Western Australia.

Jennings, G. (2020). An exploration of policy knowledge-seeking on high-volume, low carbon transport: Findings from expert interviews in selected African and South Asian countries. *Transportation Research Interdisciplinary Perspectives, 5,* 100117. https://doi.org/10.1016/j.trip.2020.100117

Jennings, G., Petzer, B., & Goldman, E. (2017). When bicycle lanes are not enough: Growing mode share in Cape Town, South Africa: An analysis of policy and practice. In W. V. Mitullah, M. Vanderschuren, & M. Khayesi (Eds.), *Non-motorized transport integration into urban transport planning in Africa* (pp. 224–235). Routledge.

Jobanputra, R., & Jennings, G. (2021). Learning from COVID-19 tactical urbanism: Challenges and opportunities for 'infrastructure-lite' in sub-Saharan African cities. In *39th Annual Southern*

African Transport Conference. https://transport-links.com/hvt-publications/learning-from-covid-19-tactical-urbanism-challenges-and-opportunities-for-%CB%9Cinfrastructure-lite-in-sub-saharan-african-cities

Johnson, T. G., Brusseau, T. A., Darst, W. P., Kulinna, P. H., & WhiteTaylor, J. (2010). Step counts of non-white minority children and youth by gender, grade level, race/ethnicity, and mode of school transportation. *Journal of Physical Activity and Health, 7*(6), 730–736. http://dx.doi.org/10.1123/jpah.7.6.730

Khan, O. (2007). *Modelling passenger mode choice behavior using computer aided stated data.* Unpublished Ph.D thesis. Queens University of Technology.

Krizek, K. (2003). Neighbourhood services, trip purpose, and tour-based travel. *Transportation Journal, 30*(4), 387–410. http://dx.doi.org/10.1023/A:1024768007730

Kunert, U., Kloas, J., & Kuhfeld, H. (2002). Design characteristics of national travel surveys: International comparison for 10 countries. *Transportation Research Record Journal of the Transportation Research, 1804,* 107–116.

Lagos Non-Motorised Transport Policy. (2018). *Empowering pedestrians and cyclists for a better city.* https://bicycleinfrastructuremanuals.com/manuals4/Lagos_NMTPolicy_2018.pdf

Loo, B. P. Y., & Siiba, A. (2019). Active transport in Africa and beyond: Towards a strategic framework. *Transport Reviews, 39*(2019), 181–203. https://doi.org/10.1080/01441647.2018.1442889

Luoma, J., & Sivak, M. (2014). Why is road safety in the U.S. not on par with Sweden, the U.K., and the Netherlands? Lessons to be learned. *European Transport Research Review, 6,* 295–302.

McDonald, N. C. (2012). Is there a gender gap in school travel? An examination of US children and adolescents. *Journal of Transport Geography, 20*(1), 80–86. http://dx.doi.org/10.1016/j.jtran

McMillan, T., Day, K., Boarnet, M., Alfonzo, M., & Anderson, C. (2006). Johnny walks to school (-) does Jane? Sex differences in children's active travel to school. *Children, Youth, and Environments, 16*(2006), 75–89.

Melbye, D. C., Møller-Jensen, L., Andreasen, M. H., Kiduanga, J., & Busck, A. G. (2015). Accessibility, congestion and travel delays in Dar Es Salaam time-distance perspective. *Habitat International, 46,* 178–186.

Møller-Jensen, L., Kofie, R. Y., & Allotey, A. N. (2012). Measuring accessibility and congestion in Accra. *Norsk Geografisk Tidsskrift, 66*(1), 52–60.

NPC (National Population Commission). (2006). *Population and housing census: population distribution by sex, state, LGA, and Senatorial district.* http://www.population.gov.ng/images

Netherlands Ministry of Transport. (2017). *Dutch national travel survey.* Ministry of Transport, Public Works, and Water Management.

New York City. (2019). *Mobility report.* Department of Transportation.

Okoko, E. (Ed.). (1998). *Transportation planning as an integral part of the master planning exercise: The utility of traffic forecasting models in Master planning approach to physical development: The Nigerian experience.* Paraclete Publishers.

Okoko, E. E. (2006). *Urban transportation planning and modelling.* Millennium Publishers Akure, Ondo State.

Olarenwaju, D. O. (1996). Social and economic deprivation in a medium-sized urban centre in Nigeria. *Habitual Interntional, 20*(2), 229–240.

Olojede, O., Yoadeb, A., & Olufemia, B. (2017). Determinants of walking as an active travel mode in a Nigerian city. *Journal of Transport & Health, 6*(8), 1–8. http://dx.doi.org/10.1016/j.jth.2017.06.008:1-8

Olvera, L. D., Plat, D., & Pochet, P. (2013). The puzzle of mobility and access to the city in Sub-Saharan Africa. *Journal of Transport Geography, 32,* 56–64.

Ortuzar, J. D. D., & Willumsen, L. G. (2011). *Modelling transport.* Wiley and Sons.

Oyesiku, K. (2021). *Transportation and logistics in Nigeria.* HEBN Publisher Plc Jericho.

Porter, G., Abane, A., & Lucas, K. (2020). *User diversity and mobility practices in Sub-Saharan African cities: Understanding the needs of vulnerable populations. The state of knowledge and research.* VREF.

Ramayah, T., Ahmad, N. H., Abdul Halim, H., Mohamed Zaina, S. R., & Lo, M. (2010). Discriminant analysis: An illustrated example. *African Journal of Business Management, 4*(9), 1654–1667.

Roberts, I., Wentz, R., & Edwards, P. (2006). Car manufacturers and global road safety: A word frequency analysis of road safety documents. *Injury Prevention, 12*, 320–322.

Sagaris, L., Costa-Roldan, I., Rimbaud, A., & Jennings, G. (2022). *Walking, the invisible transport mode, research on walking and walkability today*. https://vref.se/wp-content/uploads/2022/09/Sagaris-et-al-2022-Bibliometric-study-walking_220630.pdf

Schneider, R. J., Wiers, H., & Schmitz, A. (2022). Perceived safety and security barriers to walking and bicycling: Insights from Milwaukee. *Transportation Research Record Journal of the Transportation Research, 2676*, 325–338.

SDES. (2022). *National transport and travel survey (ENTD)*. SDES.

Sharples, J. M., & Fletcher, J. P. (2000). *Pedestrian perceptions of road crossing facilities*. Scottish Executive Central Research Unit.

State of Victoria. (2016). *Cycling – Health benefits*. www.betterhealth.vic.gov.au/health/healthyliving/cycling-health-benefits

Statistician Commuters. (2020). *Using sustainable transportation in census metropolitan areas*. Statistics Canada.

Stradling, S. (2002). Transport user needs and marketing public transport. *Municipal Engineer, 151*(1), 1–9. http://dx.doi.org/10.1680/muen.2002.151.1.23

Streets, L. (2001). *Streets are for living, and the importance of streets and public spaces for community life*. Pedestrians Association. http://www.pedestrians.org

Tiwari, G., Khayesi, M., Mitullah, W. V., & Kobusingye, O. (2020). *Road traffic injury and transport-related air quality in Sub-Saharan Africa: The extent of the challenge*. https://vref.se/wp-content/uploads/2024/01/Tiwari-et-al-2020-Road-Traffic-Injury-and-Transport-Related-Air-Quality-VREF.pdf

Traffic Analysis. (2020). *Swedish travel habits*. Traffic Analysis.

UNEP. (2017). *NMT policy development: Lessons learned from the "share the road" programme*. https://wedocs.unep.org/bitstream/handle/20.500.11822/22500/NMT_Policy_Development%2520.pdf?sequence=1&isAllowed=y#:~:text=An%20NMT%20policy%20(either%20stand,this%20negative%20investment%20cycle%20through%3A&text=Setting%20out%20the%20intent%20of%20a%20Government%20regarding%20NMT

Ungvarai, A. (2019). Modal split: Different approaches to a common term. *Materials Science and Engineering, 603*, 042091.

United Kingdom Department for Transport. (2020). *Walking and cycling statistics 2000, 2010, 2019/national travel survey*. United Kingdom Department for Transport. https://assets.publishing.service.gov.uk/media/5f294c478fa8f57acebf6792/walking-and-cycling-statistics-england-2019.pdf

United Nation Environment. (2021). *Walking and cycling global outlook report: African Edition*. https://www.unep.org/topics/transport/active-mobility/global-outlook-walking-and-cycling-report-update

United Nation Habitat. (2013). *Planning and design for sustainable urban mobility: Global report on human settlements*. Routledge. https://unhabitat.org/planning-and-design-for-sustainable-urban-mobility-global-report-on-human-settlements-2013

United Nations Environment Programme and United Nations Human Settlements Programme. (2022). *Walking and cycling in Africa: Evidence and good practice to inspire action*. https://www.unep.org/resources/report/walking-and-cycling-africa-evidence-and-good-practice-inspire-action

United Nations Environmental Programme. (2022). *Walking and cycling in Africa – Evidence and good practice to inspire action*. Walking and Cycling in Africa – Evidence and Good Practice to Inspire Action. UNEP – UN Environment Programme on 7th July, 2023.

United States Department of Transportation. (2018). *National household travel survey*. US Department of Transportation. https://nhts.ornl.gov/

United States Department of Transportation. (2019). *Traffic safety facts 2017*. U.S. Department of Transportation, National Highway Traffic Safety Administration. https://crashstats.nhtsa.dot.gov/Api/Public/ViewPublication/813141

Vanderschuren, M., Jennings, G., Khayesi, M., & Mitullah, W. V. (2017). Challenges and opportunities for non-motorized transport in urban Africa. In W. V. Mitullah, M. Vanderschuren, &

M. Khayesi (Eds.), *Non-motorized transport integration into urban transport planning in Africa* (pp. 1–10). Routledge.

Wang, Y. P., & Kintrea, K. (2019). Sustainable, healthy and learning cities and neighbourhoods. *Environment and Urbanization ASIA, 10*, 146–150.

Wardlaw, M. J. (2014). History, risk, infrastructure: Perspectives on bicycling in the Netherlands and the UK. *Journal of Transport & Health, 1*, 243–250.

Wilson, J. E., Marshall, J., Wilson, R., & Krizek, J. K. (2010). By foot, bus or car: 4 children's school travel and school choice policy. *Environment and Planning, 42*(5), 4–9.

Yaser, H., Meeghat, H., & Ali, K. (2016). Walking behaviour across genders in school trips, a case study of Rasht. *Journal of Transport & Health, 8*(11), 1405–2214. https://doi.org/10.1016/j.jth.2016.08.011

CULTURE AND DEVELOPMENT: THE TRAUMA OF THE TRAFFICKED SEEKING REMITTANCES

Ahmed Abidur Razzaque Khan[a], Garry J. Stevens[b], Nichole Georgeou[b], Dianne Bolton[b] and Terry Landells[c]

[a]*University of Liberal Arts (ULAB), Bangladesh*
[b]*Western Sydney University, Australia*
[c]*Bolton Landells Consulting, Australia*

ABSTRACT

This chapter examines the plight of Bangladeshi labourers after experiencing labour trafficking during irregular migration via a perilous maritime route to Malaysia in 2015, most of them involved in the Andaman Sea crisis. Their journey and their experiences of trauma are examined at four stages of their journey; pre-commencement/commencement; being trafficked and sold as a batch; at the transfer point when extortion of their families at home occurs, and at the end of their journey as returnees to Bangladesh (the large majority never reaching their destination). The theoretical framework helps highlight the significance of culture on the trauma experienced by the returnees in the broad context of economic and social pressures. It also leverages the individual/collectivism model from cultural psychology, self-discrepancy and resiliency theory to explain how individuals respond to and deal with such trauma, with implications for government policy and NGO support (both pro-active and re-active responses).

Keywords: Irregular migration; labour trafficking; trauma; resource-risk; resilience; self-discrepancy; economic survival; cultural psychology; collectivist culture; Bangladesh

---

Society and Sustainability
Developments in Corporate Governance and Responsibility, Volume 24, 123–151
Copyright © 2025 Ahmed Abidur Razzaque Khan, Garry J. Stevens, Nichole Georgeou, Dianne Bolton and Terry Landells
Published under exclusive licence by Emerald Publishing Limited
ISSN: 2043-0523/doi:10.1108/S2043-052320240000024006

1. BACKGROUND AND CONTEXT

The focus of this chapter is on the plight and rehabilitation of Bangladeshi male labourers who were trafficked consequent upon their embarking on irregular migration via a perilous maritime route, seeking alternative work opportunities overseas. Undocumented migration from Bangladesh has occurred since the late 1980s with Bangladeshis migrating to Japan via Thailand. After strict visa requirements closed the labour market in Japan in the early 1990s, potential migrants turned to Malaysia and Singapore, undocumented migrants crossing Thailand and Singapore as transit points, entering Malaysia by air, cars, trucks and boats, international networks becoming significant players. The irregular migration flows in the Bay of Bengal and Andaman Sea reached new heights in 2014 and 2015 culminating in the Andaman Sea crisis.[1] Between 2013 and 2016, these irregular migration boat journeys claimed approximately 2,000 Bangladeshi and Rohingya lives (IOM, 2017; UNHCR, 2021). Twenty-five of the 2,813 survivors repatriated by the International Organization for Migration (IOM) to Bangladesh after the 2015 Andaman Sea crisis were interviewed in this study, all survivors of labour trafficking. The aim was to better understand the nature of their experience and their response to associated trauma.[2]

The approach taken to understanding their motivation to undertake such a journey and their responses to their experiences is informed by the literature on development, culture, motivation, risk and trauma. We provide a multidisciplinary approach to defining the drivers of such irregular migration, highlighting that household strategy, largely determined by household heads, is a vital *collective* economic strategy in the decision-making process for migration in Bangladesh (Ullah, 2010). These labour migrants often risk meagre existing resources through irregular migration, perceiving they have few options for transforming existing family resources within a more structured accumulation strategy consistent with the notion of 'development' (Bernards, 2022). The fraught nature of family decisions to invest meagre and often borrowed resources in a transition plan to fund irregular migration is exposed here within the in-depth data provided.

The interpretation of opportunities and risks associated with facilitating family members to work overseas also reflects government policy that normalises and encourages the development path of labour migration and remittance, which has contributed to Bangladesh's economic success. For many Bangladeshis living in poverty, labour migration (whether sanctioned or irregular and undocumented) is regarded as an important pathway to improve their family's economic outcomes, even though undocumented labour migration carries significant risks, including that of being trafficked. A report of the United Nations Office on Drugs and Crime (UNODC, 2022a) identified risk factors giving rise to trafficking as including '... economic need, harmful traditional practices, internal and cross-border displacement, irregular migration and climate change'.

The complexities associated with government appraisal of economic growth patterns and social fallout is captured in the *First national study on trafficking in persons in Bangladesh* (UNODC, 2022a) where the Bangladesh Ministry of Home

Affairs stated '[t]he country's ability to handle social issues is growing as a direct result of its economic success'.

Remittances from exported labour contribute significantly to Bangladesh's economy, even though as a result of COVID they fell from 6% of GDP in 2021 to 4.6% in 2022 (Bangladesh Bank, 2022). The IOM (2022) noted the importance of remittances in increasing household disposable income and stimulating the local economy and their significance for economic development when transformed into investment, including small and medium-sized business. Thus, remittance revenue has been broadly accepted as a critical dimension of development resourcing, particularly for the transformation of assets towards more productive futures, particularly in rural areas.

However, critical challenges exist for developing nations seeking access to international labour markets as a growth strategy through remittance. Bernards (2022) suggested '[m]arketisation often founders on the messy confrontation between neoliberal fantasies of efficient, socially beneficial markets and the contradictory, spatial, material and social conditions of actually-existing capital accumulation' (p. 7). The reality and complexity of this challenge is also consistent with Sanyal's (2014) contribution to the 'development' discourse. He describes the original stages of primitive accumulation of capital, including the annihilation of pre-capital, as excluding a 'surplus population' from the development trajectory. This exclusion, in turn, poses a legitimation crisis for the government of the day, manifest in the continued existence of absolute poverty for many. As a result, the notion of 'basic needs' becomes foregrounded in a way that obscures development as a clear transition path. Sanyal suggests that

> The tension between need and accumulation ...remains at the heart of the development discourse until they both are turned into parts of a new *complex* totality produced by the market... With the rise of neo-liberalism, post-colonial capitalist development is now being posited as a market-driven process within a system of meanings that can accommodate accumulation and need as two apparently non-contradictory nodal points residing within a single space defined by the market. (2014, p. 98)

This chapter, in its discussion of the trafficking experience, highlights Sanyal's (2014) tensions between the pressure on governments to address the fulfilment of both basic needs and accumulation through market-based labour migration strategies. It is also concerned with the tensions for the Bangladeshi state in supporting a regulated labour export strategy that meets its commitments to national and international political institutions, including the UN's Sustainable Development Goals (SDGs). Regarding labour migration, it is challenged therefore to manage tensions between promoting means of employment and economic growth (including supporting labour migration as a viable option for capital accumulation) and ensuring more regulated labour market practices around migration in a manner consistent with SDGs, especially SDG 1: End poverty in all its forms everywhere and SDG 8: Promote sustained, inclusive and sustainable economic growth, full and productive employment and decent work for all. Accordingly, it is also challenged to reduce risk factors giving rise to trafficking, especially economic need and irregular migration, consistent with

SDG16 and its Target 16.2: End abuse, exploitation, trafficking and all forms of violence against and torture of children.

This paper explores the experience of survivors of trafficking at each stage of their journey, seeking to throw light on the nature of their trauma and their responses to it, highlighting the psycho-socio-economic aspects of the challenge that trafficking poses for both participants and the state.[3] It describes the business model of traffickers and their attempts to asset strip persons who are seeking pathways to utilise existing but inadequate resources as investment to access new forms of household income through remittances. It also highlights the challenges for the state in dealing with this complex reality, focussing on participants' perspectives of the economic and social constraints they face, the level of risk they perceive in undocumented migration, their propensity to learn from the trauma experienced and the significance of that trauma in a developing nation context in which all participants feel pressured to better meet the needs of their families and communities. These insights have value for policymakers and support services. They suggest that in collectivist cultures there is need for a more holistic appraisal of such trauma in the context of economic and cultural perceptions of opportunity, risk and resiliency, with implications for interventions to limit the deleterious consequences for well-being, poverty alleviation and employability of individuals and their families in the broader context of SDGs 1, 8 and 16.

2. MOTIVATION FOR UNDERTAKING UNDOCUMENTED LABOUR MIGRATION

In Bangladesh, many families believe it is within their grasp to build resources through labour migration to countries where higher wages can enhance opportunities for resource acquisition through remittances. Both individuals and the community tend to underestimate potential risk when the goal is overcoming immediate forms of poverty. The Dalal (migration agents and brokers who are themselves often a trusted community member – whilst some operate within trafficking networks) often instigate the trafficking experience and misinform community members about risks concerning labour migration and trafficking networks. In some cases, the journey is promoted as an enjoyable, quasi-holiday trip (Khan, 2020).

Khan et al. (2024) identify that perceptions of risk associated with labour migration are often heavily influenced by expectations and pressures of family and community. Whilst pursuing remittances, the local community often lacks information concerning risks associated with undocumented labour migration, the sinister nature of networks that support this process (including the role of Dalal), the threat to health and life and the consequences of an unsuccessful initiative. The results of 'naive' engagement in undocumented labour migration is often intensely traumatic for those involved, resulting in diminished current and future asset bases, health and status in the community.

In Bangladesh, as elsewhere, Government messaging has highlighted and normalised labour migration as a source of contribution to GDP, development investment and economic success for people with limited access to other forms of capital or employment options (UNODC, 2022a). However, impoverished and desperate groups often do not have access to information that differentiates between risks associated with formal and undocumented migration which are often only apparent post-event and even then, this does not always deter them from repeating desperate acts. Siddiqui (2017) provided important insight into the decision-making of trafficked labour on the sea route to Malaysia:

> Failed first-time migrants ... often repeatedly attempt to migrate. The underlying assumption is that this particular *Dalal* was bad and cheated them and they would do better with a different *Dalal*. One cannot blame them because there is a quite a number of examples of migrants becoming successful only after their third or fourth venture. (p. 7)

However, perceptions of risk are intrinsically influenced by culture. In turn, this has implications for the notion of trauma and culturally appropriate interventions in the context of preventative and reactive measures. Below we explore frameworks that support deeper insight into the relationship between culture and trauma and the ways it might influence individual decisions concerning resource enhancement options.

2.1 Collectivist Culture, Trauma and the Self-Concept

Shaler (2005) asserts that a traumatic event is interpreted in the context of emotional and personal meaning, culture providing this context. Engelbrecht and Jobson's (2016) study of trauma appraisals in trauma survivors from collectivist cultures identified themes (a number of which also emerged in this study) including: trauma and adjustment, cultural and social roles, the traumatised self, relationships with others, external attribution and education. A key theme throughout their study, and the data presented here, was the primacy of family and community expectations when evaluating and responding to trauma (such as that associated with trafficking), defining success and failure, and risk parameters.

Engelbrecht and Jobson (2016) noted the extent to which interdependence versus independence is promoted in a cultural setting, contrasting the perception of 'the self' and associated decision-making in more individualistic and collectivist cultures. Relevant to the nature of trauma associated with trafficking, they suggested that collectivist cultures do not appraise individual success in such ventures as importantly as success that reflects the interdependence of an individual and their social environment. They also emphasise that there has been little research investigating the impact of culture through self-construal in trauma-related appraisals of trauma survivors in non-Western collectivist societies, noting the need for the '... use of qualitative methodologies to understand the interplay of culture and trauma (i.e., trauma appraisals)' and emphasising the importance of the meaning that community members from collectivistic cultures attach to trauma. Such psychological insights are described as important in providing appropriate care and access to support services post-trauma given the challenge of meeting cultural obligations. Danailova-Trainor and Laczko (2010) and Jesperson et al. (2022) add that policy frameworks to combat trafficking might seek a better understanding of the relationship between development policy, labour migration and trafficking.

Engelbrecht and Jobson (2016) add that '... following traumatic events ... cognitive understandings of the world are called into question and have the potential to have ... detrimental effects on an individual; namely PTSD [post-traumatic stress disorder]' (p. 2). Their later work in 2020 highlights the importance of self-concept and self-appraisals in interpreting potentially traumatic events and determining post-traumatic psychological adjustment. In a post-traumatic situation, psychological disruptions can result in structural changes in the self-concept because the trauma experienced cannot be accommodated, resulting in negative self-appraisals that can influence future decisions. They leverage Higgins' (1996) self-discrepancy theory in describing three domains which might become discrepant and constitute sources of tension and anxiety for the individual after having experienced trauma. These are:

> The 'Actual' (representation of the attributes that one believes they possess and is one's basic self-concept), the 'Ideal' (representation of the attributes that someone would like to possess) and the 'Ought' (representation of the attributes that someone believes they should or ought to possess such as duty, obligations and responsibilities). (Engelbrecht & Jobson, 2020, p. 464)

The search for meaning can be catalytic in redefining or re-evaluating the self-concept and self-evaluation in sense-making the experience of trauma, culture influencing an individual's understanding of the self in experiencing trauma.

> ... Asian cultures tend to perceive the self to be interdependent with others and emphasize relatedness of group norms and group harmony ... a consistent self-concept [being] less valued in Eastern cultures ... an interdependent self-focus [having] a more flexible, inconsistent and discrepant self-concept than their Western counterparts ... more tolerant of apparent contradictions in self-concept. (2020, p. 464)

Engelbrecht and Jobson (2020) also note that although self-discrepancies have less impact on well-being in Eastern cultures, endorsing negative self-characteristics results in poorer psychological adjustment across cultures.

Jayawickreme et al. (2013), apply the individualism/collectivism model from cultural psychology, to emphasise the importance of understanding ethno-cultural variations in the manifestation of PTSD and argue for more insights into the varied expressions of psychological distress. They draw upon Friedman and Marsella (1996) noting that

> ...[s]ince cultural differences are tied to variations in the social construction of reality – which is in turn influenced by cultural differences in cognition and the experience and expression of emotion – the perception of what is a traumatic experience as well as the individual and social response to it can conceivably vary greatly. (p. 4)

Thus, cultural critique is also important in considering the concept of resilience. Resiliency behaviours cover a spectrum from springing back from trauma and regaining previous positions, associated assets and benefits, through to transformational resilience in which hardships become a learning exercise that acts as a springboard into alternative behaviours and aspirations more adapted to the conditions experienced (Bolton et al., 2023). In the context of the trafficking case reported below, families and community helped facilitate participants undertake irregular migration to improve their respective well-being in line with traditional communitarian networks, value sets and traditions, often underestimating risk and trauma to the participant and community. Emergent forms of resilience reported by the trafficked situate resilient behaviours in this context.

3. THE STAGES OF THE JOURNEY, THE EXPERIENCE OF TRAUMA

In investigating the cultural nature of trauma and its implications for policy, we analyse and discuss the journey undertaken by the Bangladeshi male labourers in four stages. These are illustrated in Fig. 1 below. The first stage is pre-commencement/commencement in which undocumented labour migrants are largely well-treated, although misinformed of the dangers. The second is 'Being sold in "batches"' in which the journey takes an unexpected and unimaginable direction when these labour migrants are sold to traffickers, abused, confined, restrained, held under armed guard, starved, beaten and some meet their death. The third is 'Transfer points' in which threats and demand for money can result in torture or death if not met. The fourth and final stage is 'Completion of journey'. For those who reached the destination, new threats emerged as undocumented labour, for example, violence on work sites, immigration detention, deportation and jail. The victims who failed to complete the journey returned home after significant resource loss and faced rehabilitation in extreme poverty and often ill health.

4. STAGES OF THE JOURNEY

4.1 Stage One: Pre-Commencement and Commencing the Journey

This stage includes labourers identifying expectations of their families and support networks, responding to overtures of brokers and commencing the journey on land prior to boarding sea vessels. Migration opportunities as pathways to 'development' are reinforced by government policy, local community and family. Paid work overseas promises increased financial security, improved lifestyle and the opportunity to diversify family resources that for many were becoming increasingly inadequate in maintaining or improving social and economic circumstances. Family support was often shaped by limited understanding of risk in the re-employment of family resources and incurred debt to fund the venture.

Participants had used funding mechanisms including debt financing (a common and accepted cultural practice) as well as selling land, property and other productive assets such as livestock, agricultural crops and small home businesses. Other sources of funding included NGOs (particularly microcredit agencies), traditional moneylenders, relatives and friends. Joarder and Miller (2014) reported that selling agricultural land was the primary funding strategy

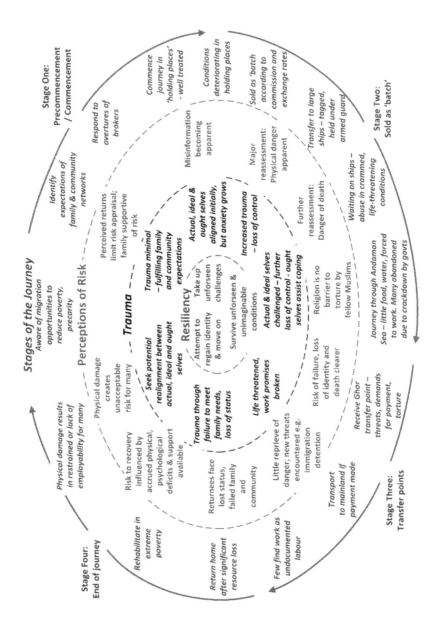

Fig. 1. Stages of the Undocumented Labour Migration/Trafficked Journey: Culture, Risk, Trauma and Resilience.

reported by 60% of irregular migrants. Study participants reported they drew on such tangible assets, 10 out of 25 reported using loans or debt financing as the principle means of funding. Although this might appear to be an extraordinary risk when considering the size of financial outlays against current assets and salaries, when set against perceived lucrative returns to be gained in Malaysia and implications for additional family income and future investment, the risk was considered low.

In addition, family and community networks were involved in shaping introductions and responses to the Dalal. Thus, in these early stages, the perception of risk was diluted by confidence that Dalal had their interests at heart, and there was limited evidence to challenge this assumption. Participants demonstrated a fundamental trust in family and community assessments of the need for urgent and alternative strategies to improve economic and social prospects. Limited information about risks associated with undocumented migration by sea were supplemented by fantasies promulgated by Dalal about the trip.

Shaed Ali (40 y.o.) recalled:[4]

> He (the Dalal) informed me that he would send me within 10 days in exchange for 220K Taka. He told that "There are football grounds in the ship. They will provide a lot of good quality food. I will provide you my cell number, so if there is any issue you can talk to me directly." The broker tricked me . . .he entrapped me in such a way that I could not break the chains.

Similarly, Mohobbot Miah (18–19 y.o.) was deceived:

> While working as a power loom operator, the broker used to visit me each day and convinced me [by saying]: "my dear nephew, would you like to ruin your life by doing this job! Go to Malaysia, I will arrange the trip. You will be in good shape. The trip will be by ship; you will reach the destination watching TV, within 5 days". He told me to collect more passengers, so I arranged five more persons. The Dalal told us that he would bear all costs and that we would enjoy the 'dolphin visa'!

The initial treatment was good with 40% of respondents stating that brokers paid for their travel, food and hotels and even for cigarettes, tea and betel nut. A migration expert interviewed commented on the innovative marketing strategies of grassroots brokers:

> These brokers are really shrewd – they do not gather people or young fellows from Comilla or Noakhali area, the reason being the people from these areas are quite smart. They used to do their marketing in areas where people are less smart, for example Sirajganj and Sathkhira, where they recruit many people. The reason is these areas have had comparatively less migration campaigning. NGOs are less active in these areas, and the local people know much less about such things as legal migration and the risks of irregular migration. Therefore, whatever [Dalal] tell people works.

Shahedali, (28 y.o.) explained how he was convinced by his colleague who had a link with the broker:

> . . .the broker instructed my colleague earlier, and then both of them met me. So, he tried his best and convinced me according to the Dalal's instruction. He had been well prepared by the Dalal to motivate me because the Dalal knew that we were close friends.

At this stage, individuals had firm expectations of benefits to self and family. However, some anxiety was generated by the requirement to maintain secrecy around the process, 14 of the respondents being aware of this condition, having been advised by Dalal not to inform family members, not even wives, of their imminent departure. However, the secrecy was a surprise for some, anxiety increasing when the chains of secret networks became apparent.

Doria Sek (20 y.o.) noted:

> There are Dalal everywhere, [and change] at every point... even in the villages one Dalal will escort people to a certain place, and another will move them... to another. They brought us from the village of Sirajganj to a police station suburb, and then escorted ...us to Chittagong. There they kept the 12 of us locked in a house. 10 more joined us in that room...22 men in a single room. It was the holy month of Ramadan; we had travelled 17 hours... Then they sent us to a small trawler at 2 in the morning.

Resiliency at this stage of the journey was manifest as the capacity for most participants to cope with the realisation that they were possibly trapped under the guise of maintaining secrecy, experiencing a loss of control and the inability to turn back.

A Madrassa student (who had been abducted) coped by calling on religious support:

> We attended Maghreb [evening] prayer there. Then I told an elderly person, "Uncle, we are all about to take a troublesome journey. We are in trouble. You people who joined voluntarily cannot turn back, and myself who had to join this trip unwillingly, I could not go back as well. Certainly not." Then I requested him, "You are the elderly person here, you call to Allah. I could not call to Allah as I am merely a lad, I do not have the language to talk to Allah yet." (Poran Miah, 18 y.o)

Poran also befriended a boy close to his age who was part of the trafficking gang, convincing him to let him use his mobile phone to send a text message to his sister informing her that he had been trafficked and was confined in a cave. This relationship potentially saved his life later when finally abandoned by the traffickers on a small island off Thailand. The young trafficker provided Poran with water, helping him survive.

Goribullah (35 y.o.), a fish vendor, demonstrated resilient behaviour that helped his cohort survive. To avoid suffocating under a tarpaulin in the transport truck, he managed to collect blades to cut holes so the labourers could breathe. Also, he carried dry foods on his head along the difficult route before finally boarding the ship. These foods helped survival on board.

4.2 Stage Two: Being Sold as 'Batches'

As groups of migrants were assembled, they were sold to trafficking syndicates in batches for fees or commissions and locked up in holding places before boarding small boats to commence the sea journey. Participants who had believed their journey was voluntary now began to sense their loss of control over the process, 8 of the 25 respondents reporting they were locked up between 2 to 7 days in remote houses or secured flats. Four respondents reported being kept under armed guard in a cave in a hillside or in an underground shelter in a jungle, to maintain secrecy and prevent any turning back.

Goribullah described being forced to board a small boat at the beginning of the trip:

> We were told [originally] that we won't go by this small boat. [But] you see, they showed up with big knives, locally made sharpened instruments. They ordered us "get boarded right away! If you don't we will chop you down [here] and throw you in the ocean" ... Due to fear all of us boarded.

Seven respondents identified they were forced to board boats by traffickers. Some were duped and were never voluntary undocumented migrants:

> ...my friend Rafiq invited me to hang out by the sea. I went with him. I didn't know, my fellow friend sold me to the trafficker and left for Sylhet. When I wanted to get back they told me that they would break one of my limbs if I tried to leave. They beat me a lot and boarded me on the boat forcefully. (Joinal Bibagi, 23 y.o)

The Bangeldeshi labourers were transferred to larger ships run by international or transnational traffickers anchored in the national waters of Bangladesh or Myanmar. Rohingya escaping persecution sometimes travelled with their families and were also on the boat. On most ships, armed traffickers distributed colour coded wrist bands to identify the boss who 'owned' the wearer. Others said they had been tagged on the small transfer boats. Over a couple of weeks for small vessels (minimum 200 passengers) to 6 weeks or more for large vessels (collecting 400–500 people), the undocumented migrants were held until the loads were viable (Poran Miah noted it took 35 days to gather 400 people). The perception of risk increased when people became sick during the waiting period. A 20-year-old participant noted that this '...was a perilous situation'.

Others in this study described verbal and physical abuse, including torture, as starting when they were being transferred to a holding place and continuing during the waiting period. Once on board the larger vessels, all participants experienced verbal abuse and forms of physical torture.

> ...[they] put us on another boat, a larger fishing trawler. They put us inside a cabin and closed its entrance cover ...they told us there is CCTV, so they can watch us, and scolded us with names, kicked us at the same time. Watching such torture, we were scared...totally panicked. (Rupban Miah, 32 y.o.)

Jahalam Box (56 y.o.) further described the abuse:

> Inside the ship, boys used to quarrel over drinking water... 250 grams of water was provided to four people to drink... the stress for water was high. For food it was ok as they provided molasses, flatten and dried rice, including oral saline... If anyone asked for water, they started beating them. And if someone was going to prevent the beating then they used to get beaten by a group. Once I asked the Magh [Burmese or Rohingya trafficker] for water and got kicked in return, and then they threw me out from the first floor of the ship. The Chinese people [who controlled the ship] told us that we were not good people. Many times, I was beaten to prevent others from beatings. They treated us like animals. The used to beat us with a fat pipe, and I got hurt on my neck.

The limited capacity to communicate increased the lack of control. They were forbidden to talk to each other.

> They keep a surveillance. If they see that some people were talking then they start beating from that side and beat all the people to other side, without any mercy. If we looked around, we were beaten. They ordered "Be seated on your space, if you move, you will be beaten." Forty-five days total we were confined like this. (Tej Ali, 36 y.o.)

The traffickers interpreted the language barrier as a form of insubordination:

> As we did not know their language, we could not ask [for what we needed]. Even when we asked [in our language] we were beaten in turn... If someone complained, then they beat us severely like kicking and punching. They beat us severely, inhumanly. The people from Dhaka area were beaten most, as they do not get the Burmese language. When the Majhi [sailors] told them not to go for a pee, they didn't get it and they went for a call of nature...So they got beaten. Because most of the Majhis were from Myanmar and Cox's Bazar, it was a problem for the people from Dhaka and Mymensing areas. (Mamud Mondol, 18 y.o.)

More than 35% of participants in the study were wounded, beaten by plastic pipes, belts, sticks, iron or steel rods, hammers and other blunt instruments. One suffered a broken hand on the ship, with permanent loss of function. Another became paralysed:

> They hit me 36 times with a pipe on this side of my hand and leg. I got sick after that beating and lost my senses. Taking my beaten-up state into consideration they gave me some juice with sleeping drugs in it. I slept nineteen days onwards. I developed sores on my side... My hand and leg became numb during that time. (Falu Boks, 30 y.o.)

For most of the participants, coping with very little food and water, not moving for weeks, insufficient clothing, suffering heat stress (from both other people's bodies and the heat of the day) created a suffocating and deadly environment. Many became sick, grew weak and developed severe skin diseases. Others, unable even to move their limbs, became unconscious. The lack of control was fuelled by constant fear of dying through weakness, illness, suffocation or execution by shooting or being thrown into the sea by the traffickers.

The participants were severely traumatised by witnessing the torture, illness, killing and suicide of others. Eight respondents described witnessing about two dozen persons committing suicide, and at least half a dozen being killed by traffickers with firearms.

> [Whilst] having a meal a person asked for some water and was kicked in response. He died out of strangulation, just in front of me. I moved aside after watching it. They threw the body into the sea immediately. People suffered a lot and died. Around fifty to sixty people died there. Some were thrown into the sea, getting their stomach opened by knives. Some others committed suicide as they could not bear it anymore. (Mohobbot Miah, 18 y.o.)

> When the number of people reached five hundred, they stopped providing food. Days passed by... and they did not give us food. Whatever provided was not enough, and we got beaten if we asked for drinking water... They forbid us to go to the toilet. All the time was spent sitting like a sack, there was no room to even move your legs. Our head had to keep inside our knees. We spent 2 months 13 days on that boat, all five hundred and seven people. They killed a lot of people for sure. They bring them inside the ship and shot them down. Then they cut the belly

and threw the dead body from the deck (into the sea) so the body easily sank... I felt so down. I thought if I die, they will throw my body same way! (Rafiqul, 19 y.o.)

Chandu Hosen (18 y.o.) recalled being sold to another ship by the ship owner and, after having been attacked by pirates, being moved to another ship by climbing a rope and jumping on board. Some people died or were killed on the spot as they could not manage this feat.

The trafficking syndicates comprised people from Myanmar, Thailand and Malaysia. The trafficking trade was carried out mainly by Myanmar nationals but included some Thai, most of whom were Buddhists, and some Chinese operators who controlled or operated ships and vessels. Severe tensions were reported as having risen between the Bangladeshi labourers and Rohingya migrants on these ships, the Rohingyans being better able to speak Burmese or other languages used by traffickers.

> Once on board the Rohingya received better treatment than us. They used to get food regularly. We wouldn't get food like them. They know their languages, [so] they could ask for their needs ...We did not know their language so we were not be able to ask for our needs, and if we ask, they beat us. (Shahedali, 28 y.o.)

Fourteen respondents identified that Rohingya helped the traffickers. Goribullah recalled that Rohingya beat and tortured some Bangladeshis to extract money:

> ... they forced us to give them money and said, "We are people of the ship, and you are Bengali". They prepared cane sticks to whip [us]. Then they dragged us [inside the ship] and if people could not pay or contest then they would kill them and throw their bodies in the sea.

Most of the respondents reported that the Rohingya acted opportunistically and failed to display the core values they expected from a Muslim community.

> They used to quarrel with Bengalis the whole night... [and] would beat up the Bengalis. The navigators of the ship listened to [the Rohingya] because they offered their children and wife to the navigators. What should I say, [the navigators] did whatever they liked. And the Rohingya had fun after sending their mothers and wives [to the traffickers]. The Rohingya would commit wrongs and then blame the Bengalis. They would then beat up the Bengalis, first tying our hands with handcuffs to the poles of the ship. Rohingya know almost all the state languages; thus, they could comply with other nationals. Such smart/bad people they are! (Mukul Miah, 35 y.o.)

Tej Ali (36 y.o.) narrated how he, along with his Bangladeshi friends, were mistreated by the Rohingya on board when they were abandoned by the traffickers after the strengthening of measures by the Thai and Malaysian governments to prevent landings.

> A few Indonesian fishing boats found us... we all looked like skeletons; they felt for us and showed sympathy... they gave us some rice, lentils and oil for the machine. However, Rohingya ate all the food and told us they would kill us all. They had seized all the arms of the ship and stabbed other Bangladeshi migrants and threw them in to sea. I was even thrown out as well, then I had to swim for half an hour to survive. Whoever could survive by swimming, they were alive; those who could not, they drowned.

Most of the Bangladeshi respondents were shocked to receive such treatment from fellow Muslims. Another example of religious trauma was experienced by a young Buddhist, escaping religious persecution in Cox's Bazar. He was mistreated throughout the journey by a Muslim cleric and his followers who tried to convert him to Islam, ultimately delivering a *fatwa* to kill him.

Thus, traumatic events during this stage of the journey included: restriction of movement, denial of water and food, forced labour, witnessing suicide and murder by traffickers and witnessing sexual misconduct and murder from fellow Muslims. Such experiences challenged their 'actual-selves' and 'ideal-selves' (Engelbrecht & Jobson, 2020; Higgins, 1996) when confronting unimaginable conditions and loss of control. Their 'ought-selves' struggled to maintain a sense of identity previously based on shared community and religious values. Yet resilience as a survival strategy was manifest by many in the face of unprecedented, shocking and incomprehensible experiences, some of which had generated despair in others leading to suicide.

4.3 Stage Three: Transfer Points

Many respondents did not reach this third stage. In April 2015, the Thai and Malaysian governments clamped down on trafficking activities after a mass grave of informal migrants was found near the Thai-Malaysia border. As a result, thousands of people were stranded at sea and abandoned in their vessels, awaiting rescue. Normally, this third stage involved transfers at the Thai-Malaysia border or at a Receive Ghor and was the most mentioned example of stress and trauma.[5]

> They could not send us [to Malaysia], rather they beat us on reaching Thailand. We were imprisoned at their hand... They beat us and ordered us to call family at home and ask our family members to send money to a specific place. We had to ask or otherwise they did not even say anything, just beat us. (Salam Mian, 25 y.o.)

It has been reported elsewhere that those who could not pay ransoms could be held for around 4 months in ships, where they had to work as cooks and were ill-treated (UNHCR, 2016). Twelve participants reported abuse and torture at Receive Ghor and were only released when their families were able to transfer money to the trafficking agents. The torture was not limited to the participants but also included mental stress for the victim's family, listening to the voice or sounds of the tortured person over mobile phones:

> I told the trafficker I won't pay a single coin until I reach Malaysia, and I didn't keep any savings at home. If I could reach my destination, my livestock is there and my brothers will give me loans. So, I would give money after reaching the destination. But I didn't give money at that place. Because of that they started torturing me. They beat me in many ways, and the sound of that torture was heard by my family [by phone]. (Jahalam Box, 56 y.o.)

Similarly, Goribullah reported that:

> They took me in Receive Ghor where they punched me and beat for over two days... Someone thought that they were going cut me into pieces. [I urged my family over the phone] "whatever amount of ransom they ask, please provide it to them and release me. Otherwise my life is at risk." ...my parents provided the money... release[ing] me from Receive Ghor.

However, there was still no guarantee that the traffickers would send them to mainland Malaysia after getting the money. Salam Miah was forced to ask his family to send money to the traffickers through the local Dalal, but even after paying, he did not reach his destination.

Crossing the border and reaching the mainland were both very dangerous:

> Next night they transported us by speed boat. We were taken to the main broker directly and then we were put in trawler set for Singapore! They turned back to Malaysia on the way. Then they disembarked us in a place of quicksand... I jumped into quicksand and sank ...The water was cold, it was a really dangerous situation. I didn't know what to do, and at that time I thought I would die. [I thought] "I won't make it to Malaysia anymore." They threw out my belongings and clothes. I even left my underwear [behind] when I crawled out. Then I went to the traffickers' residence. I got torn pants from them to wear. After putting on the pants, they put me in a narrow space in a building. It did not have even the space of one hand. I was given a bottle to pee in. They transferred us in such away. (Jahalam Box, 56 y.o.)

Transfer arrangements became more difficult after the Thai government clampdown. Ratan Shah (33 y.o.) and another labourer survived being transferred from their ship to the Thai jungle in small boats. They were without food and water in the traffickers' camp for 7 days, with only a tarpaulin as cover. The traffickers could not send them to mainland Malaysia. When released in small groups, they had to walk through the jungle, reach a main road and negotiate their own fate. In such situations, immigration detention and jail were high risks, 8 out of the 25 experiencing jails in Indonesia, Thailand or Malaysia for between 1 month and a year.

> After getting four months jail I was sent to juvenile camp. There was no regular food and bathing facilities. We had to stock water at night in a plastic pot. They provided a small amount of rice around 10 a.m. in the morning and provided 1 piece of bread before that. They added some hot water and gourd with rice. These items were served in morning and evening... People died in camps mostly out of starvation, the possibility of death is more there. If someone died, they threw the dead body [to the sea]. (Soikot Sek, 19 y.o.)

Some escaped jail and were recaptured. A 23-year-old participant, having escaped from jail was killed in a motor accident. Paklu Borua (32 y.o.) received a jail sentence of 20 days but was detained for 10 and a half months in Thai immigration.

Other forms of unanticipated risk, stress and trauma were associated with being undocumented labour. Fourteen out of 25 respondents landed in Malaysia, but only four entered the job market through trafficking networks. All four reported ongoing risk. Two were caught by immigration police and were sent back within 3 to 6 months and the remaining two, after working more than 2 years had to return due to health problems or incapacitating injuries.

Jahalam Box described how the tensions between workers themselves generated insecurity, feelings of vulnerability and superstitious thoughts of ill fate, all producing mental stress.

> I arrived at a 44-story market in Penang. My friend had given me hope that if I went there I would be able to earn 70k/month. I worked there for one month and my bills were 1,205 ringgit. Suddenly I noticed the conflict with Bangladeshi and Vietnamese workers, two [Bangladeshi

workers] were in very critical condition, one of their heads had been broken and he was bleeding severely. We fled to a two hundred to three hundred feet high hill nearby in fear of police ... a boss said "the police could release you after a few days. However, if Vietnamese get you then you are finished, they will eat you up!" Then he told us [they]are short of workers too [for] two more 44-story buildings under construction. He gave me a key ... and told me that we will stay on the 36th floor. We were fifty-three Bengalis staying in that space. Eight of us had a fight (with the Vietnamese) however it brought suffering on fifty-three of us. Suddenly two people died. One of them was from Vietnam and other one from Jessore; I worked with the other [Bengali] guy just before the day of his death. He went up in a lift to clean and someone dropped a brick or heavy stuff from an upper level and he died on the spot. A rumour spread that Bangla [people] had died. We fled again to the hill. Then another rumour started that the 44-story building got two people and it would eat up another two. Then what we can do? It is not possible to stay here. We were in fear ...I left the place without getting salary.

Some of these conditions had been rumoured prior to the migrant journey, whilst others, such as the tensions between different nationalities of labourers, were not anticipated. The Receive Ghor was known to exist and was

...typically understood as a place of physical and mental torture [that] may occur as part of a trafficker's process. Most of these migrants have heard stories about Receive Ghor prior to their departure and approach[ed] it with some dread but typically also with a resolve that they must endure it... to reach their final destination and its opportunities. (Khan, 2020, p. 111)

Under these conditions, participants needed to manage discrepancies between the actual-, ideal- and ought-selves to meet family and community expectations. For many, the clarity of family expectations and goals appeared to be a coping aid. The fear of failing to meet family expectations appeared to push some participants beyond normal levels of endurance.

In some cases, family members urged continuation despite the stress of being an illegal migrant, the success of arrival appearing to outweigh any other concerns. The discrepancy between the actual- and the ought-self is clearly demonstrated in one participant's decision:

Despite lots of problems, I continued to work. However, I fell ill in the meantime. All [my friends and relatives] told me "People are so keen to come here [Malaysia] and you want to go back!" I told them, "It is better I beg for my livelihood in my country, I won't stay in this country anymore. There is no way to stay as an illegal migrant here!". (Montaj Munshi)

Demonstrations of resiliency reflected the collectivist culture, as when Mukul Miah (35 y.o.) mobilised 10 people from his area at a critical time of the journey to swim to reach the Malaysian shore.

I told them that we are from one community, one family, and I am the elder of us. I would like a promise from all of you... "We do not leave anyone behind. If we die, we die together. We must stick together to live. The thing is all of us won't die, one of us must be alive. So, if one person survives, he can send the information to our home that they died, at that place." They all agreed.

4.4 Stage Four: Completion of the Journey

Participants had sold agricultural land as a primary funding strategy and also had accessed micro-credit and loans from traditional money lenders, relatives and friends. Other productive assets sold had included livestock, agricultural crops and small businesses. Ten out of the 25 respondents reportedly used loans or debt financing paid directly to traffickers, an extraordinarily high risk given the size of such financial outlays against assets and salaries. Four respondents leveraged initial financing or 'pay later offers' provided by traffickers, family members often being required to make these payments urgently under extreme duress.

Selling property urgently reduced its actual value. For example, Sek's family lost their land at half its value (500k Taka US$6,000) and spent 300k Taka on the journey, losing US$9,500 the equivalent of 8 years of salary. This was a common occurrence with negative flow-on effects for work, income and children's education. Sixteen out of those interviewed returned to Bangladesh through the direct intervention of the IOM after the Andaman Sea crisis. Eleven returnees received US$1,000 support payments, the remainder around US$200. The dream of earning around 20K Taka per month ended as economic disaster for most participants.

Participants detailed the levels of indebtedness and the impact on relationships with relatives, feeling less welcome and more vulnerable in their communities. They also reported that Dalal took advantage of their situation in the network and the ignorance of those trafficked to collect additional monies from families for unanticipated circumstances or elements of the process, such as securing a job (initially anticipated as part of the deal), monitoring their progress or arranging the return home. Further costs emanated from medical treatment after their return to deal with health issues incurred on the journey.

> I spent 135K for treatment in Mitford hospital. To pay for this my parents had to take microcredit loans from four organisations. Say for example my mother took one loan, let me say Sir, I arranged to draw from one organisation by my mother, my sister did another, and my brother's wife did another one, thus I arranged 135K from four microcredit agencies. I now have to pay a 2K [$US 25] per week as interest [on all four loans]. My brother is working. My daughter worked in a garment factory sewing mosquito nets, where she can make 4K per month. The rest of the money is paid by my parents and my brother and I do beg around five villages and arrange 4/5K from that. Thus I am paying the interest. (Goribullah, 36 y.o.)

This account concurs with Khan's (2020) conclusion that the business model of labour trafficking is based on acquiring current and future collective family assets. This has psychological implications for all concerned, including the understanding that this outcome represents the end of future opportunities for children's education and dealing with accrued pressure from families, friends, money lenders, micro-credit agencies and banks for loan repayment. Jahalam Box reported he became a 'broken person' and 'the poorest of the poor'. Before the journey, most of the returnees had earned 7–10k Taka per month, and as such were part of the 52% of Bangladesh's working poor living beneath the poverty line. After returning, many reported being able to earn 5k Taka or less per month, having entered the socio-economic strata of extreme poverty, 13% of the Bangladeshi community.

A major driver of discrepancies between actual-, ideal- and ought-selves of participants appeared to be shame and loss of social standing associated with community awareness of the unsuccessful return. Some perceived themselves as becoming non-persons in their communities, some abandoned by their wives or life partners living isolated existences within their communities, having lost health, wealth, social dignity and self-esteem.

Twelve out of 25 reported minor and major health conditions as a result of trauma experienced on the journey including physical and psychological violence and deprivation of food, water, sanitation and movement. Seven out of 25 noted subsequent weakness affecting manual labour and sleep. Twenty out of 25 believed their physical health was worse following migration, 6 out of 25 developed skin diseases and others urinal and sexual health disorders, the latter subject to social taboos and stigma. A community leader described how these people did not have the ability to bear the costs of treatment for sustained physical injuries.

Montaj Munshi, diagnosed with a malignant growth on his throat, returned to Bangladesh for treatment. Despite working abroad for 2 years in Malaysia, he still could not afford treatment for a life-threatening condition.

> I was a strong/ well-built person. When I was sick for seven to eight months, I reduced to a half [my size] already. I need treatment to be alive. I told my mother [the four decimals] of residential land I have now, if I want to continue the treatment, is not enough at all ...If I got to doctor ...I will be diagnosed with much disease. If I die without treatment that's ok. However for my four sons if they do not have a shelter on their head, it would be very difficult for them to live. I will die sooner or later.

Four men with chronic injuries incurred through assaults on ships lost physical capacity to return to full time paid work. Altogether, 9 out of the 25 returnees needed health treatment, the costs having to be covered by their family, and as a result of disability, they often became non-persons in the community, losing the capacity for active social and economic participation.

An IOM study (Connell, 2017) into the needs of returnees from the Andaman Sea crisis evidenced the long-term psychological impact on the returnees, especially those who had been physically beaten and abused on the journey and had witnessed the death of other migrants. In this study, 4 of the 25 reported a significant loss of self-confidence and peace of mind. They had been unable to return to full-time paid work, two being in restricted work and two unable to perform any paid work. Three other respondents reported anxiety-related conditions, for example, fear, avoidance and nightmares, the local term being 'dorai', a fear-related state associated with mental shock or trauma. Only one of these persons was able to return to paid work, the others found employment in restricted roles. Those suffering dorai are generally considered mentally sound, may recover with time and are employable. Two others experienced more serious conditions referred to locally as 'pagol' (mentally disturbed and unbalanced), having thought disturbance, potentially impulsive and largely not considered employable. Johor Ali (32 y.o.) lost his capacity to support his family on return and may have suffered pagol, setting his house on fire, divorcing his wife and attempting to kill himself. He attributes these responses to the mental stress, anxiety and tension resulting from his failed trip:

I feel panicked due to my tension. I used to hate myself. I was really annoyed with myself too. The reason for all this is that there was a family in my area which has now managed to go to America. But I have to lead a miserable life as I am in dire tension. So, I had poison [to kill myself] for the same reason. I am in a dire condition to feed my family. Life is full of struggle. Dawn to dusk I have to think about managing meals. My life has been destroyed due to my trip overseas. I could not lead a normal life. My mind is filled with sorrows.

Kiss et al.'s (2015) report found that 50 out of 1,015 (5.2%) male trafficked labourers in South East Asia claimed a suicide attempt in the month previous to survey. Our data reveal that 8 respondents had witnessed people murdered whilst onboard ship, and this was a common focus of dreams and memories; several had also experienced torture. The Human Rights Commission of Malaysia (2019) also identified it is common for individuals who are sick or restricted in their movements on these densely packed ships to be killed and thrown overboard, bodies often being cut open at the abdomen so that they sink and will not attract attention of authorities. Aladin (28 y.o.) described haunting memories, persistent nightmares and distress:

I wake up and I find myself in the ship...someone is talking inside, and I see they are slicing up the tummy. You see, recalling such scenes makes me more uncomfortable, helpless. Those [memories] get back in the dream ...Though I do not shout in my dream I can see when I wake up it is around Fazar [before sun rise] ...my sleep ends there.

Poran Miah (18, Cox's Bazar) faced similar experiences, still living in fear:

Sometimes I revisit those [times] in dreams. The way they tortured us, this haunts my mind ... they come back and forth as cycles [and] ... it has an impact on my mind. Earlier I had confidence .... I could do this and that. After getting home from overseas I lost that strength of mind ... I even feel uncomfortable while sleeping ... and I live in fear.

Kiss et al. (2015) found that 60.7 % of trafficked labourers reported symptoms of depression, 48.4 % anxiety and 46.3 % reported symptoms consistent with PTSD. In our data, Mohobbot Miah (18 y.o.) suffering a hearing problem and leg injury, revealed that memories and fear continued to haunt him:

A lot of people ask me [about my trip]. I request that they do not ask me about this incident, as I feel down when I remember it. I do recall it though, every now and then. I was so panicked there [and] lost my courage. When I recall all these in my absent mind my body turns cold in fear. I live in fear.

These responses seem consistent with trauma-related conditions. Although in interview he identified his leg injury as the primary cause of his current inability to work, these fears exacerbated his problems.

A community leader interviewed suggested that:

They are not getting the right treatment for the physical damages they had during their trip. They are not getting any type of treatment as they need money for their treatment. Eventually he becomes penniless and vulnerable. He lost his assets, how he will get money? However, he needs treatment. I've seen some of them unable to work firmly and they could not even stand. The young man used to work 8–16 hours at power loom by standing constantly. At present he lost all his energy to work.

Another returnee spoke of his need for better treatment assistance: 'I need to lead a healthy life, and for that I need some support, especially treatment support' (Doria Sek). Many face this paradox, to be able to work they need treatment, yet treatment is unaffordable as they have little income, resources have been dissipated and the government and NGOs offer inadequate support for treatment.

Many participants demonstrated resilience through the process of returning home itself. Four of the respondents described the inner strength of mind and hope that was needed, but nevertheless this also tended to depend again on financial help from family for air tickets, reinforcing the sense of dependency and failure.

5. RESILIENCE IN CULTURAL CONTEXT

The literature suggests a need for a more integrated understanding of culturally specific perceptions and reflections in relation to the experience of trafficked victims, as a basis for refining policy interventions specific to a Global South context. Danailova-Trainor and Laczko (2010) noted data on reintegration of trafficked victims are very sparse with little in-depth information available to support more integrated policy. This paper adds important insights to help close these gaps. In Fig. 1, forms of trauma and resiliency associated with the Andaman Sea crisis are demonstrated at different stages of the journey. Specific forms of resiliency include: participants taking up unforeseen challenges, surviving unforeseen and unimaginable conditions and adapting to circumstances on their completion of the journey to regain identity and move on. The capacity to make sense of the trauma appeared critical to moving on and appears relevant to future life choices of participants in fulfiling community goals by creating development options.

We discuss below the themes identified by Engelbrecht and Jobson (2016) from their study of trauma survivors from collectivist cultures, relating them to the actual-, ideal- and ought-self concepts to help interpret the experiences reported by participants, perceived through the lens of collectivist culture.

5.1 Dimensions of Collectivist Perceptions of Trauma

Cultural and social roles: When individuals fail to meet societal expectations, in this case expectations of family and local community networks, they are traumatised. In the cognitive appraisal of the risk to life of a son or daughter given responsibility for family support and future opportunities, the risk of trauma experienced in grasping an opportunity, for example, in the unregulated and non-documented labour force, is measured against failure to fulfil perceived family obligations on which many life chances depend. In other words, there can be a tendency to normalise such risk. Poverty has a significant influence on the notion of 'acceptance' of risk.

Our data suggest that the participants' actual-self trusted in family and community networks; the ideal-self was courageous enough to take advantage of opportunities; and the ought-self accepted obligations to fulfil the plans of the family to invest its meagre resources in the transformation of economic and social well-being, at the same time increasing family status in the community. When these assumptions proved to be errant in the context of the opportunity sought, discrepancies between the lived experience and one, more or all of these selves were unavoidable, potentially leading to trauma.

For some participants, the trauma of failure was experienced with unreconcilable shifts in self-concept, from a provider meeting community expectations to a dependant, especially when the physical trauma incurred was inconsistent with the recovery of traditional roles and status. Such experiences of trauma generate a sense of hopelessness and failure, individuals 'think[ing] of themselves as very weak and not very strong to face these problems [resultant from the trauma event]' (Engelbrecht & Jobson, 2016, p. 6).

These findings stress the importance of ensuring that remote communities are made aware of the real risks in following uncritically the advice of trusted community members such as Dalal.

Relationships with others: Deshingkar (2019) critiques the culturally specific role that brokers play '. . . in the subjectivation and precarisation of migrant men and women from marginalised classes and ethnicities in the Global South' (p. 2638). She draws attention to the need for richly textured accounts underpinning processes of precarisation that shed light on the complex role of brokers and their claims to help individuals fulfil obligations by transcending the constraints of local power and development inequalities.

Thus, the relationships between the family and community networks, including placing trust in brokers, might be challenged given exploitation and trauma incurred. The data reflect the extent to which family and community networks, as influential social groups, are *actually* trusted as superior forms of insight, can *ideally* ensure the viability of opportunities recommended and *ought* to be respected and leveraged, particularly given ignorance of or perceived lack of access to formal migration programs. When lived experience challenges these actual-, ideal- and ought-selves, discrepancy and trauma can result, although Engelbrecht and Jobson (2020) noted a greater tolerance of apparent contradictions in self-concept in collectivist cultures.

Again, community education through a range of media channels appears to be critical in countering the misinformation spread by Dalal and other trusted community members that leads to the exploitation and asset stripping of poor families seeking alternative forms of income.

Trauma and adjustment: As noted above, trauma has its genesis in the false information from community sources that is often accepted unquestionably by the victims of trafficking, that is, the actual-self is a member of a trusted community that should supply appropriate information that often becomes discrepant, resulting in unexpected and irreconcilable trauma. However, the experience of trauma envisaged in collectivist cultures is primarily in terms of physical health deficits from trauma, rather than mental or psychological health (Engelbrecht & Jobson, 2016). The ideal-self is physically able, physical health being a precondition for meeting obligations to family and community, especially for unskilled male labour seeking migration. Physical strength and capability are core to perceptions and behaviours that define the 'ought'. Psychological trauma is associated with the discrepant-self no longer having capacity to meet family, group and community expectations, often causing a breakdown of relationships within these networks, the latter often being essential for psychological well-being through a sense of belongingness when facing hardship and trauma. Regaining such strength depends on community reconnections, and physical health appears critical for rebuilding and regenerating an effective self-concept and meeting community expectations.

Thus, rehabilitation needs to consider medical assistance to support reintegration into the community as an active and able member.

The traumatised self: In collectivist cultures, concern for specific others often rates above concern for self, though often these are inextricably linked. Thus, a sense of failure in achieving community expectations generates self-blame and guilt despite the exogenous challenges and impediments characterising the migration journey in this case. Our data suggest that participants' actual-self sees failure and resultant losses as his responsibility, the ideal-self as achieving desired outcomes despite obstacles, and the ought-self as being responsible for reversing losses and regaining status after the journey. Community stories of the heroic achievement by some who had taken a journey previously and changed family fortunes were often seen as the norm and reinforced a sense of failure, despite the circumstances. In this study, it appears that the trafficked person tends to shoulder blame, with little retribution for the unrealistic expectations of family and community despite the level of trauma experienced. As noted below, external attribution often takes primacy over blame of others.

External attribution: Engelbrecht and Jobson (2016) identify that in collective cultures, events can be seen as arbitrary and random, causality networks often being difficult to conceptualise. This mindset can also have implications for the discrepant-self in that trauma might be seen as less contingent upon personal choices than as the result of fate. Superstitious and religious beliefs can also cast trauma and failure as punishment from a previous life, and it can also occur when an individual is alienated from their religion after experiencing trauma. Nevertheless, in line with strong community beliefs and values, many survivors of trauma revert to cultural beliefs, rituals and ceremonies to help them recover.

The data collected from participants suggest that some trauma survivors found it difficult to explain the nature of traumatic events given their adherence to fulfiling community expectations, their ideal-selves accepting and managing the 'fates' and their ought-selves perhaps believing that family, religion and community would protect them in adverse circumstances despite the danger and the problematic nature of choices made. Thus, some participants saw their trauma as the cruelty of fate. The trauma was increased for some by the experience that the assumed protection inherent in their social and religious ties and communities had not shielded them from suffering. For example, many seemed to have been traumatised by their perception that the values underpinning Islamic brotherhood had no influence on some Rohingya on this journey. Rather, they saw Rohingya gaining favour by carrying out the traffickers' directions in suppressing or abusing trafficking victims.

In the case of the role of Dalal, some believed that their actions were pernicious because of their lack of inside intelligence rather than intent, assuming that improved community intelligence could ensure more successful outcomes. Others however recognised they had been duped by trusted community representatives.

Again, this suggests a broad and comprehensive information and education programme might be needed to explain the prevalence of this situation and the nature of networks that operate towards that end (including the roles of certain Dalals).

Future: Engelbrecht and Jobson (2016) suggest '... trauma can cause a reflection on attitudes concerning life choices and how one pursues their future ... the trauma event can perpetuate uncertainty appraisals and potentially influences appraisal of future events' (p. 7). The data here suggest that the legacy of physical damage incurred throughout the journey heavily influenced perceived futures. Shame and despair often ensued, associated with the lack of capacity to recover labouring employment, their ought-selves requiring those trafficked to redress the adversity experienced in pursuing family goals intrepidly. Not being able to reinstate their positions in their communities seemed to engender psychological symptoms often associated with ongoing PTSD, such as recurring nightmares, terrors and depression.

6. MEANING MAKING BY PARTICIPANTS CONCERNING THE NATURE OF INDIVIDUAL TRAUMA

Ehlers and Clark (2000) define PTSD, as '... a common reaction to traumatic events such as assault, disaster or severe accidents ...persistent PTSD occur[ing] only if individuals process the traumatic event and/or its sequelae in a way which produces a sense of serious current threat' (pp. 319–320) Persistent PTSD occurs when '... the trauma memory is poorly elaborated and inadequately integrated into its context in time, place, subsequent and previous information and other autobiographical memories' (p. 325). The extreme and unanticipated trauma of the Andaman Sea crisis appeared to heighten such risk, further unprecedented trauma being experienced by labourers who did gain employment in Malaysia. Given that many returnees still see no other way to improve their economic circumstances, achieving a sense that they are no longer under threat of trafficking and its evils might be a difficult challenge in such economic and social contexts.

Accordingly, Bryant-Davis (2019, p. 400) suggests that '... culture plays a significant role in the vulnerability to, experience of, and recovery from mental health sources of distress, including interpersonal trauma' such as PTSD, calling for cultural awareness and cultural humility in psychological practice. Ehlers and Clark (2000) identify maladaptive cognitive processing styles associated with PTSD such as thinking about the trauma, the need to control feelings about the event tightly, rumination about how the event could have been prevented, the need for punishment of the assailant, the need to avoid actions or contingencies that could cause reoccurrence of the trauma, the need to take extra precaution and avoid normal activities that might be stressful and regenerate trauma.

Thought patterns of participants concerning trauma merit cultural critique. Victims' perceptions of the ought-self and its obligations potentially reinforce intentionality of action and purpose that could influence conceptual processing in the retelling of the trauma, as could broad community support for such initiatives, by adding a normative or inevitable dimension to traumatic experience.

The data suggest that the collectivist nature of the initiative fed a firm sense of purpose and control at the beginning of the journey. However, into the journey, trauma increases as the situation becomes largely uncontrollable. In these circumstances, family and sometimes community networks are called upon to rescue their agent from torture and facilitate the next stage of the plan.

Meaning attributed to psychological and physical damage also deserves consideration. 'Traumas that leave the individual with permanent health problems are more likely to lead to appraisals such as "my life is ruined" than traumas which inflicted reversible injuries. The quality of other people's reactions in the aftermath of the trauma (social support versus negative reactions) [also] influences the probability of appraisals such as "Nobody cares about me"' (2000, pp. 332–333).

In the accounts of trafficking survivors here, physical damage that prevented the trafficked person meet family and community expectations and needs was a dominant source of trauma and appeared to influence negative community reactions such as abandonment by spouses and loss of community status, leaving some individuals with a sense of total loss of control. In one instance, a psychological condition appeared to lead to attempted destruction of self and family, leading to the abandonment of the returnee.

Ehlers and Clark (2000) also suggest that elaboration of the trauma memory can reduce the probability of reexperiencing symptoms through fostering '... better discrimination between those stimuli that occurred around the time of the trauma and those encountered currently' (p. 341). In the case of the trafficked participants not only might some anticipate a re-occurrence, but many experience, as a consequence of failure, further trauma related to community rejection and humiliation.

Alternatively, a cultural response to a trauma can contextualise it as part of a process leading to a greater good, and thus the impact of cultural influences and interventions in interpreting trauma can assist (or impede) recovery and influence subsequent behaviours. Thus, the intention to repeat the journey is not uncommon (Siddiqui, 2017). The likelihood of the normalisation of such behaviours appears entirely probable in the tenuous alignment of the needs of economy and the accumulation strategy in the development discourse (Sanyal, 2014).

Shepherd and Lewis-Fernandez (2016) note the inappropriateness of ...

> ...the assumption of universality, which holds that human behaviors are alike across ethnic or cultural groups and that any differences are superficial and scientifically uninteresting ...

[whereas] culture can markedly influence the behaviors of an individual so the appeal to universality requires some unpacking. (p. 432)

Thus, we have argued that interpretations of trauma and related mental health issues associated with rehabilitation deserve culturally specific consideration. We have also explored the perceptions of risk by the individual at each stage of the journey taking into account the importance of the accrued loss of control. Third, the nature of the trauma experienced has been considered from the perspective of expectations and obligations derived from a collectivist culture, highlighting trauma derived from potential discrepancies between the actual-, ideal- and ought-selves. Fourth, we have identified emergent forms of resiliency at each stage of the journey.

7. CONCLUSION

Our introduction recognised Bangladesh's claim that the country's ability to handle social issues such as trafficking will grow as a direct result of its economic success. Bernards (2022. p. 7) warns against assumptions of growth based on '...the messy confrontation between neoliberal fantasies of efficient, socially beneficial markets [including labour markets] and the contradictory, spatial, material and social conditions of actually-existing capital accumulation' which underpin economic success. We have illustrated trauma experienced by undocumented labour migrants that is part of this 'messy confrontation', detailing the reality underpinning certain migration dynamics, whilst suggesting a more critical appraisal of the process of gaining remittances and the nexus between labour migration and more sustainable forms of development in less developed nations. In 2007, Kaye and McQuade made the critical observation that an

...increasing number of people are migrating both internally and across borders in search of work as a means of survival rather than as a means of improving their incomes. It is this group which is particularly vulnerable to traffickers ...Those who were trafficked invariably struggled to regain the economic position they had before leaving ...their exposure to trafficking has left them further impoverished upon their return and more vulnerable to exploitative or coercive labour practices.

In 2023, these observations are even more pertinent. In its *Trade and Development Report Update (April 2023)*, UNCTAD expanded on its previous report on structural transformation for LDCs in which is stated the

...pandemic abruptly revealed deficiencies in development paradigms that have severely reduced the capacity of the State to generate domestic resources for economic, social and environmental investment ...LDC populations have experienced a sharp decline in living standards and increasing inequality... hav[ing] come under additional pressure from rising external debt payments and soaring international energy and food prices. (2022, p. 3)

The 2023 report highlights continuous problems for developing nations that will potentially exacerbate the drivers of labour migration and challenge the achievement of more sustainable development.

We explored cultural influence on the meaning ascribed to trauma and risk associated with undocumented labour migration and the trafficked experience in collectivist cultures characterised by increasingly inadequate resources being stretched to fulfil family and community expectations for relief of poverty. We also used self-discrepancy theory to understand key forms of trauma and loss in collectivist cultures and suggested various manifestations of discrepancies in the self-concept that led to trauma at various stages of the trafficked journey. It was demonstrated that trauma was primarily understood by the participant group in terms of family and community let down, shame and loss of status, the impact particularly severe when physical loss of function resulted in the inability to gain employment that had previously supported a lifestyle as the working poor, rather than living in extreme poverty.

Bangladesh's Minister of Home Affairs has stated that the UNODC (2022a) report, '...will act as the baseline for all our future reporting on human trafficking in Bangladesh' (UNODC, 2022b). The report acknowledges the difficulties in dealing comprehensively with this phenomenon. This chapter's contribution is its analysis of perspectives of survivors of maritime trafficking, able to report personally on its impact, both physically and psychologically, and provide nuanced insights into how appraisals of the opportunities and risks around undocumented labour migration and its consequences were made. The rich description provides insights into social and cultural filters influencing perspectives and behaviours when seeking alternative development pathways to break through poverty barriers.

The 2021 World Day Against Trafficking in Persons suggested that 'Victims voices lead the way' (UN Sustainable Development Group, 2021) in better informing risks and thus discouraging what often dissipates resources rather than helps accumulate them. We believe our findings might facilitate the hearing of these voices and have relevance across a range of government policies including: communication and information services for vulnerable people concerning the dangers and evils of trafficking; interventions to support the victims of trafficking; improved international agreements and facilitation of migration opportunities; and coherent and consistent cross-portfolio initiatives in response to SDGs (particularly 1, 8 and 16).

In such a complex, dynamic and culturally nuanced context, we do not intend to be overly prescriptive. Rather we seek to promote shared understanding and consistency across relevant national and international portfolios concerning the drivers, perceptions and experiences of unskilled labour seeking migration as a means of gaining greater returns on increasingly inadequate assets in largely incomprehensible international and global environments. We suggest that insights presented here have nuanced significance for local initiatives across the public, private and NGO sectors in the spirit of working towards the fulfilment of SDGs.

NOTES

1. The Andaman Sea crisis was a humanitarian disaster that occurred between May and June 2015. About 8,000 aspiring migrants from Bangladesh and Myanmar were left stranded at sea by human traffickers when regional states ramped up maritime surveillance and interception of trafficking vessels, and an estimated 815 people died.

2. This study details the accounts of 25 survivors of labour trafficking from three major trafficking hubs in Bangladesh and other stakeholders with insights into this industry and its business model. Three local NGOs, the Ovibashi Karmi Unnayan Program (OKUP), the Young Powers Social Action (YPSA) and the Development for Disadvantaged People (DDP), helped identify and contact respondents from the field by sharing their data and networks. Only adult males (over 18 years at time of interview) who had survived maritime trafficking and were known or registered with the local organisation were selected for inclusion in the study.

3. The qualitative study was conducted from January to April 2018 in three major maritime trafficking-prone areas of Bangladesh: Narayanganj-Narshingdi (Central districts), Sirajganj (North-Central) and Cox's Bazar (South-Eastern). Twenty-five returnees and four specialist stakeholders were interviewed. Interpretative Phenomenological Analysis (Smith & Osborn, 2004) facilitated interpretation of cultural influence on the meaning ascribed to trauma associated with labour migration and the trafficked experience, requiring researcher – interviewee interpretation of lived experiences.

4. All participants were assigned pseudonyms to protect identity.

5. Receive Ghor is a trafficking term meaning a 'clearing house' where traffickers hold trafficked people (either on a boat or on land) while awaiting payment of money from migrants' families.

REFERENCES

Bangladesh Bank. (2022). *Quarterly report on remittance inflows in Bangladesh: October–December 2022*. Research Department (External Economics Wing) Bangladesh Bank. https://www.bb.org.bd/pub/quaterly/remittance_earnings/remittance%20october-december%202022%20pdf.pdf. Accessed on November 8, 2023.

Bernards, N. (2022). *A critical history of poverty finance: Colonial roots and neoliberal failures*. Pluto Press.

Bolton, D., Habib, M., & Landells, T. (2023). Resilience, dynamism and sustainable development: Adaptive organisational capability through learning in recurrent crises. In S. Seifi & D. Crowther (Eds.), *Corporate resilience: Risk, sustainability and future crises* (pp. 3–32). Emerald Publishing Limited. https://doi.org/10.1108/S2043-052320230000021001

Bryant-Davis, T. (2019). The cultural context of trauma recovery: Considering the posttraumatic stress disorder practice guideline and intersectionality. *Psychotherapy*, *56*(3), 400–408. https://doi.org/10.1037/pst0000241

Connell, J. (Ed.). (2017). *Community study on the needs of returned migrants following the Andaman Sea crisis*. International Organization for Migration (IOM). https://publications.iom.int/books/community-study-needs-returned-migrants-following-andaman-sea-crisis. Accessed on November 8, 2023.

Danailova-Trainor, G., & Laczko, F. (2010). Trafficking in persons and development: Towards greater policy coherence. *International Migration*, *48*(4), 38–83. https://doi.org/10.1111/j.1468-2435.2010.00625.x

Deshingkar, P. (2019). The making and unmaking of precarious, ideal subjects – Migration brokerage in the Global South. *Journal of Ethnic and Migration Studies*, *45*(14), 2638–2654. https://doi.org/10.1080/1369183X.2018.1528094

Ehlers, A., & Clark, D. M. (2000). A cognitive model of posttraumatic stress disorder. *Behaviour Research and Therapy*, *38*(4), 319–345. https://doi.org/10.1016/s0005-7967(99)00123-0

Engelbrecht, A., & Jobson, L. (2016). Exploring trauma associated appraisals in trauma survivors from collectivist cultures. *SpringerPlus*, *5*, 1565. https://doi.org/10.1186/s40064-016-3043-2

Engelbrecht, A., & Jobson, L. (2020). Self-concept, post-traumatic self-appraisals and post-traumatic psychological adjustment: What are the relationships? *Behavioural and Cognitive Psychotherapy, 48*, 463–480. https://doi.org/10.1017/S1352465820000156

Friedman, M. J., & Marsella, A. J. (1996). Posttraumatic stress disorder: An overview of the concept. In A. J. Marsella, M. J. Friedman, E. T. Gerrity, & R. M. Scurfield (Eds.), *Ethnocultural aspects of posttraumatic stress disorder: Issue, research, and clinical applications* (pp. 11–32). American Psychological Association.

Higgins, E. T. (1996). The "self digest": Self-knowledge serving self-regulatory functions. *Journal of Personality and Social Psychology, 71*(6), 1062–1083. https://doi.org/10.1037/0022-3514.71.6.1062

Human Rights Commission of Malaysia (SUHAKAM) and Fortify Rights. (2019). "Sold like fish": Crimes against humanity, mass graves, and human trafficking from Myanmar and Bangladesh to Malaysia from 2012 to 2015, 27 March. https://www.fortifyrights.org/downloads/Fortify%20Rights-SUHAKAM%20-%20Sold%20Like%20Fish.pdf. Accessed on April 10, 2023.

IOM (International Organization for Migration). (2017, March). *Migrant deaths and disappearances worldwide: 2016 analysis* (Issue No. 8). Global Migration Data Analysis Centre: Data Briefing Series. https://publications.iom.int/system/files/pdf/gmdac_data_briefing_series_issue_8.pdf. Accessed on April 12, 2023.

IOM (International Organization for Migration). (2022, February). *Migrants' remittances have potential to stimulate economic development.* https://belarus.iom.int/news/migrants-remittances-have-potential-stimulate-economic-development#:~:text=Remittances%20stimulate%20aggregate%20demand%2C%20increase,increase%20investment%20in%20human%20capital. Accessed on Accessed on July 14, 2024.

Jayawickreme, N., Jayawickreme, E., & Foa, E. B. (2013). Using the individualism-collectivism construct to understand cultural differences in PTSD. In K. Gow & M. Celinski (Eds.), *Mass trauma: Impact and recovery issues* (pp. 55–76). Nova Science Publishers.

Jesperson, S., Alffram, H., Denney, L., & Domingo, P. (2022). *Labour migration in Cambodia, Laos, Thailand and Vietnam: Migrants' vulnerabilities and capacities across the labour migration cycle.* ODI Thematic brief. ODI. https://odi.org/en/publications/labour-migration-in-cambodia-laos-thailand-and-vietnam-migrants-vulnerabilities-and-capacities-across-the-labour-migration-cycle/. Accessed on November 8, 2023.

Joarder, M. A. M., & Miller, P. W. (2014). The experiences of migrants trafficked from Bangladesh. *The Annals of the American Academy of Political and Social Science, 653*(1), 141–161. http://www.jstor.org/stable/24541779

Kaye, M., & McQuade, A. (2007). A discussion paper on poverty, development and the elimination of slavery. *Anti Slavery International.* https://www.antislavery.org/wp-content/uploads/2017/01/fco_full_dfid_meeting_background_paper_2oct2007.pdf. Accessed on November 8, 2023.

Khan, A. A. R. (2020). *The psychosocial impact of labour trafficking in Asia: A study of returned Bangladeshi survivors.* PhD Thesis, Western Sydney University. https://researchdirect.westernsydney.edu.au/islandora/object/uws%3A60875. Accessed on November 8, 2023.

Khan, A. A. R., Stevens, G. J., Georgeou, N., Bolton, D., & Landells, T. (2024). Economic, social and psychological drivers of labor trafficking and its impacts: A case study on returned Bangladeshi survivors. *Asian and Pacific Migration Journal, 33*(1), 191–218. https://doi.org/10.1177/01171968241242144

Kiss, L., Pocock, N. S., Naisanguansri, V., Suos, S., Dickson, B., Thuy, D., Koehler, J., Sirisup, K., Pongrungsee, V., Nguyen, V. A., Borland, R., Dhavan, P., . . . Zimmerman, C. (2015). Health of men, women, and children in post-trafficking services in Cambodia, Thailand, and Vietnam: An observational cross-sectional study. *Lancet Global Health, 3*(3), e154–e161. https://doi.org/10.1016/S2214-109X(15)70016-1

Sanyal, K. (2014). *Rethinking capitalist development: Primitive accumulation, governmentality & post-colonial capitalism.* Routledge.

Shaler, R. C. (2005). *Who they were: Inside the World Trade Center DNA story: The unprecedented effort to identify the missing.* Free Press.

Shepherd, S. M., & Lewis-Fernandez, R. (2016). Forensic risk assessment and cultural diversity: Contemporary challenges and future directions. *Psychology, Public Policy, and Law, 22*(4), 427–438. https://psycnet.apa.org/doiLanding?doi=10.1037%2Flaw0000102

Siddiqui, T. (Ed.). (2017). *Untold stories of migrants: Dreams and realities.* Refugee and Migratory Movements Research Unit (RMMRU). http://mfasia.org/migrantforumasia/wp-content/uploads/2016/12/Dreams-and-Realities-Untold-stories-of-migrants.pdf. Accessed on November 8, 2023.

Smith, J. A., & Osborn, M. (2004). Interpretative phenomenological analysis. In G. M. Breakwell (Ed.), *Doing social psychology research* (pp. 229–254). BPS Blackwell.

Ullah, A. K. M. A. (2010). *Rationalising migration decisions: Labour migrants in East and Southeast Asia.* Ashgate.

UN Sustainable Development Group. (2021, July 31). Victims' voices lead the way in the fight against human trafficking. https://unsdg.un.org/latest/videos/victims-voices-lead-way-fight-against-human-trafficking. Accessed on November 8, 2023.

UNCTAD. (2022). *The least developed countries report 2022: The low-carbon transition and its daunting implications for structural transformation: Overview.* https://unctad.org/system/files/official-document/ldc2022overview_en.pdf. Accessed on April 12, 2023.

UNCTAD. (2023). *Trade and development report update (April 2023).* https://unctad.org/system/files/official-document/gdsinf2023d1_en.pdf. Accessed on April 12, 2023.

UNHCR. (2016). *Mixed maritime movements in South-East Asia in 2015.* https://reporting.unhcr.org/sites/default/files/UNHCR%20-%20Mixed%20Maritime%20Movements%20in%20South-East%20Asia%20-%202015.pdf. Accessed on November 8, 2023.

UNHCR. (2021). *Left Adrift at Sea: Dangerous journeys of refugees across the Bay of Bengal and Andaman Sea.* https://www.unhcr.org/asia/publications/operations/611e15284/left-adrift-at-sea-dangerous-journeys-of-refugees-across-the-bay-of-bengal.html. Accessed on November 8, 2023.

UNODC. (2022a). *First national study on trafficking in persons in Bangladesh.* United Nations Office on Drugs and Crime. https://respect.international/first-national-study-on-trafficking-in-persons-in-bangladesh/. Accessed on November 8, 2023.

UNODC. (2022b). *GLO.ACT – Bangladesh launches the first national study on trafficking in persons in Bangladesh.* https://www.unodc.org/southasia/en/frontpage/2022/October/bangladesh_-unodc-glo-act-launches-the-first-national-study-on-trafficking-in-persons-in-bangladesh.html. Accessed on November 8, 2023.

PART 3

COMMUNITY AND CULTURE

INVESTIGATING CULTURE AND ITS INFLUENCE ON SOCIO-ECONOMIC DEVELOPMENT IN THE KINGDOM OF ESWATINI

Aaron Siboniso Gwebu[a] and Md Humayun Kabir[b]

[a]*Eswatini National Treasury, Eswatini*
[b]*Sol Plaatje University, South Africa*

ABSTRACT

Culture (traditional or organisational) has tended to be either a resource or an impediment to socio-economic development (SED) because culture plays an important role in the socio-economic sphere. This study investigates traditional culture that influences SED in light of the prevailing socio-economic situation in the Kingdom of Eswatini (Previously known as the Kingdom of Swaziland). Based on the existing demographics and political state, most people of the Kingdom live in rural areas, where traditional culture is predominant, and poverty is prevalent. That justifies their advocacy for SED influenced by cultural and traditional structures as opposed to one influenced by the internationally inclined modern democratic structures. This study used quantitative approaches and collected data from 30 'SED initiatives'. Results of the study indicate that traditional cultural influence is most prevalent in rural communities, while the adoption of the new national constitution in 2005 brought an insignificant change in the way culture influences SED. It was also noted that cultural governance, cultural tourism, customs and traditions, gender discrimination and marginalisation of people living with disabilities are the main existing components relating to the area of the central phenomenon. Further findings indicate that Eswatini culture is largely epitomised by the existence of the Monarchy authority, as a wide range of beliefs, customs and traditions are entrenched in the core values of the same. This infers that the Kingdom of Eswatini is predominated by socio-cultural values, which necessitates a telling influence on SED issues.

Society and Sustainability

Developments in Corporate Governance and Responsibility, Volume 24, 155–183

Copyright © 2025 Aaron Siboniso Gwebu and Md Humayun Kabir

Published under exclusive licence by Emerald Publishing Limited

ISSN: 2043-0523/doi:10.1108/S2043-052320240000024007

Keywords: Traditional culture; cultural influence; socio-economic development; Eswatini; rurality

1. INTRODUCTION

Eswatini is a tiny Kingdom located in the southern part of Africa, between South Africa and Mozambique. It is a landlocked country characterised by beautiful scenery consisting of tremendous mountains and valleys, a great attraction for tourists (Britannica, 2020). The national economy of the Kingdom has been primarily dependent on agriculture, particularly maize and sugar cane, as the country's natural resources are scarce (Njeim, 2018). The Kingdom has an estimated population of about 1.2 million, of which 49.2% are males and 50.8% are females (Countrymeters, 2020), while unemployment has been on an average of 25% for the past two decades (Statistica, 2019). Urban and rural population is at 29.6% and 70.4%, respectively (Eswatini Demographics, 2020). The literacy rate has been growing at a rate of 12.79%, from 55.33% to 88.42%, since 1976, while GDP growth is estimated at 1.8% on average for the past 5 years (Eswatini Data, 2019). The overall poverty line is at less than US$1.90 a day, with the rural areas predominantly affected, where 58.9% of the population on the receiving end, while income inequality is being estimated at 49% (World Food Programme, 2019).

Swaziland, now officially Eswatini, is the name the country inherited from its colonisation by the British, as Anglicised from the early king and nation builder, Mswati II (Britannica, 2020). The new name Eswatini was officially introduced on 19 April 2018, a co-incidental 50th birthday of the incumbent King of the Swazi nation, King Mswati III (British Broadcasting Corporation, 2018). The country's governance system consists of a traditional system and a Western model system; the head of both systems is the King (King Mswati III) [African Development Bank (ADB), 2005]. The Kingdom's jurisdiction system is administrated by customary law (traditional Swazi law and custom) and Roman-Dutch law (ADB, 2005; www.state.gov). The country's traditional structures (such as Swazi National Courts) are governed by customary law, and the country's constitutional courts (such as the High Court, Magistrates Courts and Industrial Court) and political system are overseen by Roman-Dutch law (ADB, 2005). The Western model is followed for the national and local government systems (ADB, 2005). The King has power over legislative, executive and judicial (ADB, 2005). The head of the State and head of the government are The King and the Prime Minister, respectively.

Eswatini is governed by a Monarchical authority with absolute power (Britannica, 2020). Relentless efforts and negotiations between the Kingdom and Britain led to independence in 1968. The late King Sobhuza II, then Paramount Chief, orchestrated and masterminded the ultimate independence (Britannica, 2020). King Sobhuza II was known for his great leadership skills, which epitomised the Kingdom with sustainable tranquillity that earned him great respect and popularity among his people and beyond borders (National Orders Booklet, 2019). This has been the main catalyst for the political stability the country has enjoyed for decades, which attracted Foreign Direct Investment (Basu & Srinivasan, 2002). This enhanced the economic conditions of the country, as more and more industries were established, and more employment opportunities were created.

While globally the political sphere has been continuously shifting towards multiparty systems of governance, Eswatini has been heavily criticised for its traditional form of democracy, where Chiefdoms and Constituencies (Tinkhundla) are used in the place of political parties (Houseland, 2015). While the progressive minority has openly but quietly decried this state of affairs, the majority of the populace has been adamant, as evidenced by the triumph of the now-defunct Imbokodvo National Party during the era of the now-banned political party system of governance (Dlamini, 2019). They argue that this system is ideal for them as it equitably supports their unique Swazi heritage and socio-economic initiatives (Boermeester, 2018). This governance system is operationalised by statutes and regulations that are culturally inclined (Southern Africa Litigation Centre, 2018), which underpins the essence of the study.

According to Williams (2007), culture was part of the factors or reasons why China, the world's most developed country in the middle ages, suddenly stagnated or even went backwards. China had a culture of self-dependence which largely entailed neglecting foreign commerce. Williams continued to point out that due to the dynamics that go with it (culture), China eventually changed and became arguably one of the leaders in socio-economic development (SED) worldwide. Concurring with Williams' assertions, Micronesian Counsellor (2009) noted that globalisation has not entirely made economic development attainable in every place of the world, attributing that to the existence of ingredients touching on national ethos and traditions termed culture. This essentially forms the basis of the argument that culture is part of the factors that influence SED in any country or society, and the Kingdom of Eswatini is no exception.

In the Kingdom of Eswatini, culture, mostly traditional, is predominantly practiced and as such, its influence on SED is inevitable. Such influence could be further promoted by the country's governance, which is cultural and traditional. The Swaziland National Administration (2016), the office responsible for the administration and recording of chieftaincy conflicts and disputes in all the country's communities, revealed that pending (unresolved) disputes are 71 out of the 161 Chiefs in the country. This infers that SED has been derailed in 44% of the country's chiefdoms, for at least a decade now. In 2005, the Kingdom adopted its national constitution (NC) which among other things, sought to also address socio-economic issues. That has also formed the basis for this study in terms of measuring culture's influence before and post its adoption.

In the socio-economic sphere, culture has become one of the influences or determinants of the same. Depending on the living environment, culture has tended to be either a resource or an impediment to SED. The Organization for Economic Co-operation and Development (OECD) (2009, p. 65) attested to that by asserting that 'a growing range of cultural elements are being employed to brand and market regions'. The purpose of this study is to investigate and identify existing cultures influencing SED in light of the prevailing socio-economic situation in the Kingdom of Eswatini. In particular, this study aims to investigate possible ways of countering the adverse influence of culture and stimulating the commendatory influences of these cultures on SED without undermining the values, beliefs and identity of the Swazi people. Based on the existing demographics, economic state and political state, Eswatini has many of its people living in rural areas, where traditional culture is predominant, and poverty is prevalent. That justifies their advocacy for SED influenced by cultural and traditional structures as opposed to one influenced by the internationally inclined modern democratic structures. This informs the practical rationale of the study and underlines the importance of this study, particularly to Swazi citizens.

1.1 Problem Statement

The Kingdom of Eswatini is well endowed with cultural beliefs and traditions that have been sustained since ancient times. These are characterised by some influence on the SED of individual citizens and communities across the Kingdom's constituencies and chiefdoms. Separating the two (culture and SED) in order to enhance the latter is what has been the challenge, both at a social and political level. Blending them for the same purpose has been much embraced, despite the risk of inevitable opportunity costs that string along. This has become a way of living for the people of the Kingdom of Eswatini.

To support the latter mentioned, the description of culture as a way of living, thinking and behaving by the Council of Europe (2016) form a synthesis of assertions by Levin (2007) who noted that King Sobhuza II, the late Swazi King succeeded by the substantive one, made the entire Swazi people one in the way they live, think and behave. Levin stated that the late King was able to create, construct and orchestrate the Swazi culture successfully like a natural phenomenon. This was largely attributed to him being perceived as a principal mobilising and unifying factor during de-colonisation, a legacy the substantive King vowed to sustain when he was enthroned in 1986.

To solidify the problem statement, it suffices to highlight what The Heritage Foundation (2016) observed about the Kingdom's state of affairs. It reported that the country's economic freedom status is 'mostly un-free' due to, among other things, an inefficient regulatory framework that continues to kerb the emergence of a dynamic private sector. The fundamental question is whether such a status quo could also be traced to cultural attributes in the Kingdom.

As part of the evidence regarding the afore-stated area of central phenomenon, Dlamini Martin Gobizandla, in his budget speech for 2017/2018 as Minister for Finance, highlighted a serious concern by the Government of Eswatini regarding the derailment of an E5 billion Swazi Rail Link Project. This project was envisaged to commence in 2015, but due to chieftaincy disputes and fragmented cultural beliefs and formalities, it could not take off. In a nutshell, the challenge related to the relocation and reburial of people from their ancestral residences is something they resisted owing to cultural beliefs. In addition, a 2017 quarterly report by a construction company (Inyatsi Construction) revealed a similar influence, where a road construction project for the Manzini City to Sikhuphe

International Airport had its costs suddenly escalated owing to ancestral (cultural) beliefs. The report highlighted causes and reasons that justified the escalation of budgeted costs of the project. Relocation of the affected Mafutseni Filling Station at E8 million extra cost (75% negative variance) ahead of the much cheaper option of demolishing a particular tree that had always been perceived as an important national symbol for its being a resting place (during the ancient hunting culture-*butimba*) for the traditionally highly regarded late King Sobhuza II, sums up the problem.

The study intends to establish whether, among other cultural-linked influences, cultural governance, gender discrimination, cultural traditions and discrimination by disability form part of the influence on SED. The study also sought to identify the actual influence associated with such cultures, establishing if employment, self-sustainability, gender and economic inequality and service delivery do form part of the categories of these influences. Cultural tourism and sub-cultures such as religion, arts and hospitality are also explored in terms of their influence on SED in the Kingdom of Eswatini. Please refer to the appendix for the definition of several terms.

1.2 Gender Marginalisation

The United Nations Children's Fund (UNICEF) (2008) narrated about existing cultural barriers driven mainly by attitudes and traditions on the girl child (including early marriages) in Southern Sudan. The perpetrators included government officers, soldiers, teachers and even non-governmental organisations (NGOs) officials. The report revealed that when the girls reached a certain stage of maturity, where they could read and write, they were then withdrawn from school to be taken as wives by men who had money. These perpetrators claimed they continue doing this because their culture dictates that they must marry virgins either as their first or second wives. The girls who were expected to immediately assume duties of the traditional wife in the households and the community where they lived hence had their educational aspirations curtailed. That tended to suppress and deprive them of opportunities for better self-sustenance and potential contribution to the SED of their country.

UNICEF (2016) concurred with the above assertions highlighted in the UNICEF (2008) report, as the former revealed that the Kingdom of Eswatini is also exposed to under-age marriage, where an estimated 7% of girls are married before the age of 18. According to the Swaziland Government Gazette of 2017 which contained a newly proposed Marriage Bill, the main purpose of this piece of legislation was to find redress in, among other issues, the marrying of the school-going girl-child through Swazi Law and Custom. This was instigated by the general observation that this cultural practice has indeed continuously impeded and denied the girls their constitutional right to education. These girls end up being uneducated wives with no skills enabling them to be self-sustaining, while on the other hand, the boy-child continues to be culturally well supported in his self-development and educational aspirations. This has been viewed as grossly discriminatory and detrimental to the economic welfare of girls and women as it impedes their potential in the SED of the Kingdom.

On the same issue, UNICEF (2013) made mention of the fact that cases of this nature continued to prevail (especially in the rural areas) even after the NC which had clear prescriptions (section 29) of every child's constitutional right to education. The report further revealed that the country's traditional leadership declared that girl-child marriage is acceptable under customary law. United Nations Fund for Population Activities (2012) asserted that save for parental consent in countries where under age marriage is allowed, such marriage became a traditional belief that was also propelled by economic gains envisaged from the 'cattle wealthy' proposer. The report revealed that this was aggravated by the fact that the affected girls' families were usually poverty-stricken with less education. United Nations Fund for Population Activities continued to report about the high state of poverty, especially in rural communities, and the high prevalence of cultural practices. This situation therefore makes the Kingdom of Eswatini prone to the practice of under-age marriage. Hands at Work in Africa (2014) provided supporting evidence by revealing that cultural pressure has driven many Swazi men to take on wives and children who are subjected to abject poverty. Hands at Work in Africa continued to report that desperate families volunteer to give their daughters (as young as 12–14 years) away for money.

The incumbent leader in traditional affairs in the Kingdom, who is also referred to as the traditional Prime Minister, rejected the amended girl-child protection bill and was adamant that *kwendzisa* (the custom of a man marrying an underage girl) is a culture that should not be abolished. This is despite the existence of the most recent Child Protection and Welfare Act of 2012, which was partially for the same course. He emphasised that he and his compatriots (Royal Council) would review this Act to counter it.

This culmination shows that the country is faced with a resilient influence of Swazi traditional culture as about 80% of the interviewed traditional leaders also remained adamant about parting ways with this practice. Their strong belief is despite the dictates of the NC as provided under section 29 which specifically spells out the right of every child to be protected from practices that may constitute an impediment to his/her health, education and development.

1.3 Cultural Governance

Rojek (2007) argued that 'one of the greatest challenges facing a modern British government is the task of reconciling nationalism with multiculturalism, multi-ethnicity and globalisation' (p. 10). He elaborated that the Britons found such a proposed policy to be undermining and fragmenting their national cultures and shared national values.

Rojek further viewed that this was an indication of a shift from ideological legacies of race towards disparities in cultural differences. Like the British, the Kingdom of Eswatini appears to be so inclined to its cultural beliefs. Sy and Lewis (2014) highlighted about the severity of the economic injury the Kingdom was likely to experience due to the imminent revocation of its African Growth and Opportunity Act status. African Growth and Opportunity Act is a United States of America (US) trade initiative purported to promote SED in Sub-Saharan African countries through the provision of duty-free trade on their exports.

Sy and Lewis revealed that this state of affairs was propagated by the Kingdom's failure to meet the standard benchmarks imposed by the US government. According to Sy and Lewis, these benchmarks evolved much from the failure of the Kingdom to uphold the rule of law, an aspect the US Government considered an integral part of the fundamental concept of the African Growth and Opportunity Act initiative. This condition was viewed by the GOS as a call to change national cultures and shared national values which are the backbone of the nature of its governance. Apparently, this was something they were not prepared to do because, in the context of the Kingdom, it would be tantamount to degrading the power of the Monarchy. Sy and Lewis also highlighted that the Monarchy remains the final voice in judiciary matters of the Kingdom of Eswatini and the King is not viewed as just a head of state but the highest culturally unifying figure that should be accorded absolute respect and allegiance with no terms and conditions attached.

As a synthesis of the evidence by Sy and Lewis on the African Growth and Opportunity Act impasse, it suffices to add that Africa Caribbean and Pacific–European Union (2013) further mentioned that the spirit of the rule of law was based on the idea that the law should rule than one of the citizens and that even the guardian of the laws is obeying the laws. Further to that, Lee (2011) gave an insinuating report that the sacking of High Court Judge Justice Thomas Masuku, as orchestrated by the High Court Judge then, was a clear contempt of the rule of law. Lee asserted that he was being victimised for his open belief in the respect for the rule of law. This was viewed as being a result of the influence of the existing cultural type of governance, which prioritises socio-cultural ahead of socio-economic approach to national issues.

Maintaining its stance on national values, like the British did in the already cited case of Rojek (2007), the Kingdom of Eswatini refused to budge from its belief in the integration of economic development envisaged with socio-cultural values. This was confirmed by a report from the African Growth and Opportunity Act (2014) which revealed a resultant pronouncement by many apparel firms in the Kingdom to the effect that they would be closing down operations or at the least, greatly downsizing due to the potential loss of the Africa Growth and Opportunity Act rights, unless the government intervenes by subsidising the US levy on their exports. All these are alleged consequences of a society that is more cultural-inclined than SED-sensitive.

1.4 Cultural Diplomacy

A demonstration of the crucial interrelation and embracement of cultural elements and SED, the European Union Commission (2016) initiated a new strategy to put culture on top of important agendas for European Union Commission international relations. The main focus of this initiative was to embrace a diversity of cultures existing among the Commission's international partners thereby promoting and strengthening mutual understanding and respect for fundamental values. The report continues to mention that with such an agenda, which the European Union Commission otherwise terms cultural diplomacy, the Commission was optimistic to foster and realise long-term relationships with countries across the world.

This was a factor viewed as a potential enabler of success in facing the common challenges hindering the enhancement of SED. In strengthening the opinion that there was a synergy between culture and SED, the European Union Commission highlighted that cultural traditions, cultural and creative industries, small-medium enterprises and tourism, form part of the essence of this modesty. As a result, in the cultural and creative sectors, the Commission has already funded many projects such as African Caribbean Pacific Cultures programmes and programmes supporting and promoting cultural governance and intercultural dialogue. The report refers to cultural governance as having governments that embrace native cultural values and ethics, while intercultural dialogue means member countries have diplomatic relations that entrench mutual consent and understanding of cultures existing independently.

According to the European Union Commission, the aim of the initiative was primarily to harmonise the inevitable influence of culture on SED. In order to help implement it, as this was of major importance with regard to culture and its influence on SED, the European Union Commission set up what they called the Cultural Diplomacy Platform. The Cultural Diplomacy Platform was to be operated by a consortium of European Union Commission stakeholders with the concise agenda to deliver policy advice, facilitate networking, develop training programmes for cultural leadership and carry out activities with cultural stakeholders – all of which envisaged harmonising the synergy between the two social components for the benefit of the society of the Member States. A country endowed with a very rich culture like that of the Kingdom of Eswatini could benefit immensely from such an initiative as it would be exposed to the earmarked programmes such as the training of traditional leaders on matters of SED and assisting the government in making all-encompassing policy advice.

1.5 The Influence of the Monarch Authority on SED

The assumption of patronage status by Her Majesty the Queen Mother (who comes second in the Monarch authority) on several 'SED initiatives' (Refer to appendix) has created enormous motivation for many Swazis through her willingness to support them in their capabilities and competencies. Seeing one of the highest authorities in traditional structures taking a leadership role in such initiatives has created a good impression of entrepreneurship and self-development (being attributes of SED) in communities across the Kingdom. Food Agriculture and Natural Resources Policy Analysis Network (2011) revealed that the founding of the Liphupho Lendlovu Foundation, an umbrella/mother body for all poverty alleviation projects by Her Majesty the Queen Mother, has earned an award (Food Security Policy Leadership Award). The many projects that Her

Majesty the Queen Mother has embarked on are humanitarian, developmental and cultural in nature. These are intended to improve the socio-economic welfare and food security of the people of the Kingdom of Eswatini in all 55 constituencies. According to the Food Agriculture and Natural Resources Policy Analysis Network report, Her Majesty the Queen Mother decided to take up such projects to fill the gap which she foresaw could be best filled by her in her capacity as the mother of the nation. The Food Agriculture and Natural Resources Policy Analysis Network further indicated that the following form part of the already up-and-running projects under this foundation:

- *Philani Maswati Organisation:* The aim behind this initiative was to address the sad plight of the despondent elderly people and their children who had been exposed to poverty and the associated effects of the emergence of the HIV/AIDS pandemic. Through the support from the able and privileged citizens, the organisation met the food, clothing and shelter challenges faced by many senior citizens who have lost their able-bodied bread winners through death or incapability.
- *Swaziland Women's Economic Empowerment Trust:* This is a project established in 2008 with the objective of establishing a Woman Empowerment Fund or a 'Women's Bank' responsive to addressing SED challenges faced by women (especially in rural communities) owing to their less privileged backgrounds. As an apex organisation, it was envisaged that Swaziland Women's Economic Empowerment Trust would facilitate and secure financial services for women to enable the poor to borrow, save, build assets, increase incomes, and in the long run overcome poverty.
- *Swazi Secrets:* This is a commercialisation of the Marula fruits, a natural product that grows around the communities where aspiring women traders live. It is a dream that mainly targeted poor rural women to help them generate income from the Marula fruit. Some of the successfully commercialised by-products of this fruit include soap, sweets, lotion and lip balm. All of these are being produced from the Marula Oil product which is rich in anti-oxidants and vitamin E, an ingredient with anti-aging properties and effective healing of scar tissue. Women from all parts of the country bring their collection of dried fruit to strategic community collection points where they have their wares weighed for quality and paid cash on the spot if they meet the required standard of freshness. At the end of the day, the poor women have something to put on the table for their families and hence have their socio-economic challenges met.
- *Swaziland Trading House:* This is an initiative established to facilitate a coordination of rural women with local and outside markets for their handicraft products. This was propelled by the exploitation of the women by unscrupulous buyers who were taking advantage of their desperation and illiteracy, buying their wares for far less than the market value. In order to satisfy the quality and bulk requirements, the women are visited and encouraged by field officers to form groups, which enables Swaziland Trading House to buy their products at far better prices.

- *Khulisa Umnfwana Organization:* This is a project intended to assist the youth in deviating from unhealthy practices like early sex, teenage pregnancy and drug abuse to name but a few. These were viewed as a big impediment to the SED of the Kingdom as its sustainability can only be assured by a healthy youth, who are the future human resource. Its mission was to instil support and strengthen values of good behaviour on them thereby avoiding the adverse effects of, among other side effects, the HIV/AIDS pandemic, a disease known for its detrimental consequences on socio-economic endeavours by government and NGOs.

In summary, the vision and endeavours of Her Majesty the Queen Mother of the Kingdom of Eswatini are viewed to have a primary focus on improving the socio-economic status of women in the Kingdom as a group that appeared to be socially suppressed yet hard-working. To some extent, it can be said that this is a step in the right direction in terms of respecting the rights and freedoms of women as per the dictates of the NC of 2005, section 28 (1) of chapter III. Her Majesty the Queen Mother initiatives appear to be well orchestrated to give them equal opportunities in SED issues, thereby unwinding poverty acceleration in their families and communities. This indeed is a notable cultural influence on socio-economic matters as all sponsors and contributors towards their sustainability render assistance under the umbrella of *kwetfula* (presenting a gift of honour and allegiance to Her Majesty the Queen Mother), a Swazi culture of paying allegiance and respect to the Monarch by extending assets, properties or gifts. Her Majesty the Queen Mother uses the same presented items to help identified areas of need for the poverty-stricken in all the communities of the country.

1.6 Culturally Influenced Gender Inequality

Impower (2013) noted that prior to the adoption of the NC, gender was regarded as a determining factor in rural land allocation. Women were customarily not allocated land unless through the husband or male relative. Impower (2013) further highlighted that such land is held by customary tenure through customary law and is only administered by the chiefs' courts. Entitlement is only on an allotment basis as ownership remains with the King in trust for the Swazi nation. This means when allotted the land, the subject of the Chiefdom is restricted from transferring it to the next person as that remains the prerogative of the Chief who represents the King. This is different from the case of urban land, where the Title Deed Land processes were not guided by gender issues, but rather by Roman-Dutch Law courts.

Impower (2013) indicated that such a practice emanated from the customary belief that land should only be allocated to men as they are the ones who are expected to build homes for their wives and families. However, due to the change in family dynamics which gave rise to single-parenting, this cultural practice became obsolete and biased in terms of the rights of women to rural land acquisition. Seeker (2011), in his illustration about the importance of shelter, mentioned that, among other things, it helps one to have a feeling of well-being. This explains that shelter forms part of the basic accomplishment of SED and clearly, the affected women were deprived of improving their socio-economic status and well-being.

1.7 The Influence of Cultural Attractions on SED

Cultural attractions have also tended to play a significant role in SED through tourism. This sub-set of tourism, which has been widely referred to as cultural tourism, may include tourism in urban areas and also tourism in rural areas. The OECD (2009) has concurred that cultural tourists have had a significant influence on SED because of their notable general trend of spending substantially when compared to standard tourists.

Csapo (2012) introduced a standardised classification of cultural tourism in order to highlight the most important types of elements by some thematic grouping. The study observed that this can prove essential in terms of ascertaining the influence of culture on SED as far as cultural tourism is concerned. He considered Heritage Tourism, Cultural Thematic Routes, Cultural Tours, Traditions/Ethnic Tourism, Event/Festival Tourism, Religious Tourism and Creative Culture as what may constitute major cultural tourism forms or types. For purposes of this study, the focus has been on Traditions Tourism and Heritage Tourism because the two are the ones predominating in the Kingdom of Eswatini. With Traditions Tourism, he identified local cultures' traditions as the tourism product, while with Heritage Tourism, he among other things, identified cultural heritage sites as the product or activity of tourism.

Other forms of focus may be Event/Festival Tourism, in which among other things, he identified cultural festivals and events as the product of Tourism and Creative Culture. Apart from the beautiful scenery, Csapo (2012) pointed out that the Kingdom was hugely demonstrated as one very rich in culture, which helped it make up for its lack of size. Cultural heritages such as Mantenga Cultural Village showcasing various deep traditional Swazi ways of life and cultural festivities/events such as the annual reed dance portray the amount of potential the Kingdom could have if properly nurtured. A cultural event of note is the annual reed dance, an annual event where young and unmarried maidens always pitch up at Ludzidzini Royal residence for one of the most fabulous and amazing cultural scenes you can find the world over. As Euromonitor International (2013) asserted, 'cultural' tourists are always attracted and motivated to spend substantially more than they would for a normal tourist destination in the Kingdom of Eswatini. That can be viewed as having some significant influence on SED of the individual citizens benefiting from spending such as in accommodation, transport, shopping and handcraft to name but a few.

Swaziland Tourism Authority (2013) revealed that the Southern Africa Tourism Services Association, to whom the government entity is a subscribing member, has actually 'branded' the Kingdom of Eswatini as 'A Royal Experience' for tourists. Southern Africa Tourism Services Association substantiated the 'branding' by singling out the Kingdom's uniqueness of its governance (Executive

Monarchy), as characterised by a high practice and embodiment of culture and heritage that is effectively influencing almost all aspects of Swazi life. Supporting that assertion, Euromonitor further illustrated that this is a traditional kind culture coupled with a sub-culture of respect, friendliness and hospitality, all of which are major attributes of an attractive tourism-based SED. Such features have propelled Southern Africa Tourism Services Association to symbolise a visit by tourists to the Kingdom as a 'magical experience'. The 'magical experience' denotation inferred an experience rare to find as the Kingdom is a destination that has adequate attractions in terms of both the natural environment interaction and human interaction aspects.

Further empirical evidence by the OECD (2009) on tourism revealed that the growing relationship between tourism and culture has become a major co-driver of destination attractiveness and competitiveness, which economists would want to call comparative advantage, a thing the Kingdom could strive to achieve. As tourism in the Kingdom of Eswatini is a highly regarded form of SED, culture being a sub-set of the same therefore has the potential of significantly influencing the latter, which fact is alluded to by Kukreja et al., 2012. Kukreja et al. continued to point out that the number of tourists worldwide has doubled from 565.4 million in 1995 to 1006.4 million in 2010, with an expected rise estimated at 1.56 billion by 2020, where such rate of increase will be largest in developing countries. Clearly, by virtue of being one of the developing countries, the Kingdom of Eswatini can be said to be practically poised to have her SED reasonably enhanced. The current NC adopted in 2005, wherein section 60 (11) provides that places of historical interest, artefacts and the environment ought to be preserved and protected, could also play a big role in enhancing tourism-based SED.

In summary, what can be noted from the literature section is that a larger context of the empirical evidence recorded reflects that culture could have had an adverse influence on SED in the Kingdom of Eswatini, where themes such as Gender Marginalisation, People Living with Disability, Cultural Governance and Culturally Influenced Gender Inequality have concurring indications. On the other hand, themes like Cultural Diplomacy, the Influence of the Monarch Authority on SED and the Influence of Cultural Attractions on SED show a favourable influence on the same in the Kingdom as many have benefited from either working in the cultural industry or selling their wares to tourists.

2. RESEARCH METHODS

The quantitative method was applied to capture the different aspects of the influence of culture. In the context of this study, the study employed the survey research approach to interrogate the influence of culture on socio economic development in the Kingdom of Eswatini. Delecce (2017) described survey design as the method for collecting information or data as reported by individuals. This entailed the use of semi-structured questionnaires, which were completed by government development practitioners, and development officers from government organisations and NGOs.

2.1 Population and Sampling

The population of this study included 30 institutions and they were chosen based on their SED projects which are susceptible to the influence of the Kingdom's cultures by nature and magnitude. The study used a stratified random sampling technique to target 30 institutions tasked with SED in the Kingdom. These institutions were UNICEF, Micro-projects – Regional Development Fund, Swaziland (Eswatini) Investment Promotion Authority, Swaziland (Eswatini) Association of Savings and Credit Cooperative, Ministry of Economic Planning and Development, Federation of Organization of Disable People in Swaziland (Eswatini), Swaziland (Eswatini) Financial Corporation, National Emergency Response Care against HIV AIDS, Ekululameni Skills and Development Training Centre, Gone Rural, Mantenga Cultural Village, Swaziland (Eswatini) National Trust Commission, Ministry of Home Affairs, Ministry of Tinkhundla and Administration, Ministry of Commerce, Industry and Trade, Ministry of Education and Training, EU, Government Security Forces, Swaziland (Eswatini) Meat Industries, Co-ordinating Assembly for Non-governmental Organizations, Khulisuntfwana, Ezulwini Handcraft Centre, Swaziland (Eswatini) Water and Agricultural Development Enterprise, National Disaster Management Agency, Women and Law, Swazi National Administration, Swaziland (Eswatini) Electricity Company, House of Parliament Archives Department, Swaziland (Eswatini) National Council of Arts and Culture and Swaziland (Eswatini) Tourism Authority. Most of them do have a corporate social responsibility policy that is geared towards developing the under-privileged directly, which is something they have not stopped doing. They generate profits that are publicly declared and attract substantial government tax which further contributes to the Kingdom's SED.

The study employed 120 development practitioners from 30 'SED initiatives'. The Slovene's sampling technique was adopted, where n represents sample size, N represents population size and e represents the margin error, to calculate the total sample of the study.

$$n = \frac{N}{1 + N(e^2)}$$

$n = 120/(1 + 120)\ 0.0025$
$n = 120/1 + 0.3$
$n = 92$

The 92 development practitioners formed the sample of the study. The total sample of 92 development practitioners was further apportioned using stratum weights (proportions) which were calculated based on the total number of SED

Table 1. Samples per Strata.

Strata	Weight	Sample
Government departments	0.423077	39
Government organisations	0.384615	35
NGOs	0.192308	18
Total		92

institutions in each category or stratum (government departments, government organisations and NGOs). The numbers of development practitioners to be selected in each stratum are shown in Table 1.

In each stratum, development practitioners were selected using simple random sampling technique. Furthermore, the numbers assigned to each employee were used together with the table of random numbers to select the total number of respondents required in each stratum as per the determined weights.

3. RESULTS AND DISCUSSIONS

While the Kingdom is administratively partitioned into four regions, which have their respective Regional Administrators for development purposes, it is further divided into sub-regions called constituencies (Tinkhundla), all with their Heads called *Tindvuna teTinkhundla*. Furthermore, as it might be normal that the Kingdom is governed by the three arms of government (Legislature, Judiciary and Executive), it happens to be also traditionally controlled, as manifested by the existence of chiefdoms within the constituencies which are headed by traditional leaders called Chiefs. While the former report through the Regional Administrators' line of authority, the latter are subordinated directly to the Monarch authority only.

According to the existing national governance structure, the Chiefs are the ones mandated with the authority of consenting to any SED by virtue of being the ultimate custodians of all land in the various communities of the Kingdom. Precisely, they carry out that duty on behalf of and in representation of the Monarch Authority (the King). On the other hand, the constituency heads' is to operationalise SED and ensure that it is accordingly expedited. The third participants, who are the development practitioners, are responsible for delivering and coordinating 'SED initiatives' to the two (Chiefs and constitutional heads), whose Offices fall in parallel hierarchical structures.

Procedurally, the former is concerned with the proper allocation of the land resource for SED and accounts to the Monarch Authority, while the latter is expected to ensure proper utilisation of the other material resources like building materials allocated and accounts to the Government. This is a conflict of interest not easy to resolve as both Offices prove to be equally important for the roles they play. However, if the Monarch Authority could establish and empower a Board of Trustees per region to have a unified power of full execution of SED ear-marked. Such a board could comprise a membership that is all encompassing in terms of matters that are both socio-cultural and socio-economic at the same time. The resources for SED sanctioned are delivered at the constituency centres (Tinkhundla), which by the design of the *Tinkhundla* concept seek to facilitate the intended decentralisation of services. That further strains the relationship of the two participants as most of the Chiefs feel these should be delivered to them because culturally, they are superior to the constituency heads and as such, as traditional leaders, they are the ones that oversee everything (including SED) that takes place in the communities they lead. The idea of Board of Trustees could even help bridge a possible de-link in terms of the relationship between the Monarch Authority and the Government Authority which impacts on the con-stituency heads to whom the SED resources are delivered.

3.1 Analysis of the Survey

This section of the results quantifies the perceptions of development practitioners so as to statistically deduce the 'main' and 'other' cultural factors that influence SED. The sample of 92 development practitioners had the composition of development initiatives as shown in Table 2.

The analysis was based on periods prior to and posts the Kingdom of Eswatini National Constitution, for both urban and rural areas. An analysis of their perceptions of the 'main' cultural influence prior to the NC is shown in Table 3.

Table 3 shows respondents' perceptions on the influence of the main cultural influence, wherein, girl-child early marriage, ancestral belief, livestock wealth beliefs, Chiefs' consent to development, cultural governance and Chiefs' mar-ginalisation in accessing SED funds are perceived as having a negative influence on SED.

This was supported by the fact that a significant 77% (71 respondents) in urban areas and 64% (59 respondents) in rural areas to total respondents to the survey believed that the factor mentioned above had a negative influence on SED prior to the NC. Furthermore, it is worth observing that 34 respondents considering the urban setting believed that girl-child early marriage influenced SED negatively. On the contrary, Christianity and cultural education were seen to be contributing positively to SED by all respondents covered by the survey (15 respondents in all) and were answering the questions looking at events before the constitution.

The rural setting was also not different from the urban setting as most responses were on the negative side. Approximately 83% (20 respondents) of respondents in the rural setting were for the view that girl-child marriage contributed negatively to SED, whilst Christianity, cultural education, respect and hospitality, and cultural events were seen by 79% of respondents surveyed (26 respondents all together) to be contributing positively to SED prior to the NC.

Table 4 shows that results even post the NC in urban area settings were still similar to those prior to the NC. This was evident as respondents who partici-pated in the survey and answered the various questions still perceived the

170 — Culture and Its Influence on Socio-Economic Development

Table 2. Major Development Initiatives.

SED Initiative	Number of Development Practitioners Interviewed	Proportions of Total Sample
UNICEF	2	2%
Micro-project – Regional Development Fund	2	2%
Swaziland (Eswatini) Investment Promotion Authority	2	2%
Swaziland (Eswatini) Association of Savings and Credit Cooperative	2	2%
Ministry of Economic Planning and Development	2	2%
Federation of Organization of Disable People in Swaziland (Eswatini)	2	2%
Swaziland (Eswatini) Financial Corporation	2	2%
Swaziland (Eswatini) Tourism Authority	2	2%
National Emergency Response Care against HIV AIDS	2	2%
Ekululameni Skills and Development Training Centre	2	2%
Ezulwini Handicraft Centre	2	2%
Gone Rural	2	2%
Mantenga Cultural Village	2	2%
Swazi National Administration	5	5%
Women and Law	5	5%
Ministry of Home Affairs	5	5%
National Disaster Management Agency	5	5%
Ministry of Tinkhundla and Administration	5	5%
Ministry of Commerce, Industry and Trade	5	5%
Ministry of Education and Training	6	7%
EU	6	7%
Khulisumntfwana	6	7%
Swaziland (Eswatini) Water and Agricultural Development Enterprise	6	7%
Swaziland (Eswatini) Meat Industries	6	7%
Co-ordinating Assembly for Non-governmental Organisations	6	7%
Total	**92**	**100%**

girl-child early marriage (88%), ancestral belief (56%), livestock wealth belief (100%), Chief's consent to development (100%), cultural governance (100%), Chiefs' marginalisation in accessing SED funds (100%) to have a negative influence on SED. These influenced SED negatively since the tradition hindered the girl child's education and prevented females not to accessing income through formal employment and self-employment income-generating projects. This had a multiplier effect on poverty as most women in the country have a lot of dependencies. Secondly, livestock wealth has impacted negatively on SED by hindering both subsistence and commercial production and the supply of beef commodities.

AARON SIBONISO GWEBU AND MD HUMAYUN KABIR 171

Table 3. Perceptions of Development Practitioners on the Main Cultural Influence Prior to the National Constitution.

| Time | Setting | Main Cultural Factor | Influence | | |
			Positive	Negative	Total
Prior to National Constitution	Urban	Girl-child early marriage	0	34	34
		Ancestral belief	6	10	16
		Livestock wealth/ancestral belief	0	9	9
		Christianity	6	0	6
		Chiefs consent to development	0	6	6
		Cultural education	9	0	9
		Cultural governance	0	6	6
		Chiefs' marginalisation in accessing SED funds	0	6	6
		Total	**21**	**71**	**92**
	Rural	Girl-child early marriage	4	20	24
		Ancestral belief	3	3	6
		Livestock wealth belief	0	3	3
		Christianity	3	0	3
		Chiefs consent to development	0	3	3
		Cultural education	3	0	3
		Chieftaincy power disputes	0	4	4
		Cultural governance	0	11	11
		Women power undermined	0	4	4
		Disability considered taboo	0	4	4
		Polygamy conflicts	0	4	4
		Respect and hospitality	4	0	4
		Cultural events	16	0	16
		Chiefs' marginalisation in accessing SED funds	0	3	3
		Total	**33**	**59**	**92**

Table 4 also shows results from respondents in the rural setting, from which it can be noted that there is not much difference from results prior to the constitution, as still livestock wealth belief, chief's consent, chieftaincy power disputes, cultural governance, women power undermined, disability considered taboo, polygamy conflicts and chief's marginalisation in accessing SED funds were perceived to have a negative influence to SED by 78% of total respondents (72 respondents).

The rural setting was also not different from the urban setting as most responses were on the negative side. 26% of 92 respondents (24 respondents) in the rural setting were for the view that girl-child marriage contributes negatively to SED, whilst 20 respondents (22% of 92 respondents) viewed that Christianity, cultural education, respect and hospitality, and cultural events contribute positively to SED post to the constitution, results of which are similar to those for the

172 Culture and Its Influence on Socio-Economic Development

Table 4. Perceptions of Development Practitioners on the Main Cultural Influence Post the National Constitution.

			Influence		
Time	Setting	Main Cultural Factors	Positive	Negative	Total
Post National Constitution	Urban	Girl-child early marriage	4	30	34
		Ancestral belief	7	9	16
		Livestock wealth belief	0	9	9
		Christianity	6	0	6
		Chiefs consent to development	0	6	6
		Cultural education	9	0	9
		Cultural governance	0	6	6
		Chiefs' marginalisation in accessing SED funds	0	6	6
		Total	**26**	**66**	**92**
	Rural	Girl-child early marriage	0	24	24
		Ancestral belief	0	6	6
		Livestock wealth belief	0	3	3
		Christianity	3	0	3
		Chiefs consent to development	0	3	3
		Cultural education	3	0	3
		Chieftaincy power disputes	0	4	4
		Cultural governance	0	11	11
		Women power undermined	0	4	4
		Disability considered taboo	0	4	4
		Polygamy conflicts	0	4	4
		Respect and hospitality	4	0	4
		Cultural events	10	6	16
		Chiefs' marginalisation in accessing SED funds	0	3	3
		Total	**20**	**72**	**92**

survey of prior the constitution. The survey also sought to investigate 'other' cultural influences (other than the main ones) that influenced SED in the Kingdom of Eswatini. Table 5 below shows the results of the survey.

3.1.1 Urban Setting Prior to the National Constitution

From Table 5, it can be noted that prior to the *NC* in the urban setting, 30 (41% of total respondents) respondents perceived the boy-child afforded education tradition to have a positive influence on SED, whilst 44 respondents (59% of total respondents) perceived Monarchy power abuse, Traditional Swazi Nation Land disputes, land disputes and Muslim religion influence SED negatively prior to the constitution.

AARON SIBONISO GWEBU AND MD HUMAYUN KABIR

Table 5. Perceptions of Development Practitioners on 'Other' Cultural Influence Prior to National Constitution.

| Time | Setting | Other Cultural Factors | Influence | | |
			Positive	Negative	Total
Prior to National Constitution	Urban	Boy-child afforded education	30	13	43
		Monarchy power (abused)	0	6	6
		Traditional Swazi Nation Land disputes	0	9	9
		Land disputes	0	10	10
		Muslim	0	6	6
		Total	**30**	**44**	**74**
	Rural	Boy-child afforded education	16	3	19
		Monarchy power (abused)	5	10	15
		Peace and tranquillity	4	0	4
		Chiefs consent to development	0	4	4
		Disability considered inability	4	4	8
		Traditional Swazi Nation Land disputes	0	7	7
		Cultural events	4	0	4
		Cultural education	16	0	16
		Land disputes	0	3	3
		Muslim religion	0	3	3
		Total	**49**	**34**	**83**

3.1.2 Rural Setting Prior to the National Constitution

In the rural setting, prior to the constitution, 49 respondents (59% of total respondents) believed that boy-child afforded education, peace and tranquillity, disability considered inability, cultural events and cultural education factors contribute SED positively. These factors are dominated by the boy-child afforded education and cultural education, which form 32 (39%) of the 49 (59%) total under 'positive influence'. On the other hand, 34 respondents (41% of total respondents) believed that Monarchy power abuse, Chiefs consent to development, disability considered inability, traditional Swazi Nation Land disputes, land disputes and Muslim religion had a negative influence on SED. These are dominated by the Monarchy power abuse and traditional Swazi Nation Land dispute factors which form 17 (21%) of the 34 (41%) total under 'negative influence'.

Post-NC also depicted no relative change in 'other' cultural influence, and the responses are shown in Table 6.

3.1.3 Urban Setting Post National Constitution

The boy-child factor 34 (46%) was perceived to be immensely influencing SED, as it completely dominated the other factors under 'positive influence'. Furthermore,

174   *Culture and Its Influence on Socio-Economic Development*

Table 6. Perceptions of Development Practitioners on 'Other' Cultural Influence Post National Constitution.

			Influence		
Time	Setting	Other Cultural Influence	Positive	Negative	Total
Post National Constitution	Urban	Boy-child afforded education	34	9	43
		Monarchy power abuse	0	6	6
		Traditional SNL disputes	0	9	9
		Land disputes	0	10	10
		Muslim religion	0	6	6
		Total	**34**	**40**	**74**
	Rural	Boy-child afforded education	16	3	19
		Monarchy power abuse	0	15	15
		Peace and tranquillity	4	0	4
		Chiefs' consent to development	0	4	4
		Disability considered inability	4	4	8
		Traditional SNL disputes	0	7	7
		Cultural events	4	0	4
		Cultural education	16	0	16
		Land disputes	0	3	3
		Muslim religion	0	3	3
		Total	**44**	**39**	**83**

Monarchy power abuse, traditional Swazi Nation Land disputes, land disputes and the Muslim religion factors were perceived to be hampering SED, as shown by the enormous number of respondents attesting to its negative influence on urban SED.

3.1.4 Rural Setting Post National Constitution

Table 6, shows that even post NC in rural settings, the boy-child afforded education tradition, peace and tranquillity, cultural events and cultural education 44 (53%) were perceived to influence SED positively. These positively influencing factors are dominated by the by-child afforded education and cultural education factors which form 32 (39%) of the 44 (53%) total under 'positive influence'. Monarchy power abuse, Muslim religion, land disputes and traditional Swazi Nation Land disputes 39 (47%) were noted in the rural areas as 'other' factors exacerbating the negative influence on SED. These are dominated by the Monarchy power abuse and traditional Swazi Nation Land disputes factors which form 22 (26%) of the 39 (47%) total under 'negative influence'.

The subsequent graphs (Figs. 1 and 2) show a brief and summarised comparison of the main and other cultural influences identified in this part of the study, prior to and post the NC. This influence was not different from that cited by the Constituency Heads and traditional leaders who also cited chieftaincy

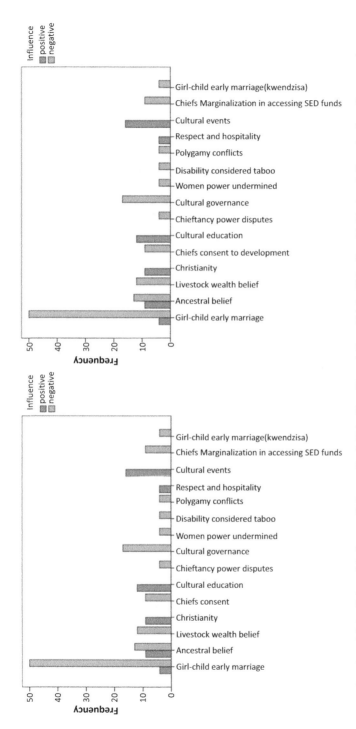

Fig. 1. Main Cultural Influence Prior to (Left-Side Graph) and Post (Right-Side Graph) National Constitution Compared.

176 Culture and Its Influence on Socio-Economic Development

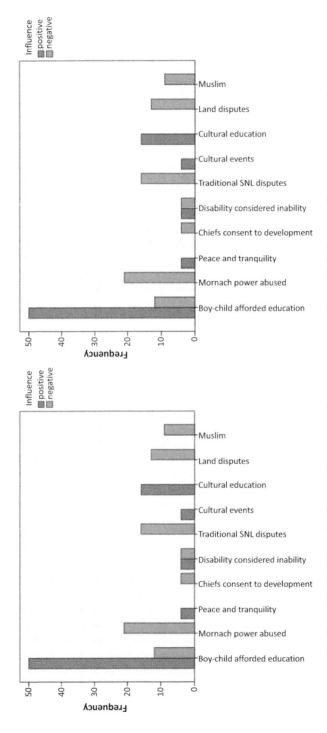

Fig. 2. 'Other' Cultural Influences Prior to (Left-Side) and Post (Right-Side) National Constitution Comparison.

Table 7. Summary of Qualitative and Quantitative Responses.

Main Cultural Influence	Other Influence
1. Girl-child early marriage	1. Boy-child afforded education
2. Ancestral belief	2. Monarchy power abused
3. Livestock wealth belief	3. Peace and tranquillity
4. Christianity	4. Chiefs consent to development
5. Chiefs consent to development	5. Disability considered inability
6. Cultural education	6. Traditional SNL disputes
7. Chieftaincy power disputes	7. Cultural events
8. Cultural governance	8. Cultural education
9. Women power undermined	9. Land disputes
10. Disability considered taboo	10. Muslim
11. Polygamy conflicts	
12. Respect and hospitality	
13. Cultural events	
14. Chiefs' marginalisation in accessing SED funds	

disputes, chiefdom boundary disputes, girl-child early marriages and isolation of disabled people as the main cultural influence influencing rural and urban SED in the Kingdom of Eswatini.

In summary, the ultimate aim of the study was to triangulate the qualitative and quantitative findings, so as to comprehensively deduce the influence of culture on SED in the Kingdom of Eswatini. The summarised responses from the qualitative and quantitative survey are presented in Table 7, as the study identified the following as forming part of the cultural influence on SED in the Kingdom.

The final consolidated cultural influences identified by the study on SED are presented in Table 8.

To conclude the summary, the above summaries illustrated in Table 8 indicate that the negative cultural influence identified by the study outweighs the positive influence in the study, suggesting an overall negative influence of culture on SED in the Kingdom of Eswatini.

4. CONCLUSIONS

The study investigated and identified existing cultures influencing SED in the Kingdom of Eswatini. Cultures like girl-child early marriages, boundary disputes, chieftaincy disputes, women mourning period and isolation of the disabled have been identified as those that influence SED in the Kingdom of Eswatini. The findings of the study uncovered most of the identified cultures that have a negative influence on SED as depicted in Table 8. The study further revealed 'other' cultures that were perceived by development practitioners to influence

Table 8. Summary of Identified Cultural Influence and Influence on SED.

Identified Cultural Influence	Influence on SED
Girl-child early marriage	NEGATIVE
Ancestral belief	NEGATIVE
Livestock wealth/ancestral belief	NEGATIVE
Chiefs consent to development	NEGATIVE
Chieftaincy power disputes	NEGATIVE
Cultural governance	NEGATIVE
Women power undermined	NEGATIVE
Disability considered taboo	NEGATIVE
Polygamy conflicts	NEGATIVE
Chiefs' marginalisation in accessing SED funds	NEGATIVE
Monarchy power abused	NEGATIVE
Disability considered inability	NEGATIVE
Traditional SNL disputes	NEGATIVE
Land disputes	NEGATIVE
Muslim religion	NEGATIVE
Christianity	POSITIVE
Cultural education	POSITIVE
Respect and hospitality	POSITIVE
Cultural events	POSITIVE
Boy child afforded education	POSITIVE
Peace and tranquillity	POSITIVE

SED in the Kingdom. These are summarised in Table 7. Predominance of the influential cultures was notable in the rural areas, while their overall practice was noted to have been insignificantly varied when comparing periods prior to and post the adoption of the NC. While these cultures were seen to be imposing such influence independently, most of them are importantly linked to the overall Monarch authority (traditional authority), hence the cultural-inclined overall governance of the country. These results can also be said to depict a country with a low cultural heterogeneity (culturally homogeneous) despite the influence of the inevitable globalisation factor. An augmented analysis of the study suggests that such a state of affairs has created a detrimental influence that outweighs the existing favourable influence on the SED of the Kingdom. The dominant cultures closely linked to the traditional authority include that of Chiefs being born (not appointed), underage marriages on the girl-child and discrimination of women in leadership positions, to name but a few. Efforts to find redress on these have not yet yielded significant impact and as such they continue to be impediments to socio-economic advancements linked to them.

The drawn conclusions of the study, based on the findings, confirmed the reality of culture's influence on SED of the Kingdom. It also highlighted the existence and effectiveness of government programmes aimed at improving the socio-economic status of the people in the communities. Some are notably backed by the NC and some not. Clearly, most have not been able to reach their intended potential effectiveness-wise. The cultural-associated impediments have overall not been successfully mitigated. To achieve that, the primary recommendation would be the formulation of a more actionable policy seeking to bridge the glaring gap between socio-economic and socio-cultural perceptions. This will not only harmonise the traditional system currently predominating the Kingdom's governance with the internal economic-driven systems in place but will also actualise the Kingdom's slogan which says 'Swaziland, the New Promise for Africa'. This is a slogan purported to mean that the Kingdom possesses qualities of potential growth in SED than any other country in Africa.

4.1 Significance of the Study

The study articulates the awareness among the citizenry on the existing cultural influence on SED, which is something that should stimulate willingness to change their current mind-set and perceptions about culture and SED for the better. It will further contribute immeasurably towards the Kingdom's vision of first-world status as contained in the NDS. Consequently, this is envisaged to create awareness of the existing challenges relating to the dynamics of both culture and SED, thereby appreciating and recognising the importance of all the relevant stakeholders.

The study is also important in creating an understanding to policy and decision-makers on the importance of formulating a well-consulted statute, with subsidiary policies seeking to harmonise and consolidate the interrelation of the two (culture and SED). References drawn from provisions of section 60 (10) of the NC of 2005, which dictates that the government ought to make efforts to ensure that customary and cultural values form an integral part of SED also proved imperative. Lastly, the findings of the study could have an important role to play in raising the voice of the marginalised in matters of SED, not only in principle, as section 30 of the NC already depicts, but also in practice.

4.2 Limitation of the Study

The study is limited by the fact that culture is associated with the Monarchy, and so any research on it could easily be misconstrued or politicised.

REFERENCES

African Caribbean Pacific-European Union. (2013). *Respect for the rule of law and the role of an impartial and independent judiciary*. ACP-EU Joint Parliament Assembly Committee on Political Affairs. www.europarl.europa.eu. Accessed on June 24, 2017.

African Development Bank (ADB). (2005). *Kingdom of Swaziland – Country governance profile*. Operations Department, ONCB, ADB.

African Growth and Opportunity Act. (2014). *Swaziland braces itself for AGOA exit*. www.agoa.info. Accessed on June 21, 2017.

Basu, A., & Srinivasan, K. (2002). *Foreign direct investment in Africa – Some case studies*. International Monetary Fund. https://www.imf.org/external/pubs/ft/wp/2002/wp0261.pdf

Boermeester, S. (2018). *Best of Eswatini*. ISSUU. https://issuu.com/svengvp/docs/ebook_llres

Britannica. (2020). *Sobhuza II, King of Eswatini*. www.britannica.com

British Broadcasting Corporation (BBC). (2018). Eswatini king renames country 'the Kingdom of eSwatini'. www.bbc.com

Council of Europe. (2016). *Socio-economic impact of culture*. Compendium of Cultural Policies and Trends in Europe. http://www.culturalpolicies.net. Accessed on November 10, 2016.

Countrymeters. (2020). *Eswatini population*. www.countrymeters.info

Csapo, J. (2012). *The role and importance of cultural tourism in modern tourism industry* (pp. 1–50). www.intechopen.com. Accessed on July 15, 2017.

Delecce, T. (2017). *Definition and design* (pp. 1–15). www.study.com. Accessed on October 07, 2017.

Dlamini, H. P. (2019). *A constitutional history of the Kingdom of Eswatini (Eswatini), 1960–1982* (pp. 339–347). www.link.springer.com

Eswatini Data. (2019). *Eswatini adult literacy rate*. www.knoema.com

Eswatini Demographics. (2020). Population of Eswatini. *Worldometer*. www.worldometers.info

Euromonitor International. (2013). *Travel and tourism in Swaziland*. www.euromonitor.com. Accessed on July 12, 2017.

European Union Commission. (2016). *A new strategy to put culture at the heart of EU international relations* (pp. 1–40). www.europa.eu. Accessed on July 14, 2017.

Food Agriculture and Natural Resources Policy Analysis Network. (2011). *The food security policy leadership award*. www.dialogue.fanrpan.org. Accessed on July 19, 2017.

Hands at Work in Africa. (2014). *About Swaziland*. www.handsatwork.org. Accessed on February 9, 2018.

Houseland, C. (2015). *Labor protests in Eswatini: When no news is not good news*. www.africasacountry.com

Impower. (2013). *Grow the talent that will grow your company*. www.women-unlimited.com. Accessed on June 24, 2017.

Kukreja, S., Sharma, A., & Sharma, A. (2012). Role of tourism in social and economic. *Development and Society, 3*(1), 10–31.

Lee, R. (2011). *Swaziland abandons rule of law* (pp. 1–24). www.osisa.org. Accessed on June 24, 2017.

Levin, R. (2007). Swaziland Tinkhundla and the myth of Swazi tradition. *2*(10), 1–23. www.tandfonline.com. Accessed on October 7, 2017.

Micronesian Counselor. (2009). *The role of culture in economic development*. www.micsem.org. Accessed on May 8, 2017.

National Orders Booklet. (2019). *King Sobhuza II (1899–1982)*. The Presidency, Republic of South Africa. www.thepresidency.gov.za

Njeim, N. (2018). *Socioeconomic impacts of infrastructure investment in Eswatini: The case of LUSIP*. University of Arkansas. https://scholarworks.uark.edu/cgi/viewcontent.cgi?article=4493&context

Organisation for Economic Co-operation and Development. (2009). *The impact of culture on tourism*. www.oecd.org. Accessed on May 22, 2017.

Rojek, C. (2007). *Cultural studies*. Sage Publication.

Seeker. (2011). *Why you need shelter to survive* (pp. 1–20). www.seeker.com. Accessed on February 8, 2018.

Southern Africa Litigation Centre. (2018). Alignment of Eswatini's domestic laws with recommendations of United Nations human rights mechanisms. *COSPE*. http://www.southernafricalitigationcentre.org/wp-content/uploads/2018/

Statistica. (2019). *Eswatini – Unemployment rate 1999–2019*. www.statistica.com

Swaziland National Administration. (2016). *Unresolved chieftancy disputes and conflicts*.

Swaziland Tourism Authority. (2013). *The Kingdom of Swaziland*. Ministry of Tourism. www.thekingdomofswaziland.com. Accessed on July 11, 2017.

Sy, & Lewis (2014). *Swaziland's AGOA status Revoked*. Accessed on July 10, 2017.

The Heritage Foundation. (2016). *Economy: Population, GDP, inflation*. Business,Trade. www.heritage.org. Accessed on June 24, 2017.

United Nation Children's Fund. (2008). *Socio-economic and cultural barriers to schooling in southern Sudan*. www.unicef.org. Accessed on March 12, 2017.

United Nations Children's Fund. (2013). *In Swaziland, child marriage is still a grey area*. www.irinnews.org. Accessed on July 7, 2017.

United Nations Children's Fund. (2016). *State of the world's children, Swaziland*. www.girlsnotbribes.org. Accessed on July 6, 2017.

United Nations Fund for Population Activities. (2012). *Marrying too young; end child marriage*. www.unfpa.org. Accessed on July 5, 2017.

Williams, J. (2007). *Cultural and social factors that affect development*. https://makewealthhistory.org. Accessed on March 11, 2017.

World Food Programme. (2019). *Eswatini*. www.wfp.org

www.state.gov. *Investment climate statement – Swaziland*. http://www.state.gov/e/eeb/rls/othr/ics/2011/157363.htm. Accessed on March 17, 2001.Appendix

APPENDIX: ADDENDUM

Boundary disputes – refers to the case of two or more chiefdoms claiming jurisdiction over a particular territory within their areas of authority.

Chief – in the context of the Kingdom of Eswatini, refers to a born male within a family duly empowered by the Monarch, who takes over ruler ship from his father and is given the authority to rule chiefdom as a birth right and not by election.

Chiefdom – in the context of the study, refers to an area marked as a territory for the ruling Chief.

Chieftaincy disputes – refer to situations where the rightfulness of the one given the power and authority to be the leader of a chiefdom is being challenged or disputed.

Constituency – in the context of the study or of the Kingdom of Eswatini, it refers to a sub-division of land (sub-region) instituted by the government with the intention of making boundary demarcations for electoral and service delivery purposes.

Cultural governance – refers to the system of governance which is largely controlled by the traditional structures of authority in the Kingdom of Eswatini.

Cultural tourism – refers to tourism being largely promoted by cultural heritage and practices taking place in the Kingdom of Eswatini.

Culture – in the context of the study, refers to the behavioural patterns and practices in terms of the beliefs, events, traditions, customs and values of the people in the Kingdom of Eswatini.

Kubutseka – is a process of initiation for a new member joining into the traditional men regiments, where he is then sworn in after being tested for total loyalty, allegiance and respect for the Monarch's authority.

Livestock wealth/ancestral belief – in the context of the study, refers to the belief by Swazi farmers in keeping and not disposing of livestock citing that it is either 'wealth given to them by their ancestors' or such is 'purely for the ancestors' and cannot be tempered except for ritual purposes only.

Lobola – is a Siswati name for dowry which is in a form of an average of 17 cattle, or an equivalent amount of cash paid to the family of the woman or girl who is being married the Swazi traditional way.

Long mourning period for women – this is a culture practiced in the Kingdom of Eswatini, where a woman is expected to wear black mourning attire *(inzilo)* and have limited public appearance for 2 years in respect for her late husband.

Ludzidzini – the name given to the main Royal Residence where the traditional line of authority is based or controlled and the place where most cultural events and customary rituals take place.

Lusekwane – a shrub tree used for performing rituals during the sacred Incwala, and is also a name used to refer to the cultural ceremony where throngs of young males are gathered to go and cut it for the same purpose.

Socio-economic development initiatives – in the context of the study, this refers to government departments, government organisations and NGOs given the necessary resources to operationalise socio-economic development as proficiently and efficient as possible.

Tindvuna teTinkhundla – refers to constituency heads in Siswati.

Tinkhundla – a Swazi name referring to a constituency centre where decentralisation of all government services and secondary elections take place.

Traditional leaders – refers to the people entrusted to be custodians of culture, customs and traditions, where in most cases are given the authority to be leaders of communities on behalf of the Monarch's authority.

Umbutfo – a Swazi traditional warrior affiliated to a regiment after having gone through a formal cultural initiation process that normally tests his loyalty, patriotism and respect for the Monarch. It is also a name given to the defence force of the Kingdom of Eswatini.

Umhlanga – a Siswati name for the reed plant that is cut by the young maidens during the Umhlanga Reed Dance cultural ceremony, which is a cultural ceremony where throngs of them converge to dance and celebrate their virginity before the Monarch.

Ummiso – a slow-pace cultural dance for women which is done during any cultural event in the Kingdom of Eswatini.

THE EFFECT OF COMMUNITY-BASED TOURISM AND REGIONAL DEVELOPMENT: A BIBLIOMETRIC STUDY

Philipe Lira de Carvalho[a], Mariana Lima Bandeira[b] and Airton Cardoso Cançado[a]

[a]*Federal University of Tocantins, Brazil*
[b]*Universidad Andina Simón Bolívar, Ecuador*

ABSTRACT

Community-based tourism (CBT) is a management model that prioritises the sustainable use of natural resources while valuing local history and culture in the tourism entrepreneurship business. It has received attention from academics and society worldwide due to its potential to contribute to sustainability frameworks but has some gaps and challenges that need addressing. Studies have highlighted weaknesses in projects, risks of losing community essence through partnerships with the tourism industry and a lack of preparation for community governance. This chapter presents findings from bibliometric studies of publications on CBT and its impact on sustainable regional development indexed by Web of Science (WOS) and Scopus databases over 5 years (2018–2022). The study uses Lotka and Bradford's Laws to review the frequency of citations, the experience and background of cited authors, main subjects, concerns and the most used methodological design. The findings revealed three major concern areas: sustainable development, CBT and the development of tourism. These clusters were further categorised into four subcategories: community participation, sustainability, sustainable tourism and governance. The research papers were published in high-impact factor journals, indicating their relevance and significance in the scientific community. Qualitative results suggest CBT is closely linked to local development issues. There remain challenges that need to be addressed, including the need

---

Society and Sustainability

Developments in Corporate Governance and Responsibility, Volume 24, 185–213

Copyright © 2025 Philipe Lira de Carvalho, Mariana Lima Bandeira and Airton Cardoso Cançado

Published under exclusive licence by Emerald Publishing Limited

ISSN: 2043-0523/doi:10.1108/S2043-052320240000024008

to associate economic, social and cultural aspects with sustainability issues. It is also essential to improve participation of the local community in governance aspects and expand communication and public policies to motivate and ensure the success of CBT.

Keywords: Community-based tourism; regional development; bibliometric study; sustainable tourism; tourism governance

1. INTRODUCTION

This work aims to connect community-based tourism (CBT) with regional development. CBT refers to a management model that is controlled by the community and involves the participation of visitors and locals that generate collective benefits. So, it promotes the sustainable use of natural resources for recreational and educational purposes, facilitates intercultural experiences, improves the quality of life of the community and fosters an appreciation of the history and culture of these populations (Souza, 2018). Apart from that, regional development is understood as a result of the effort of communities, government and the private sector to formulate regional policies, to discuss matters related to the development process of a region (Xavier et al., 2013).

Indeed, regional development involves numerous initiatives and is a subject of debate that combines multiple disciplines in this scope: studies associate regional development with the community's perspective on tourism (Alibio Oppliger & Morbeck de Oliveira, 2022) or highlight the connection between CBT in the Brazilian Amazon and its impact on regional development (Figueiredo, 2022); and others discuss regional development policies, based on the identification of regional growth patterns, seeking a more localised approach (Silva et al., 2019).

The research question is centred around the limitations of CBT implementation. One of the major concerns is the potential for the industry to dominate the community, as well as the lack of preparedness among community members for governance. Teixeira et al. (2019) presented these weaknesses, mentioning that initiatives of CBT, with these characteristics, are unsustainable in long term. Considering these arguments, what are the most important learnings about the CBT for the regional development?

It is important to highlight the increased interest of the academic community in the theme of community tourism or CBT, which is observed in approximately 2,000 articles that were published in the last 5 years in the Web of Science – WoS and Scopus databases. This number was the result of a random exploratory search made in the year 2022 to justify the importance that the theme has acquired in the academic community in the context of regional development. Recent research indicates that these publications, despite this growth in number, also address different themes, methodologies and theoretical and epistemological perspectives (Graciano & Holanda, 2020).

On the other hand, tourism activity has become one of the fundamental sources of wealth for many developing countries, and sometimes CBT is considered as a pillar of regional development (Teixeira et al., 2019). It should be noted that the agenda of the UN World Tourism Organization (UNWTO) includes actions to generate knowledge about the tourism market and disseminate the World Code of Ethics for Tourism with a view to maximising the socioeconomic contribution of tourism and minimising possible negative impacts. It is a regulatory dynamic that intends to contribute in a sustainable way to regional development.

In terms of methodology, this study uses bibliometric analysis in combination with content analysis of the most significant articles published in the WOS and Scopus databases in the last 5 years, that is, from 2018 to 2022. This approach provides both quantitative and qualitative insights into the main lessons learnt from practice and theory related to regional development.

In this research, it is assumed that CBT contributes to regional development, in line with Furtado's (1967) perspective, which recognises the multidimensionality of the subject. Furthermore, the surveyed works will be related to the four major advances or overcoming's proposed by the author for the pillars of the Theory of Regional Development: those associated with the spatial structure, the structuring of territories, modern technologies and the complexity of spatial phenomena. In this path, it is assumed that regional development has precarious resonance in matters related to the economic and political situation of a country (Monteiro Neto et al., 2017). Therefore, it is understood that the visibility of community tourism could also contribute to this legitimacy and that regional development could be part of the political and economic agenda.

This chapter is structured into four main sections, apart from the introduction. The first section is the literature review, which provides an overview of CBT in the context of regional development. The second section details the methodology used in the research, followed by a discussion of the results in the third section. Finally, the fourth section presents the conclusions drawn from the research findings.

2. THE CONTEXT OF COMMUNITY-BASED TOURISM IN REGIONAL DEVELOPMENT

In 2003, the World Tourism Organization (UNWTO) named itself a specialised agency of the United Nations, whose mission is to promote 'sustainable, responsible and universally accessible tourism as an inducer of inclusive development' (WTO, 2012, s/p). Thus, in this expansion of tourism as an economic activity, responsibility for regional development is included, based on the promotion of policies and instruments to support tourism, the increase in formal employment, eradication of poverty, gender equality, promotion, and protection of cultural heritage, encouraging education and training, offering training and technical assistance (WTO, 2012).

CBT practiced in Brazil is recognised as a development strategy for the national government (Teixeira et al., 2019), as it seeks to make the connection with sustainable development, which encompasses multiple dimensions, namely:

economic, social, cultural, environmental, ecological, territorial and political (Sachs, 2009).

Teixeira et al. (2019) point out that sustainable tourism should consider an economic development model that allows: (1) improvement in the quality of life of local communities and visitors; (2) maintenance of environmental quality; (3) equitable distribution of local benefits and costs; (4) awareness of the impacts of tourism and (5) improving social and health infrastructure.

That said, CBT, in the context of sustainable tourism, aims to generate favourable impacts in the economic and social dimensions, in harmony with the environment, territory and local cultures, as it is constituted as 'an important instrument of local development policy, focussing on generating jobs and income, and expanding social inclusion' (Teixeira et al., 2019, p. 6).

Thus, it can be said that the CBT depends on the participation of the community, with the aim of generating collective benefits from the resources of the Conservation Unit. It turns out that in order to avoid the depletion of these resources, this tourism must also be aligned with sustainability issues.

For this, it is fundamental that the community join forces for the practice of teamwork and the centrality of collaboration to support the implementation; increase community potential; define common goals; democratise opportunities and benefits; to finally achieve the development expected by all (Faxina & Freitas, 2021).

Conversely, Teixeira et al. (2019) state that, in Brazil, CBT still has problems and does not generate the expected results. As a rule, most of the projects undertaken have weaknesses and/or are unsustainable in the long term, with great challenges and the search for external technical assistance; there are risks in linking CBT initiatives to the tourism industry; and the lack of preparation of individuals in the community for governance, or leadership, regarding decision-making, must be legitimised.

The main cause of inconsistencies and problems in the community is the difficulty of interaction among participants, which is reflected in governance issues, but even knowing how to correct it, no research was found that dared to suggest improvements (Graciano & Holanda, 2020).

In the absence of clear objectives on the part of the community to be achieved through the CBT, there are no conditions to plan or get partners for the project. Management must rely on the participation of partner companies, suppliers, community representatives, potential customers and support and promotion institutions linked to public authorities (Teixeira et al., 2019).

The associations trend plays an important role. Through them, the community starts to claim, together with public sector entities, improvements for local development; they are constituted as an 'instance of participation legitimized by the whole, by bringing together residents and discussing agendas of collective interests. In this sense, they must provide a democratic flow and be active' (Faxina & Freitas, 2021, p. 253), which depends on the performance of the board of these associations and residents.

This proposal corroborates the idea that participation in associations would be one of the indicators to assess the strength of social capital in a community (Portes, 2000; Ballesteros, 2017), and that it would be directly related to the local protagonist in the tourism activity, being this determinant to assess whether that experience is CBT or not (Faxina & Freitas, 2021).

From a practical point of view, Graciano and Holanda (2020) compare several studies that demonstrate that CBT is an activity that does not always involve all community participants, given its heterogeneity and divergence among members; however, it needs participatory management and, above all, the formation of a national network to support development and, above all, that strives for sustainability.

In practical studies, the authors detected little evolution in knowledge between 2013 and 2018, given that the same difficulties had been discussed previously and new research only pointed to the same challenges without deepening the discussions, nor proposing solutions, including the main cause of the Community problems are due to the lack of interaction between members, reflecting a governance issue, in which the studies presented did not propose to propose improvements (Graciano & Holanda, 2020).

Finally, it is apprehended that the CBT must be aligned with the objectives of sustainable tourism provided by the WTO, with proposals that aim to promote the improvement of the quality of life of the receiving communities, the visitor's experience, the natural environment, as well as to ensure an equitable distribution of benefits and costs.

2.1 The Other Side of Tourism and Community

Tourism activities inevitably impact the environment of ecological nature reserves, but with proper planning and management, it can promote sustainable development while protecting the environment. In a study that examines the impact of tourism activities on the environmental carrying capacity, plant landscape and atmospheric environment of Wuyishan National Nature Reserve, Han (2019) develops a set of recommendations. The author concludes the overall environmental quality is excellent, but the total suspended particle content of the Jiuqu River exceeds first-class standards. Ultimately, we should create meaningful tourism activities that prioritise eco-environmental protection and sustainable development in all tourism activities.

In this sense, Han (2019) observes the current laws and regulations on tourism management in Wuyishan National Nature Reserve are inadequate, resulting in severe destruction of natural resources and a lack of supervision. To achieve ecological sustainability, the author suggests the urgent need to strengthen the management competences of managers, operators and tourists. As tourists are direct participants in tourism activities, the suggestions also are directed to them: tourists must adopt responsible behaviour and refrain from uncivilised actions such as littering, picking and painting in reserves. Additionally, the research results point to the need of providing adequate facilities and services to ensure that tourists do not harm the environment. For the author, we must standardise tourism behaviour, educate tourists on ecological science and ensure harmony between tourism activities and the ecological environment. This is particularly shared by Zhang et al. (2021).

Wise (2020) has similar concerns. In today's competitive landscape, economic sustainability is of utmost importance for destinations looking to attract tourists, consumers and new customers. To meet the evolving demands of consumers, destinations must showcase their latest offerings and host events (Wise, 2020). However, it's crucial to balance these changes with a growing emphasis on social and community impacts. Social and community impacts are also important to consider, as they relate to local attitudes about places as well as quality of life for residents and businesses in destinations (Zhang et al., 2021). The intangible impacts of tourism are closely linked to local attitudes towards destinations and the quality of life for residents and businesses, which are constantly evolving. As a result, new forms of participation and evaluation are needed to understand these impacts fully.

Xiong et al. (2023) show that environmental impacts of tourism are mostly measured by CO_2 emissions, while other pollutants such as SO_2, NH_3, VOC, N_2O and PM 2.5 are often ignored. The USA, due to its extensive use of fossil fuels for energy production and consumption, is the second largest greenhouse gas (GHG) emitter after China. Their study aims to fill the knowledge gap by analysing the impact of four LH sectors on three GHG emissions and six air pollutants at the sub-industry level. They also considered economic growth, energy consumption and globalisation in their analysis as they are crucial elements and should not be ignored. Their findings suggest that analysing the LH sub-industry level provides comprehensive information for sustainable policies and offers a new direction for academia and practitioners.

Over 15,000 research articles have been published on the correlation between tourism and the environment, yet they fail to take into account the environmental impact of tourism at a sectoral level, as Xiong et al. (2023) highlight in their paper. It is evident that tourism development contributes heavily to CO_2 emissions due to its high energy consumption, both directly through operations and indirectly through related services. Evidence supporting this belief comes from Katircioglu (2014, cited by Xiong et al., 2023), who confirmed that tourism development is responsible for CO_2 emissions and climate change in Turkey. The accommodation sector, casino and gaming facilities, restaurants and similar services consume energy to carry out day-to-day operations that emit CO_2 and other gases. The long-term expansion of tourist activities leads to increased transport, high production in the leisure and accommodation sectors, and greater fuel consumption, resulting in environmental pollution.

3. METHODOLOGICAL PROCEDURES

This study is exploratory in nature and uses bibliometric with quantitative techniques and content analysis. Its aim is to gain insight into the subject by analysing its historical mapping and metric trends, and also to discuss the most relevant texts in the context of socio-political factors.

Bibliometric analysis has been a popular method in the last years that aims to explore a large volume of scientific data to be analysed and unveil the evolutionary nuances of a specific field, while also highlighting emerging areas of this field (Donthu et al., 2021). Through bibliometric analysis, it is possible to decipher and map the evolutionary nuances and cumulative scientific knowledge on a given topic, making sense of the large volume of data and building solid foundations for the advancement of the specific field in significant and innovative ways. Thus, it allows and enables scholars to: (a) obtain a broad view of the subject; (b) identify existing gaps; and (c) forming new ideas in research; and (d) direct the intended contributions to a given area of study (Donthu et al., 2021).

It is important to point out that bibliometrics has combined statistical techniques with content analysis to deepen the analysis of the investigative path, trends and emerging themes in the field. There is evidence that the combined use of these techniques is becoming common (Galvagno, 2017; Duque & Cervantes-Cervantes, 2019; Oliveira & Teodósio, 2020). In this sense, scholars should elaborate insightful discussions involving equivalent justifications and relevant trends, rather than simply describing a bibliometric summary (Donthu et al., 2021).

In the bibliometric review, figures and tables are used for descriptive demonstration of the publications found in the selected databases, through which it is possible to observe the historical trajectory and the thematic and methodological trends on the subject. In addition, by approaching the content of each thematic grouping, it is possible to interpret the results and analyse the context in relation to the events that form this axis for a good understanding of the content, following the suggestions of Donthu et al. (2021).

As a research model, bibliometrics is part of the field of information sciences (Gouveia, 2013; Carvalho & Gouveia, 2017; Rodrigues-da-Silva, 2019), although it has currently been used by other areas of knowledge. In addition to providing knowledge about 'the performance and impact of scientific activity in a given region' (Dávila Rodríguez et al., 2009, p. 321), showing trends in academic productivity, the ability to contribute to knowledge and innovation in science, it can also offer inputs for the construction of public policies and various decision-making processes related to substantive dimensions of CBT. For this reason, the decision to combine the quantitative results with the qualitative analysis of trends and results presented from the bibliometric study is justified.

For data collection, two internationally recognised bibliographic databases were chosen: *Web of Science* – WoS and *Scopus*, using the Brazilian scientific platform called Capes/Café, with the aim of including publications in high-impact journals, and also because the export of texts has an interface with the software used.

As the surveys were carried out, reports were generated and exported in *BibTex* for the purpose of statistical analysis in the Bibliometrix package of *R Studio*. This software was used to identify the combination of different structures and to analyse the selected bibliography and, in addition, to visualise the metrics and graphs of the relationships between authors and the concepts that are associated.

The relationships between terms and connections between citations, in the results, provide guidelines on the main assumptions and arguments about CBT and its influence on local development.

For the analysis of bibliometrics, which corresponds to the quantitative part of this research, the most common bibliometric indicators were used, namely, citation analysis and co-citation analysis (Zupic & Cater, 2015). The first method is based on the assumption that the most cited authors are the most influential and relevant to the topic; in the second case, it is assumed that while two or more academic works are cited at the same time, their contents are closely related to each other, which leads to the belief that the documents are similar.

Content analysis was applied in a combination of the method proposed by Bardin (2016) and Piñuel-Raigada (2002). The latter defines that the main objective of the technique is: 'to achieve the emergence of a latent meaning that comes from social and cognitive practices that instrumentally resort to communication to facilitate the interaction between communication and text' (Piñuel-Raigada, 2002, p. 4). The texts went through the three stages that Bardin (2016) proposes, namely: pre-analysis, coding and categorisation. From then on, the meanings were considered in terms of the theoretical framework developed in this research.

4. RESULTS AND ANALYSIS

4.1 Bibliometric Data of CBT

The bibliometric survey was carried out during the month of October 2022 on the *WoS* and *Scopus bases*, as already mentioned. In each one, the following terms were used: 'community tourism' and 'community-based tourism' in the title, abstract or keywords of the articles. As a result, we reached the amount of 247 and 383 articles, respectively, in the *WoS* and Scopus database with the term 'community tourism'. Subsequently, 545 and 812 articles were reached, respectively, in the same databases with the term 'community-based tourism'.

It is important to highlight that given the similarity of the terms 'community tourism' and 'community-based tourism', it was necessary to use each term individually to take advantage of the scope of the research, considering that they are the same concept.

In addition, a filter of articles from the last 5 years was carried out, whichever is from 2018. The use of this filter is justified to enable the qualitative analysis of bibliometrics, as refinement reduces the bibliographic survey to the most relevant, delimiting the collected bibliography. From this filter, 131 results were obtained in the *WoS* Database and 155 results in *Scopus* with the term 'community tourism'. Then, a total of 348 articles and 491 articles were reached, respectively, in the databases with the term 'community-based tourism'. Therefore, it was possible to compute a total of 1,125 articles, which through specific software (*R Studio*) it was possible to detect 321 articles as duplicates, with this the amount was reduced to 804 articles. Fig. 1 illustrates the path taken in the survey and selection of texts:

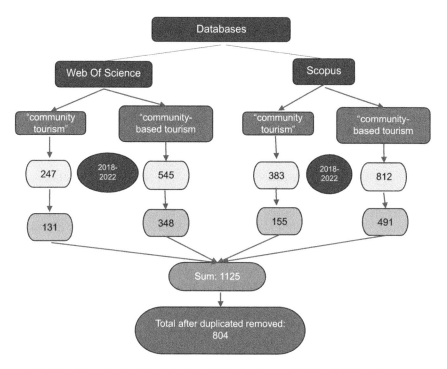

Fig. 1. Flowchart of the Selection of Texts. *Source:* Elaborated based on our methodological design and the results of the searches (2022).

As shown in the flowchart, from a total of almost 2000 articles, after applying the indicated filters and removing duplicates, a set of 804 articles was obtained, which were analysed below.

From these results, it was possible to visualise the evolution of the production of articles in the last 5 years, specifically between 2018 and 2022, years chosen in the research, as shown in Fig. 2.

The numbers show that CBT has attracted interest from the academy and is on the rise, considering that the data collected in 2022 are until the month of September and already totalled 142 (Table 1). The total number of publications in 2018 was 143 articles and it shows an increasing growing. In 2021, there were 189 articles published in the databases studied. This number is supported by the number of citations per year, as shown in Table 1, the average number of citations per article each year.

The most relevant academic journals, in this bibliometric study, are those listed in Table 2, which shows the total number of articles published in the last 5 years, as well as the Journal's H *index*.

It is observed in Table 2 that from the 218 articles published, 150 were in journals that have an *H-Index* greater than five, showing the relevance of these publications and their potential impact in academia.

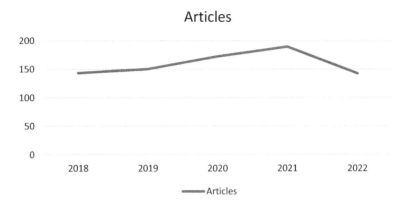

Fig. 2. Articles Published by Year. *Source:* WOS and Scopus Search Result in Bibliometrix (2022).

Table 1. Average Citations per Article and per Year.

Year	N	MeanTCperArt	MeanTCperYear	Citable Years
2018	143	8.67	2.17	4
2019	150	6.61	2.20	3
2020	172	4.97	2.48	2
2021	189	2.15	2.15	1
2022	142	0.62		0

Source: WOS and Scopus Search Result in Bibliometrix (2022).

Table 2. Articles by *Journal/H Index*.

Journal Name (Source)	Articles	H-Index
Sustainability (Switzerland)	47	10
African Journal of Hospitality, Tourism and Leisure	32	5
IOP Conference Series: Earth and Environmental Science	26	3
Journal of Sustainable Tourism	26	12
Geojournal of Tourism and Geosites	19	6
Journal of Environmental Management and Tourism	16	4
University and Society Magazine	15	1
Current Issues in Tourism	14	7
Tourism Recreation Research	12	5
Community-Based Tourism in the Developing World	11	1

Source: WOS and Scopus Search Result in Bibliometrix (2022).

The terms tourism, ecotourism, sustainability, sustainable development, tourism development, CBT, local participation, tourism management, community-based, tourist destination, among others, suggest the importance of aligning the theme with such words – Fig. 3 presents a sample of the keywords most found in the analysed articles.

Fig. 3. Most Frequent Keywords on the Topic. *Source:* WOS and Scopus Search Result in Bibliometrix (2022).

The association of these words emphasises the contextualisation of CBT with other types of tourism and the need for local community participation for environmental sustainability.

In this study, *Lotka*'s Law is also confirmed, which identifies the number of authors who have published a certain number of articles; thus, productivity is measured based on the distribution and on a model of size and frequency of a compendium of publications (Lotka, 1926). It appears that a large proportion of scientific literature is produced by a small number of authors, and this is equivalent to the production of articles by a large number of authors, as shown in Table 3.

Table 3. Author Productivity Through Lotka's Law.

Documents written	N. of Authors	Proportion of Authors
1	1671	0.882
2	164	0.087
3	41	0.022
4	5	0.003
5	6	0.003
6	5	0.003
21	1	0.001
32	1	0.001

Source: WOS and Scopus Search Result in Bibliometrix (2022).

By reading Table 3, it is observed that 1,671 authors produced only one document, corresponding to 0.882 of the total number of authors producing articles on the central theme researched. At the same time, it is observed that one author produced 21 articles and another 32 articles.

Table 4 shows the most relevant authors who published about CBT and their respective number of articles. Some of their contributions were showed in the qualitative analysis part of this chapter.

Table 4. Most Relevant Authors.

Authors	Articles	Articles Fractionalized
GIAMPICCOLI A	32	13.67
MTAPURI O	21	8.33
DŁUŻEWSKA A	6	2.08
ERNAWATI N	6	1.92
KIM S	6	1.83
NA N	6	6.00
ZIELINSKI S	6	1.83
JUGMOHAN S	5	1.58
LEE T	5	2.03
MUSAVENGANE R	5	3.00

Source: WOS and Scopus Search Result in Bibliometrix (2022).

It is important to highlight that these authors published their articles in Q1 and Q2 quartiles, such as: *Journal of Tourism and Cultural Change* (ISSN 1476-6825) and *Sustainability* (ISSN 2071-1050). The authors with more publications Giampiccoli and Mtapuri have works alluding to sustainable and community-based tourism in small islands, the impacts of COVID-19 on CBT, theories associated with the level of tourists and hosts, the importance of empowering communities to receive tourists, among others.

After analysis of institutional affiliation, South Africa (*Durban University of Technology, University of Johannesburg*), Australia (*Griffith University*), the United States (*North-West University*) and Mexico are the countries where research on CBT is very important, according to publications in the databases studied. However, the origin of the authors is diverse (Table 5).

As can be seen from the Table 5, Indonesia demonstrates a greater quantitative association of publications of articles in which there is a correspondence between the author and the country of publication.

The factorial analysis in blibliometrics represents the sets of variables that are interrelated. Fig. 4 indicates those variables that most interrelate with each other, with strong trends for the terms: conservation, tourism innovation, area protection, natural resource and residents' perceptions. Thus, it is possible to observe ways to contribute to CBT.

Table 5. Corresponding Author's Country.

Country	Articles	SCP	MCP	Freq	MCP_Ratio
	219	219	0	0.272	0.000
INDONESIA	61	60	1	0.076	0.016
SOUTH AFRICA	50	49	1	0.062	0.020
THAILAND	43	43	0	0.053	0.000
CHINA	34	29	5	0.042	0.147
SPAIN	33	29	4	0.041	0.121
BRAZIL	31	29	2	0.039	0.065
USA	30	28	2	0.037	0.067
ECUADOR	29	22	7	0.036	0.241
MALAYSIA	24	23	1	0.030	0.042

Source: WOS and Scopus Search Result in Bibliometrix (2022).

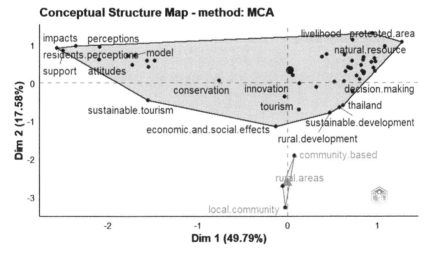

Fig. 4. Factor Analysis. *Source:* WOS and Scopus Search Result in Bibliometrix (2022).

In Table 6, the evidence shows that Brazil stands out as the country that most produced articles published on CBT, followed by Indonesia and Ecuador.

The most cited scientific productions globally referring to the subject (CBT) show that research about CBT has been consolidated, as shown in Table 7.

Table 6. Country Scientific Production.

region	Freq
BRAZIL	118
INDONESIA	106
ECUADOR	86
SOUTH AFRICA	81
SPAIN	67
THAILAND	64
MEXICO	60
CHINA	56
USA	50
MALAYSIA	46

Source: WOS and Scopus Search Result in Bibliometrix (2022).

Table 7. Most Global Cited Documents.

Paper	DOI	Total Citations	TC per Year	Normalized TC
LEE TH, 2019, TOUR MANAGE	10.1016/j.tourman.2018.09.003	178	44.50	26.94
DODDS R, 2018, CURR ISSUES TOUR	10.1080/13683500.2016.1150257	98	19.60	11.30
EUSEBIO C, 2018,	10.1080/09669582.2018.1425695	98	19.60	11.30
WONDIRAD A, 2020,	10.1016/j.tourman.2019.104024	79	26.33	15.91
RAMKISSOON H, 2020, J SUSTAINABLE TOUR	10.1080/09669582.2020.1858091	70	23.33	14.10
ROGERSON CM, 2020, DEV SOUTH AFR	10.1080/0376835X.2020.1818551	65	21.67	13.09
STONE MT, 2018, J SUSTAINABLE TOUR	10.1080/09669582.2017.1349774	56	11.20	6.46
WOOSNAM KM, 2018,	10.1016/j.tourman.2017.09.015	48	9.60	5.54
JOO D, 2020, J SUSTAINABLE TOUR	10.1080/09669582.2019.1675673	47	15.67	9.47
MAYAKA M, 2018, J SUSTAINABLE TOUR	10.1080/09669582.2017.1359278	46	9.20	5.30

Source: WOS and Scopus Search Result in Bibliometrix (2022).

Figure 5 shows the network of cowords (co-occurrence of keywords) using *biblioshiny*. The node size indicates the occurrence of the keyword, so the larger the more times the keyword occurs. The *link* between the nodes represents the correlation between the keywords. The thematic clusters show the nodes and the links that explain the topic coverage (nodes) of the theme (cluster) and the relationships (links) between the topics (nodes) that manifest under that theme (*cluster*). Tourism and development are the words that interconnect the others. Two major themes (cluster) emerge. The first one is Community-based tourism and the second one is Tourism Development, where we can see ecoturism and sustainability as subtopics.

Fig. 5. Co-occurrence Network. *Source:* WOS and Scopus Search Result in Bibliometrix (2022).

We can observe in Fig. 6 three main themes (high density and high centrality) that have a greater relationship with CBT. From our interpretation, we can inferred that:

- the first and second clusters (in the righ upper side of graph) indicate international publications that have addressed sustainable development, community-based, rural areas, followed by topics on CBT, management and impacts. These terms occupy the centre of the figure, which indicates a strong tendency of researchers to learn about tourism associated with sustainable development.
- the third cluster (in the left side down of the graph) deals with themes related to the development of tourism, tourism and ecotourism, which are seen as driving themes, that is, quite frequent in the researched scientific productions;
- the smaller cluster highlights that humans are emerging or declining themes.

It is visible that the Bradford's Law was reached in our study. Bradford's Law is one of the laws of bibliometrics that affects the set of academic journals and seeks to identify the breadth and scope that a given topic has when it appears published. In his work, Bradford (1934) noted that there was always a smaller core of journals closely related to the topic itself, and at least a larger core in which there was more dispersion.

Thus, Table 8, resulting from the survey of this research, demonstrates the grouping of sources in line with Bradford's Law. It is understood that these

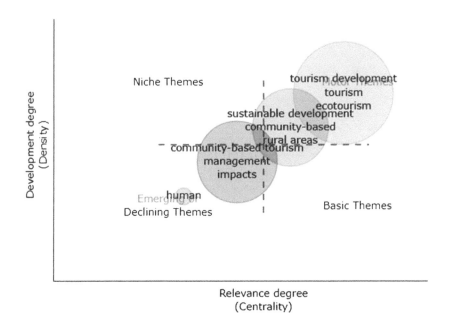

Fig. 6. Thematic Map. *Source:* WOS and Scopus Search Result in Bibliometrix (2022).

journals located in zone 1 are indicative of those that are most interested in the subject and generally have published research related to CBT, as observed in the column of accumulated frequency.

Table 8. Grouping of Sources According to Bradford's Law.

SO	Rank	Freq	cumFreq	Zone
SUSTAINABILITY (SWITZERLAND)	1	47	47	Zone 1
AFRICAN JOURNAL OF HOSPITALITY, TOURISM AND LEISURE	2	32	79	Zone 1
IOP CONFERENCE SERIES: EARTH AND ENVIRONMENTAL SCIENCE	3	26	105	Zone 1
JOURNAL OF SUSTAINABLE TOURISM	4	26	131	Zone 1
GEOJOURNAL OF TOURISM AND GEOSITES	5	19	150	Zone 1
JOURNAL OF ENVIRONMENTAL MANAGEMENT AND TOURISM	6	16	166	Zone 1
REVISTA UNIVERSIDAD Y SOCIEDAD	7	15	181	Zone 1
CURRENT ISSUES IN TOURISM	8	14	195	Zone 1
TOURISM RECREATION RESEARCH	9	12	207	Zone 1
COMMUNITY-BASED TOURISM IN THE DEVELOPING WORLD: COMMUNITY LEARNING, DEVELOPMENT & ENTERPRISE	10	11	218	Zone 1

Source: WOS and Scopus Search Result in Bibliometrix (2022).

From Fig. 7, it is possible to observe that there is a continued increase of publications in two journals with Q2 and Q1, respectively: *Sustainability* (ISSN 2071-1050) and *Journal of Sustainable Tourism* (ISSN 1476-6825).

It may be a temporary, conjunctural movement and not necessarily indicative that other journals may be losing interest in the topic. Anyway, we decided to

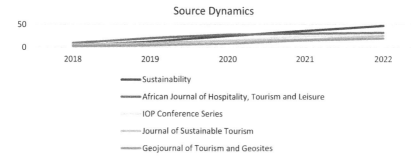

Fig. 7. Source *Dynamics. Source:* WOS and Scopus Search Result in Bibliometrix (2022).

expand this analysis, and, in addition, a new search was carried out of the texts published in these two journals in 2021 and 2022 with the same terms used in the bibliometric survey: 'Community-based tourism' and 'Community tourism', reaching a total of 68 articles after removing duplicates and selecting the articles that fix to the main objective of this paper (*Sustainability,* 40 articles and in the *Journal of Sustainable Tourism,* 28 articles).

4.2 The Qualitative Analysis

Sustainability is an open access journal with a significant number of articles published in each issue. The periodicity of publication is fortnightly, and they address different themes of sustainability, among them sustainable tourism. The *Journal of Sustainable Tourism* is a journal owned by Taylor & Francis Online, a privately based publication, and has an exclusive focus on sustainable tourism. Due to its characteristics, we were unable to access all published articles.

The word cloud presented in Fig. 8 shows the 30 most frequent words (minimum length of 5 characters and minimum 40 times used in the texts) that were automatically identified with the textual analysis software (MAXQDA) of all 68 papers.

As can be seen, tourism is closely linked to the issue of local, development, sustainable and community, and also it is evident the importance of economic, social and cultural aspects. The results also show that some instrumental aspects appear in this cloud, as management, support, knowledge, resources and impacts, for instance.

When we do the same exercise by journal, we have the result presented in the Fig. 9. In the cloud of the most 30 frequent words (minimum of 30 times that these words are used in the texts published during 2021 and 2022 in the *Sustainability* Journal), we can see that the tourism is strongly linked to local development, social dimensions and sustainability. But it is not clear how this development and sustainability are reached through the CBT. Nevertheless, some insights can be mentioned, through the suggested codes created from the word cloud. First, we can define the development in some dimensions: economic, social, cultural, community/collective, environmental, rural/urban. Secondly, the

Fig. 8. Frequent Keywords on the Topic. *Source:* Sustainability and Journal of Sustainable Tourism (2023) Research Results.

Fig. 9. Most Frequent Keywords on the Sustainability Journal. *Source:* Sustainability (2023) Research Results.

means for reach this development can be though in terms of levels of participation, type of legitimacy/power, resources employment, entrepreneurship promotion.

The following cloud (Fig. 10) shows the results of the 30 most frequent words used in the papers published in the Journal of Sustainable Tourism during the years of 2021 and 2022.

Fig. 10. Most Frequent Keywords on the Journal of Sustainable Tourism.
Source: Journal of Sustainable Tourism (2023) Research Results.

We deleted the obvious words as tourism, community, development and sustainability, and we can see the terms highlighted are linked with some relevant aspects that are explored in the texts. Local and social seem to be more relevant, followed by management and support. We also can construct some inferences through this result. For instance, we can propose that the local and social development acquire more relevance in the research, followed by the economic, environmental and cultural ones. Also, we can suggest that support, knowledge and management models are important aspects considered in the development of the CBT. This instrumental perspective could be influenced by some ethnic and gender discourse, the destination, the solidarity and the volunteer.

Following, we choose some of the most relevant texts to summarise. Many of them are authored by the most relevant authors listed in the Table 4. It is interesting to observe that most of these research are collaborative and show, also, they have a large academic experience in these subjects.

The study of Walther and da Costa (2022) uses ethnography to analyse the emergence of an art-based social enterprise and entrepreneurial ecosystem in

Southeastern Brazil, focussing on the Oficina de Agosto (OdA) and its impact on the local community, and its contributions to economic, cultural and societal development. The study discusses the local conditions that set the Small Enterprise to success, the importance of place, entrepreneurial ecosystems, local perspectives and processes, and identifies OdA's forces, boundaries, limitations and challenges. Using these results, it provides managerial recommendations that may help entrepreneurs deal with the tensions that emerge from the juxtaposition of the social and the economic, the traditional and the contemporary, the local and the global, and the insider and the outsider. The study suggests business and community practices based on long-term patience, non-hierarchical relationships and a constant effort to adopt both/and thinking. The main conclusion is that social enterprise may work as an alternative market model that could support community building, social enterprises' initial social focus may not be perennial or unshakeable, and the managerial recommendations offered might be extended to other businesses in Bichinho, in other semi-rural Brazilian towns, or even in international settings that might bear economic and social resemblance to our researched context.

Jurkus et al. (2022) discuss the history and modern interpretation of biodiversity conservation, as defined by the Convention on Biological Diversity (CBD). The CBD considers off-site and on-site measures to preserve biological diversity, including legal measures and the preservation of genetic material. Ecotourism, introduced in the 1960s, is a form of sustainable tourism that promotes conservation, has low negative visitor impact and provides for beneficially active socio-economic involvement of local populations. The precise definition of ecotourism has proven to be a tricky task, resulting in a multiplication of definitions. The article identifies three broad tenets or pillars for ecotourism development: conservation, development and experience. The research trends in biodiversity conservation and tourism sustainability involve investigating issues implied by uncontrolled visitation to protected areas, CBT development and how tourists are offered and use opportunities for learning and meaningful encounters with the environment and local community. The overarching megatrend in biodiversity conservation and sustainable tourism research is environmentally responsible travel to natural areas that conserves the environment, has low negative visitor impact and improves the wellbeing of local communities. The article concludes by highlighting the relevance of this field for meeting the UN Sustainable Development Goals until 2030 and the research directions and practical applications in protected area management.

Rural tourism is taking centre stage as an alternative to overcrowded urban tourism and is established as a lever for the recovery of small economies. Ecuador is positioned as a leader in community tourism, which is based on taking advantage of natural and cultural resources of ancestral spaces of indigenous communities. In this sense, Maldonado-Erazo et al. (2022) propose the consolidation of sustainable tourism through innovation, linking neglected groups, and investment in communities in order to generate a resilient future. Considering that Ecuador is highlighted as a leading country in CBT due to the wide variety of tourism enterprises resulting from the multiple processes of insurgency and vindication for collective rights of local communities and indigenous, Afro-Ecuadorian, and Montubio peoples and nationalities, the main object of study is CORDTUCH, a national ecuadorian network which brings together several peasant and indigenous communities in the province of Chimborazo.

The text highlights poverty as a circumstantial concept for the indigenous world-view and recognises the value of their culture and the Pachamama. CBT teaches us to work with communities through cultural encounter actions, in which differences are respected and communities begin to be understood as subjects with the capacity to bring change in their territories. CBT confirms that it is not only the generation of a business but also the definition of an organisational process, which protects the territories, strengthens the capacities of the communities and safeguards ancestral knowledge. Gender equity and generational participation have made it possible for 55% of the participants in this type of tourism to be women. The enterprises produced an important local economic revitalisation, contributed to the generation of jobs, and reduced migration to the city or to other countries. Maldonado-Erazo et al. (2022) recommend continuing to strengthen alliances between the private, public and community sectors, consolidating a marketing process that identifies specific market niches and sound investment strategies, and developing new mechanisms and tools for managing information in all areas of work. Future lines of research include volunteer tourism in the context of community tourism for the economic reactivation of communities.

The paper of Giampiccoli et al. (2022) is a critical view of CBT. The authors recognise that tourism is a rapidly growing and profitable global economic sector, but it also has negative impacts such as displacement of communities and environmental destruction. The United Nations Sustainable Development Goals propose new directions to rethink the current economic growth ideology in the context of social and environmental needs. However, current hegemonic notions of sustainable tourism often highlight the role of the industry and markets, failing to fight poverty and inequality. Considering these aspects, the article discusses the potential benefits and limitations of CBT in promoting the well-being of local communities.

Giampiccoli et al. (2022) state while CBT can contribute to community empowerment and development, its implementation can also lead to disappointment and endanger the well-being of locals. To enhance the chances of success, a collaborative framework involving policymakers, planners and other government officials is necessary. The basic principles of CBT, such as redistribution of wealth, ownership and control of the local tourism sector, and respect for local cultural contexts, are in line with promoting local community well-being.

Adopting a critical view too, the paper of Zhao et al. (2022) discusses the phenomenon of hollow villages in rural China, caused by migration to urban areas, and the government's efforts to support rural development through CBT. The study examines the impact of a tourism programme on a hollow village and explores the concept of empowerment in community transformation, recognising the positive and negative impacts of CBT on local communities and the importance of empowering residents in tourism development. The study identifies the uncertain transformation in the community resulting from tourism gentrification and local residents' self-gentrification.

Suriyankietkaew et al. (2022) examine sustainable leadership frameworks and competencies in the SME sector, using a case study of a green, social enterprise in Thailand. Their literature review identifies five essential characteristics of CBSE: community ownership, community management, profit sharing or reinvestment, social and environmental problem-solving and financial self-sustainability. Besides, it develops some aspects of the sustainability of business, as long-term perspective, focus on the human side of organisations, organisational culture, innovation, ethical behaviour and social and environmental responsibility.

Methodologically, Suriyankietkaew et al. (2022) used a qualitative case study research design to investigate sustainable leadership in a green community-based social enterprise (CBSE) in Tung Yee Peng (TYP) village in China. The research employed multi-data collection methods, including in-depth interviews, focus groups and non-participatory observations, with a multi-stakeholder perspective. Thematic analysis was used to organise the data and identify commonalities, and document analysis was employed to gain a more in-depth understanding of the CBSE context. The study aimed to validate the data, gain insights into the specific context and present reliable findings for further theoretical advancement. The research method helped to expand understanding and knowledge about sustainable leadership in the CBSE phenomenon. Findings suggest that sustainable leaders should integrate value-based practices and competencies, including care for stakeholders, ethical values, social innovation and pro-environmental behaviour. An alternative sustainable business model is proposed, with practical advice and policy implications for sustainable futures.

One of the most relevant authors published a collaborative paper in 2021 where he shows the need of empowering and preparing the community for their own development. Mtapuri et al. (2021) propose extending the Knowledge Attitude Practices (KAP) survey to include Skills (KSAP) and argue that communities need to be equipped with knowledge, attitudes, skills and practices beyond tourism. The results of this research recommend conducting surveys on CBT, tourism and livelihoods to gain a holistic understanding of these aspects among community members, tourists and stakeholders. The KSAP model is a tool that can be adapted to local conditions and used by tourism stakeholders. The paper is a conceptual one compiled using secondary data.

The paper of Li et al. (2021) explores the cultural sustainability of Jeju Island in South Korea and the importance of constructive collaboration with local communities in tourism ventures. In-depth interviews with local residents reveal negative indications of cultural sustainability due to informal power dynamics and barriers to CBT collaboration. However, there is a strong relationship between collaboration and cultural sustainability, highlighting the need for involvement of the local community in sustainable tourism development. The study provides significant implications for tourism policymakers and practitioners on how to plan and operate sustainable tourism for long-term benefit.

Guizzardi et al. (2022)´s study examines how sustainability can drive tourist demand in small areas during early stages of tourism development. The study proposes feasible methods and scales to analyse the perceived value of rural tourism and visitor perceived sustainability and compares the advantages of ordinal SEM to the standard model and finds that a good state of conservation of cultural heritage and a well-protected natural environment are the most important indicators of perceived sustainability.

The methodology of Guizzardi et al. (2022) focuses on visitor perception of sustainability in rural areas of Italy and Croatia that are at an early stage of tourism development. These areas have valuable natural and cultural heritage, but currently attract few tourists and lack accommodation, infrastructure and tourist facilities. Adapted indicators from literature review were discussed with local authorities and experts for these nine rural sites. General questions were suggested for typical visitors and Questionnaires collected via face-to-face interviews from April to December 2019. Data were analysed and the results support conclusions that good conservation of local cultural heritage and environmental protection measures are important indicators of perceived sustainability. Additionally, functional benefits are the most important dimension of perceived value. Perceived sustainability has a strong and positive indirect effect on destinations' competitiveness through perceived value.

In sum, Guizzardi et al. (2022) disentangle the relationship between tourism and sustainability, showing that sustainability is perceived as a limitation but is a driver of destinations' competitiveness due to its strong influence on perceived value, which moderates its contribution to destination image, satisfaction and intention to recommend.

In their article, Chatkaewnapanon and Lee (2022) discuss the importance of community participation in tourism development in rural areas. The authors emphasise that the community needs to decide if they want tourism, and that the development process should be based on the local community's approach. The research results suggest methods to encourage proactive participation and improve the quality of outcomes. It also highlights the need for the community to understand their tourism resources and the development process. To achieve this, foresight methodologies such as community arts and community goal-setting workshops are introduced. These workshops help the community visually evaluate their resources and understand the implications of tourism development. The authors emphasise the importance of practical implications and sustainable continuation of tourism activities. Finally, the study demonstrates how community-driven tourism development can make a difference if it involves the proactive participation of residents and their professional perceptions. The authors conclude that foresight strategies need to be applied regularly to keep community and tourism development on the right track.

4.3 Interpretation and Synthesis of Results

In the last 5 years, it is noted that the year 2021 was marked by a greater number of publications about the CBT. Also, it should be noted that the articles were cited in journals of great impact, and the two main ones are *Sustainability* and *the Journal of Sustainable Tourism*. Through these journals, it was possible to survey 82 articles in the years 2021 and 2022 focused on the theme of this article to support a qualitative analysis.

The word cloud shows there was a higher frequency in the words tourism, ecotourism, sustainability, local participation, among others. When talking about CBT, it is important to highlight these aspects of community participation, as well as sustainable development.

The articles selected for qualitative analysis were concentrated in countries as Brazil, Indonesia, Ecuador and South Africa. The CBT proved to be a development strategy for the country, which, associated with sustainable development, allows bringing improvements to the place, environmental quality, equitable distribution of wealth, awareness of social and health impacts and improvements (Teixeira et al., 2019). It turns out that there is a need for full community participation in making efforts to improve the locality, increasing the potential and benefits.

The analysed studies were intentionally chosen to demonstrate how the subject is explained. In order to summarise the main theoretical themes of the qualitative analysis of this study, Table 9 was developed.

From the qualitative analysis of the data, it is intended to find answers to the guiding questions contained in the introduction of this article. The authors Giampiccoli and Mtapuri stand out and their contributions are explored, based on this result.

Table 9. Main Theoretical Findings.

Theoretical Findings	Authors
Community participation	Chatkaewnapanon and Lee (2022), Mtapuri et al. (2021), Mizanur Rahman (2021), Fauzan et al. (2021), Giampiccoli et al. (2022), Hernández et al. (2021), Li et al. (2021), and Zhao et al. (2022)
Sustainability	Sosa et al. (2021), Zhou et al. (2021), Triarchi et al. (2021), Ciro and Toska (2020), and Jurkus et al. (2022)
Sustainable tourism	Matiku et al. (2020), McNaughton et al. (2020), Vargas (2020), Ramkissoon (2023), and Maldonado-Erazo et al. (2022)
Governance and management	Rahman et al. (2022), Suriyankietkaew et al. (2022), Guizzardi et al. (2022), Zielinski et al. (2020), Huang and Chen (2020), Sun et al. (2020), and Walther and da Costo (2022)

Source: The authors themselves (2023).

Among the relevant findings, three large clusters were found in terms of concerns: sustainable development; CBT and the development of tourism, which will be triggered in four categories: community participation, sustainability, sustainable tourism, and governance. Elsewhere, the papers were published in journals with a high impact factor, and it shows that it is effectively relevant to the scientific production.

The qualitative results point to that CBT is closely linked to local development issues, but there are some challenges that we need, as society, to face. For instance, the economic, social and cultural aspects need to be associated with sustainability issues, and this model needs some support to be in the long term.

Also, there is a great need to improve the participation of the local community in aspects of governance, and it is important to expand the communication and public policies to motivate this movement and guarantee CBT. The idealisation of a natural participation remains on a utopian plane, because this perspective of the common space, of common interests, of the collective and collaborative dynamic is not necessarily perceived in all the dynamics of collective organisations. It is an almost romanticised idea of participation or, perhaps, a necessary development for the very survival of a society and of humanity.

Difficulties in participating could be explained by the coexistence of diverse cultural capitals in our region 'the pre-Columbian, the Spanish and Portuguese colonial, in some the Afro-American presence and the contemporary modalities of capitalist development' (García Canclini, 2008, p. 70), but also it contradicts Pierre Bourdieu's vision of the possibility of a hegemony of a legitimate culture, since in the context of collective organisations, several cultures could coexist and, for this very reason, generate differences that could be integrated.

Finally, participation and collaboration depends on many factors and the studies highlight the need of knowledge – practical, technical and also cultural ones – to develop the empowerment of community about the management of tourism in their territory.

5. CONCLUSIONS

This article aimed to show the results of a bibliometric study of national and international publications in the *WOS* and *Scopus databases* in the years 2018–2022 on CBT and Regional Development to determine the growth of this field of research, identify the main ideas and concepts related to this field of research, in addition to providing recommendations for future studies.

The present study was developed through a bibliometric and qualitative review. The quantitative results were described and analysed through the Lotka and Bradford's Laws, reviewed the frequency of citations, the experience and background of the most cited authors, the mains subjects and concerns, and methodological design most used. Both bibliometric laws were confirmed.

And in the literature review it was found that CBT, also known as Community Tourism, requires the participation of the local community in partnership with tourists for the development of sustainable tourism. The following problem was raised, supported by Teixeira et al. (2019), that CBT still has problems and does not generate the expected results, due to the weaknesses of the projects being unsustainable in the long term, the risks of linkage with the industry tourism and the lack of preparation of individuals in the community for governance.

To resolve this problem, greater participation of the local community in aspects of governance is needed, that sustainable tourism projects are known to all and that there may be public policies aimed at guaranteeing CBT. In view of this, the community must become aware of the exploitation of local tourism, resolving issues of mistrust with the external environment and self-managing resources and anticipating solutions.

It is possible to see that research on CBT has attracted more attention from researchers recently, that is, over the years research has increased, with emphasis on the year 2021 with 189 articles published, in 2022, although there were only 142 articles published, but still referring to the month of September. It was found that the most cited articles come from journals with a high impact factor and Q1 or Q2, thus highlighting the publication in journals of greater renown.

In this regard, future studies have the potential to identify new research trends on CBT and Regional Development. It is noticed that CBT acts in territorial development from the interface with social, cultural and environmental dynamics, which brings challenges and, consequently, generates spaces for the production of knowledge capable of addressing these different dimensions. Specifically, it would be interesting to propose an integrative literature review, as there are journals that publish texts on multiple topics associated with CBT. The integration of themes, the systematisation of research and even the establishment of a typology of these studies could be a contribution to the area.

Future studies could also be generated with different methodologies or qualitative and mixed approaches, such as *Process Tracing* of public policies or community decisions, or ethnographies directed at local changes, for example.

REFERENCES

Alibio Oppliger, E., & Morbeck de Oliveira, A. K. (2022). Tourism as an economic possibility for the sustainable development of the quilombola Community of furnas dos baianos, Aquidauana, Mato Grosso do Sul. *Revista Brasileira de Gestão e Desenvolvimento Regional, 18*(2). https://doi.org/10.54399/rbgdr.v18i2.6498

Ballesteros, E. R. (2017). Claves del turismo de base local. Presentación. *Gazeta de Antropología, 33*(1), 1–10. https://doi.org/10.30827/Digibug.44359. http://hdl.handle.net/10481/44359

Bardin, L. (2016). *Análise de Conteúdo*. Edições 70.

Bradford, S. C. (1934). Sources of information on specific subjects. *Engineering, 137*, 85–86.

Carvalho, A. M. F. D., & Gouveia, F. C. (2017). Repositórios institucionais de acesso aberto: adequação às novas métricas da web. *Revista Eletrônica de Comunicação, Informação e Inovação em Saúde, 11*(1–14). https://www.reciis.icict.fiocruz.br/index.php/reciis/article/view/1420/pdf1420

Chatkaewnapanon, Y., & Lee, T. (2022). Planning sustainable community-based tourism in the context of Thailand: Community, development, and the foresight tools. *Sustainability, 14*(12), 1–13. https://doi.org/10.3390/su14127413

Ciro, A., & Toska, M. (2020). Entrepreneurial eco-systems for sustainable community-based tourism development in Albania: Case studies of community tourism development. *Innovation and Entrepreneurial Opportunities in Community Tourism*, 109–137. https://doi.org/10.4018/978-1-7998-4855-4.ch007

Dávila Rodríguez, M., Guzmán Sáenz, R., Arroyo, H. M., Piñeres Herera, D., Rosa Barranco, D. D. L., & Caballero-Uribe, C. V. (2009). Bibliometría: conceptos y utilidades para el estudio médico y la formación profesional. *Salud Uninorte*, *25*(2), 319–330. https://www.redalyc.org/pdf/817/81712365011.pdf

Donthu, N., Kumar, S., Mukherjee, D., Pandey, N., & Lim, W. M. (2021). How to conduct a bibliometric analysis: An overview and guidelines. *Journal of Business Research*, *133*, 285–296. https://doi.org/10.1016/j.jbusres.2021.04.070

Duque, P., & Cervantes-Cervantes, L.-S. (2019). Responsabilidad social Universitaria: una revisión sistemática y análisis bibliométrico. *Estudios Gerenciales*, *35*(153), 451–464. https://doi.org/10.18046/j.estger.2019.153.3389

Fauzan, M., Muhammad-Hapiz, A. M., Azizul, R., Rosilan, S., Hamidi, A. H., Zahari, I., Aweng, E. R., Mohamad-Faiz, M. A., Abas, M. A., Kamarul-Ariffin, H., Nor-Hizami, H., Mohammad-Firdaus, A. K., Susatya, A., & Zulhazman, H. (2021). Document details – Managing and protecting of endangered Rafflesia species in Kelantan, Peninsular Malaysia. *IOP Conference Series: Earth and Environmental Science*, *842*(1). https://doi.org/10.1088/1755-1315/842/1/012069

Faxina, F., & Freitas, L. B. A. (2021). Análise de Implantação do Turismo de Base Comunitária em Terra Caída, Sergipe, Brasil. *Turismo, Visão e Ação*, *23*(1). https://doi.org/10.14210/rtva.v23n1.p242-262

Figueiredo, S. L. (2022). Community-based tourism alternatives in the Brazilian legal Amazon. *Confins-Revue Franco-Bresilienne de Geographie*, *54*. https://doi.org/10.4000/confins.45154

Furtado, C. (1967). Intra-country discontinuities: Towards a theory of spatial structures. *Social Science Information*, *6*, 7–14.

Galvagno, M. (2017). Bibliometric literature review: An opportunity for marketing scholars. *Mercati y Competititivitá*, *4*, 7–15. https://doi.org/10.3280/MC2017-004001

García Canclini, N. (2008). *Culturas híbridas: estratégias para entrar e sair da modernidade.* Tradução Heloísa Pezza Cintrão, Ana Regina Lessa. 4. ed. 4. reimpr. São Paulo: Edusp. (Ensaios Latino-americanos, 1).

Giampiccoli, A., Dłuzewska, A., & Mnguni, E. M. (2022). Host population well-being through community-based tourism and local control: Issues and ways forward. *Sustainability*, *14*(4372), 1–17. https://doi.org/10.3390/su14074372

Gouveia, F. C. (2013). Altimetria: métricas de produção científica para além das citações. *LIINC, Revista IBICT*, *9*(1), 214–227. [Rio de Janeiro]. http://revista.ibict.br/liinc/article/view/3434/3004

Graciano, P. F., & Holanda, L. A. (2020). Análise bibliométrica da produção científica sobre turismo de base comunitária de 2013 a 2018. *Revista Brasileira de Pesquisa em Turismo, São Paulo*, *14*(1), 161–179. http://dx.doi.org/10.7784/rbtur.v14i1.1736

Guizzardi, A., Stacchini, A., & Costa, M. (2022). Can sustainability drive tourism development in small rural areas? Evidences from the Adriatic. *Journal of Sustainable Tourism*, *30*(6), 1280–1300. http://doi.org/10.1080/09669582.2021.1931256

Han, F. L. (2019). Environmental impact of tourism activities on ecological nature reserves. *Applied Ecology and Environmental Research*, *17*(4), 1–10. https://doi.org/10.15666/aeer/1704_94839492

Hernández, S. M. A., Vaca, D. M. G., Cejas, M. N., Martínez, M. F. C., Aguirre, P. E. M., & Mora, O. P. F. (2021). Document details – Quality and tourism supply: A study of enterprises linked to rural community-based tourism in the canton of Riobamba. *Academic Journal of Interdisciplinary Studies*, *10*(4), 130–140. https://doi.org/10.36941/AJIS-2021-0104

Huang, S., & Chen, G. (2020). Chapter 23: Chinese government and tourism governance. *Social and Political Science*, 339–350. https://doi.org/10.4337/9781788117531.00029

Jurkus, E., Povilanskas, R., & Taminskas, J. (2022). Current trends and issues in research on biodiversity conservation and tourism sustainability. *Sustainability*, *14*(3342), 1–14. https://doi.org/10.3390/su14063342

Li, X., Kim, J. S., & Lee, T. J. (2021). Collaboration for community-based cultural sustainability in island tourism development: A case in Korea. *Sustainability, 13*(7306), 1–17. https://doi.org/10.3390/su13137306

Lotka, A. J. (1926). The frequency distribution of scientific productivity. *Journal of the Washington Academy of Sciences, 16*(12), 317–323.

Maldonado-Erazo, C. P., del Río-Rama, M. . d.l.C., Miranda-Salazar, S. P., & Tierra-Tierra, N. P. (2022). Strengthening of community tourism enterprises as a means of sustainable development in rural areas: A case study of community tourism development in Chimborazo. *Sustainability, 14*(4314), 1–22. https://doi.org/10.3390/su14074314

Matiku, S., Zuwarimwe, J., & Tshipala, N. (2020). Document details – Community-driven tourism projects' economic contribution to community livelihoods – A case of makuleke contractual park community tourism project. *Sustainability, 12*(19). https://doi.org/10.3390/su12198230

McNaughton, M., Rao, L., & Verma, S. (2020). Document details – Building smart communities for sustainable development: Community tourism in Treasure Beach Jamaica. *Worldwide Hospitality and Tourism Themes, 12*(3), 337–352. https://doi.org/10.1108/WHATT-02-2020-0008

Mizanur Rahman, M. (2021). Biologia Futura: Can co-management protect Saint Martin's corals of Bangladesh? *Biologia Futura, 72*(4), 517–527. https://doi.org/10.1007/s42977-021-00101-4

Monteiro Neto, A., Castro, C. N., & Brandão, C. A. (2017). *Desenvolvimento regional no Brasil: políticas, estratégias e perspectivas* (p. 468). IPEA. https://www.ipea.gov.br/portal/images/stories/PDFs/livros/livros/20170213_livro_desenvolvimentoregional.pdf

Mtapuri, O., Thanh, T. D., Giampiccoli, A., & Dłuzewska, A. (2021). Expansion and specification of knowledge, skills, attitudes and practices survey model for community-based tourism development. *Sustainability, 13*(10525), 1–12. https://doi.org/10.3390/su131910525

Oliveira, V. M. D., & Teodósio, A. D. S. D. S. (2020). Consumo colaborativo: um estudo bibliométrico entre 2010 e 2019. *REAd. Revista Eletrônica de Administração (Porto Alegre), 26*(2), 300–329. https://doi.org/10.1590/1413-2311.285.988743

Piñuel-Raigada, J. l. (2002). Epistemología, metodología y técnicas de análisis de contenido. *Estudios de Sociolingüística, 3*(1), 1–42.

Portes, A. (2000). Capital social: Origens e aplicações na sociologia contemporânea. *Sociologia, Problemas e Práticas, 33*, 133–158. https://sociologiapp.iscte-iul.pt/index.o.jsp?lingua=2

Rahman, M. S.-U., Simmons, D., & Shone, M. C. ., R. (2022). Social and cultural capitals in tourism resource governance: The essential lenses for community focused co-management. *Journal of Sustainable Tourism, 30*, 2665–2685. https://doi.org/10.1080/09669582.2021.1903016

Ramkissoon, H. (2023). Perceived social impacts of tourism and quality-of-life: A new conceptual model. *Journal of Sustainable Tourism, 31*(2), 442–459. https://doi.org/10.1080/09669582.2020.1858091

Rodrigues da Silva, R. A. (2019). O patrimônio industrial no Brasil no século XXI: Um estudo bibliométrico do estado da arte. *Labor e Engenho, 13*. https://doi.org/10.20396/labore.v13i0.8655823

Sachs, I. (2009). *Caminhos para o desenvolvimento sustentável.* Garamond.

Silva, A. C. J. D., Raposo, J. G., & Bagattolli, C. (2019). Dinâmica do desenvolvimento regional brasileiro: uma discussão a partir de métodos de análise regional. *Revista Brasileira de Desenvolvimento Regional.* https://doi.org/10.7867/2317-5443.2018V6N3P049-066

Sosa, M., Aulet, S., & Mundet, L. (2021). Document details – community-based tourism through food: A proposal of sustainable tourism indicators for isolated and rural destinations in Mexico. *Sustainability, 13*(12). https://doi.org/10.3390/su13126693

Souza, T. do V. S. B. (2018). *Turismo de Base Comunitária: Princípios e Diretrizes.* ICMBio. https://uc.socioambiental.org/sites/uc/files/2020-03/turismo_de_base_comunitaria_em_uc_2017.pdf

Sun, J., Yang, Y., & de Jong, A. (2020). A geographical approach to trust in tourism. *Tourism Geographies, 22*, 768–786. https://doi.org/10.1080/14616688.2019.1652337

Suriyankietkaew, S., Krittayaruangroj, K., & Iamsawan, N. (2022). Sustainable leadership practices and competencies of SMEs for sustainability and resilience: A community-based social enterprise study. *Sustainability, 14*(5762), 1–36. https://doi.org/10.3390/su14105762

PHILIPE LIRA DE CARVALHO ET AL.

Teixeira, F. R., Vieira, F. D., & Mayr, L. R. (2019). Turismo de Base Comunitária: Uma Abordagem na Perspectiva da Análise de Clusters. 2019. *Turismo, Visão e Ação, 21*(2). https://doi.org/10.14210/rtva.v21n2.p02-21

Triarchi, E., Pappa, P., & Kypriotelis, E. (2021). Tourism destination development, a situation analysis of a Greek region. *Springer Proceedings in Business and Economics*, 53–73. https://doi.org/10.1007/978-3-030-57953-1_4

Vargas, M. R. P. (2020). Community projects, a vision of development from the rural tourist stage. *Universidad y Sociedad, 12*(3), 14–19. https://www.scopus.com/record/display.uri?eid=2-s2.0-85100891903&origin=inward&txGid=63f41ed2a1e6e909af861372a44552dc

Walther, L., & da Costa, C. E. F. (2022). The Renewal of Arts, Lives, and a Community through Social Enterprise: The Case of Oficina de Agosto. *Sustainability, 14*(125), 1–27. https://doi.org/10.3390/su14010125

Wise, N. (2020). Urban and rural event tourism and sustainability: Exploring economic, social and environmental impacts. *Sustainability, 12*(14), 5712–5717. https://doi.org/10.3390/su12145712

World Tourism Organization (WTO). (2012). *SEBRAE International Observatory*. https://ois.sebrae.com.br/comunidades/omt-organizacao-mundial-do-turismo/

Xavier, T. R., Wittmann, M. L., Inácio, R. D. O., & Kern, J. (2013). Desenvolvimento regional: uma análise sobre a estrutura de um consórcio intermunicipal Universidade Federal de Santa Maria (UFSM). *Rev. Adm. Pública – Rio de Janeiro, 47*(4), 1041–1065. https://www.scielo.br/j/rap/a/L4vNPxh9nVbvdJtQbpnTmRy/?format=pdf&lang=pt

Xiong, C., Khan, A., Bibi, S., Hayat, H., & Jiang, S. (2023). Tourism subindustry level environmental impacts in the US. *Current Issues in Tourism, 26*(6), 903–921. https://doi.org/10.1080/13683500.2022.2043835

Zhang, X., Song, C., Wang, C., Yang, Y., Ren, Z., Xie, M., Tang, Z., & Tang, H. (2021). Socioeconomic and environmental impacts on regional tourism across Chinese cities: A spatiotemporal heterogeneous perspective. *ISPRS International Journal of Geo-Information, 10*(410), 1–18. https://doi.org/10.3390/ijgi10060410

Zhao, Z., Wang, Y., Ou, Y., & Liu, L. (2022). Between empowerment and gentrification: A case study of community-based tourist program in Suichang County, China. *Sustainability, 14*(5187), 1–17. https://doi.org/10.3390/su14095187

Zhou, X., Wang, J., & Zhang, S. (2021). Evaluation of community tourism empowerment of ancient town based on analytic hierarchy process: A case study of Zhujiajiao, Shanghai. *Sustainability, 13*(5), 1–18. https://doi.org/10.3390/su13052882

Zielinski, S., Jeong, Y., Kim, S.-I., & Milanés, C. B. (2020). Why community-based tourism and rural tourism in developing and developed nations are treated differently? A review. *Sustainability, 12*(15), 5938. https://doi.org/10.3390/su12155938

Zupic, I., & Cater, T. (2015). Bibliometric methods in management and organization. *Organizational Research Methods, 18*(3), 429–472. https://doi.org/10.1177/1094428114562629

AN ANALYSIS OF CORPORATE SOCIAL RESPONSIBILITY IN CROSS-CULTURAL SCENARIO

Amit Kumar Srivastava[a], Shailja Dixit[b] and Akansha Abhi Srivastava[c]

[a]*Invertis University, India*
[b]*Amity University, India*
[c]*Institute of Hotel Management, India*

ABSTRACT

The term corporate social responsibility (CSR) is not new as it has its root in the past, but now it becomes more complicated today. It has been observed that CSR is the building block of social capital and globalisation is the main factor which has forced the market and business to interact with the people either they are from their own place or from different part of the country. At the time of interaction, people interact with the differences of their cultures, beliefs and they have different hopes from the companies and its place in society. This reality of interaction with many differences provides us a direction to explore the cross-cultural variations and to know how it helps in creating the social responsibility policy by the government in different countries and its implementation by business people, employees and other stakeholders. This theoretical review is aimed to explore the role of institutionalisation theory for increasing the social capital and ensuring positive CSR practices in cross-cultural scenario.

Keywords: Corporate social responsibility; cross-cultural CSR; institutionalisation; institutional CSR; mimetic isomorphism in CSR

Society and Sustainability
Developments in Corporate Governance and Responsibility, Volume 24, 215–233
Copyright © 2025 Amit Kumar Srivastava, Shailja Dixit and Akansha Abhi Srivastava
Published under exclusive licence by Emerald Publishing Limited
ISSN: 2043-0523/doi:10.1108/S2043-052320240000024009

1. INTRODUCTION

People are the part of any society means it is the society which provides human interaction to a firm. As per the stakeholder theory, any business or firm has interaction with the different types of people as stakeholder. So, people are the major source in the survival of firms. As society and people are complementary to each other, then firms are supposed to be responsible for them from ethical point of view. Different researches indicate the different reasons that corporate social responsibility (CSR) should be embedded in the business model.

As we all know businesses are not only financial entities but also essentially social. So, the very first reason that a business model requires CSR is that every business is established on a societal phantom to prosper in the long term. This reality is very interesting that every business comes in existence to serve the community, customers and other stakeholders for that they require the people. It is also very interesting to see that many studies have concluded that different factors like psychological biasness, unlimited urge of profit maximisation and cut throat competition in the present era companies are focusing on only financial goals. This short-term orientation of the business leaders can be avoided by adopting CSR-based business model which promptly force the business leaders to notice the social dimensions while seeing their financial goals. Their keen observation will make a balance between social dimension and financial goals. This will be helpful for the firm to maintain symmetry on both the continuum and also increase their symmetrical robustness in future in terms of social and financial goals.

It has been observed in the many studies that a good culture of the firm increases its authenticity in the society. So, the next reason of including CSR in the culture of firm will increase its legitimacy in the community and society. Authenticity is an essential factor for ensuring financial resources and obtaining costumer interest in which companies are lacking initially. So, it is significant for the new firms to earn authenticity in any ways. In the same context, maintaining socially responsible culture by the companies will create their significant authenticity in the society. A study has concluded that companies which have given importance to CSR practices from the beginning are less likely to face charges of green washing when engaging in socially responsible activities later (Park & Park, 2021). Therefore, it is important for the firms to know these reasons of adopting CSR which will be significantly important for their survival.

Different HR policies in companies are framed to boost employees' involvement and skills. Human resource practices emphasise safety programme, training, career and succession planning are aimed to improve employee relations. Multinational companies have many subsidiaries in different countries and cultures. Different studies have observed a positive impact of internationalisation on CSR activity (Attig et al., 2016). With the rise of internationalisation of firms and their employees, research on cross-cultural and religion differences attains vitality in CSR realisation and practices.

1.1 Cross-Cultural Dimension of CSR

It has been realised during the study that the government, policymakers, owners and managers from different origins provides different relative importance to CSR as different cultures promote it differently. Standards are set by people as individuals for ensuring the ethics and ethical framework in business, intervention of law, levels of corporate responsibility, role of religion in business, elements of modern corporate culture, creates an ethical corporate culture and provides servant leadership. Corporate leaders play a key role in formulation and implementation of CSR and the appropriate drivers of socially responsible decisions and actions are also undertaken by them (Sauser, 2005; Waldman & Siegel, 2008). Leader who follow all the standards are known as ethical leaders and they always think about long-term consequences, drawbacks and benefits of the decisions they make in the organisation. They follow high ethical standards set by different formal and informal institutions and act in accordance with them. They serve as role models for their followers and show them the behavioural boundaries set within an organisation. They are perceived as honest, trustworthy, courageous and demonstrating integrity towards law and order (Mihelic et al., 2010). They try to learn more about new practices, systems and organisational culture components which are important in initiating and sustaining CSR in business operations world-wide (Hargett & Williams, 2009).

It is also clear from the Corporate Rishi model overall benefit of the society is led by the individual and corporate actions (Sharma, 2002). This model also suggests that great and ethical thoughts of managers and leaders are the building block of social responsibility as well. One can observe the differences in societies. These differences exist in different forms due to which variations can be seen in the attitude of managers in various companies to comprehend and address the different issues comes under their social responsibility (Dobers & Halme, 2009). This is the reason today companies are broadening the extent of their CSR to increase productivity of employees, to attain competitive advantage and to improve its image among all stakeholders. It has been observed in many studies that due to stigmatised image of the company, employee's performance do not reach to the level of excellence and represent their low job satisfaction (Flammer & Luo, 2017). A previous study contends that to be competitive, a company must figure out a synchronised way to engage minds of employees (Buckingham & Coffman, 2014). A research in cross-cultural domain concludes that the companies that have more internationalisation are having higher score in CSR ratings (Attig et al., 2016). In the existing global scenario, cultural intelligence is necessary for the promotion of global leadership, so it is becoming important for the leaders having vision and intention of globalisation should involve in creating the cultural understanding and effects of its differences on important key performance indicators of their companies.

So, it becomes important to know how the agenda of social responsibility comes in cross-cultural scenario means who led this and how? In answer to this question, our critical analysis through hermeneutics tells that first ethical thoughts of leaders and managers motivate them to come with something new to flourish the society and then they will try to incorporate all their goodness of thoughts in their institutions like Ratan Tata. Then their goodness will move towards government and policymakers and it will get praised and approved by authorities and will inculcate in the law of country. This is the journey of social responsibility from an informal medium to formal institution led by corporate managers and leaders.

Then due to the result of mimetic isomorphism, this approved goodness of thoughts of leaders and managers will blossom in the cross-cultural scenario. The best example of this mimetic isomorphism in terms of CSR comes in our mind to highlight the efforts of Indonesian government for mandating the CSR in country and then this fragrance has been transferred to the other countries and their government established the law. By creating this type of conceptual understanding, we can move towards the institutional theory which explains the points of differences in CSR disclosure in different cultures. In this way, the strategic understanding of CSR usually manifests it in two ways by combining two different approaches – passive and active.

(1) Passive approaches consider the social responsibility as a mandatory rule.
(2) Active approaches consider social responsibility as the guidance to increase social capital and corporate reputation.

Although different religions may have a different impact on CSR, all above standards are subject to a theoretical base because geographical differences are highly prominent. Practically, it is visible that inhabitants of different geographical areas with same religion may behave differently to CSR. For example, Christians of Pakistan and the USA are different in their lifestyle. In the same context, Muslims of India and Saudi Arabia seem to give charities and donations for different purposes, implicitly and explicitly. Moreover, mere a label of religion and true practice of a religion are two different things that possibly have different impacts on CSR practices. Thus, a cross-border empirical investigation of different religions can address the questions how cultural differences affect passive assumption of CSR in the mandatory rules and how it influences the active guidance of social capital and corporate reputation.

So, to identify and create an understanding, how do cross-cultural differences affect these two approaches? Our exhaustive review of literature has identified many scholars have found a strong chemistry between culture and religion in cross-cultural scenario (Triandis, 1988). Relationship of community religion and participation of different stakeholders in company's CSR practices has also been discussed in many studies in terms of community, religion and cross-cultural scenario (Cui et al., 2016). Our analysis tells that before studying this chemistry, we have to explore the different cross-cultural dimensions and concept of CSR disclosure in this respect.

1.2 Cross-Cultural Dimensions and CSR Disclosure

Institutions are social structures. The institutional theory describes more resilient facets of social structure by considering the processes through which structures including norms, rules, routines and schemes turn established as authoritative procedures for social behaviour (Scott, 2007). There are many cross-national studies to determine the relationship of CSR and various parameters of cross-cultural difference (Farooq et al., 2019). In light of Hofstede's model, the line between individual and group is blurred in collectivistic society (Hofstede, 1984). On the other hand, individualistic find themselves differentiated and separate from others (Bochner, 1994). Different cultures have a variety of association with CSR disclosure. For instance, extant literature supports a negative correlation between CSR disclosure and power distance. According to most of the researchers, companies originated from higher power distance countries display a low level of social performance, and the relationship between power distance and environmental performance is also negative (Gallén & Peraita, 2018). However, the correlation between power distance and CSR may also be positive (Ho et al., 2019).

The rules of institutions in society differ in different countries and have a great influence on disclosure of CSR (Campbell, 2006). In countries with a high level of uncertainty avoidance culture, people make an endeavour to control or handle uncertainty through formal rules or institutions (Hofstede & Minkov, 2010). Such institutions can be divided into formal and informal formats. The rules such as laws, regulations, acts, ordinances and regulations are regarded as formal in institutionalism. On the other hand, customs, values, culture and religion in terms of socially shared rules are treated as informal institutions (Farooq et al., 2019).

2. REVIEW OF LITERATURE

2.1 Informal Institutionalism as Driver of CSR

2.1.1 Religion in Cross-Cultural Scenario of CSR

Religion is one of the factors of diversity (workforce) in global enterprises (Perez-Batres et al., 2010). In the different areas of Asian countries such as Singapore and Hong Kong, religiosity influences on CSR support with a higher proportion of CSR demand (Ramasamy et al., 2010). Researchers also summarised the beliefs of big religions which have a large number of followers regarding social support and responsibility. Buddhism, Judaism, Zoroastrian, Christianity, Hinduism, Islam, Confucianism and Taoism all works for the well-being of others (Ramasamy et al., 2010). At the same time, CSR has several benefits for the firms in response to that they got consumer's preference to purchase from socially responsible firms still on higher price. A survey of 47 countries (Pew Global Attitudes Project) tells to the Middle East, Asia and Africa placed people having faith in God, express relatively more morality and good values (Kohut et al., 2011; Ramasamy et al., 2010). However, in India, a large number of firms emphasise philanthropic activities earlier after some time companies like TATA has started long-term CSR strategies for providing the benefits to society (Srivastava et al., 2012). The philanthropic feelings in the manager's attitude can be seen in Indian scenario due to religious thoughts and feelings present in them (Srivastava et al., 2020). So, religion is also a binding force in the owners, managers, employees of Indian origin which binds them with the CSR activities and putting the preaching of their religions on real front (Srivastava et al., 2020). In any region, all internal stakeholders such as employees, executives, directors and decision-makers who believe and belong to any religion can be classified in two categories: true practitioners of original preaching of a religion and nonpractitioners of preaching and rules of a religion. Furthermore, because Asian consumers demand greater social responsibility from the firms (Ramasamy et al., 2010), the link of religiosity and CSR support may also be influenced by geographical cultural norms.

2.1.2 Hofstede's Culture Dimension at Different Levels of CSR

In the materialistic surface of secular dominance, although religion may have confronted a declining node in power assumption, the role of religious congregations, preaching and beliefs in societal moves at this stage cannot be ruled out in the study of social responsibility because millions of people are associated with religions (Farooq et al., 2019). A previous study of 3,055 corporations of countries of Europe and Eastern Asia showed that CSR performance was influenced by Hofstede's Cultural dimensions and the tendency of socially responsible practices by corporations in European countries was ahead than those in East Asian countries (Thanetsunthorn, 2015). Relationship of the institutional condition of public/private regulations and CSR is theoretically and empirically focused by researchers.

It is evident from Thanetsunthorn study that individualism and power distance indices have a significantly negative impact on the environmental performance of corporations. Moreover, a negative direction between masculinity and CSR relates to environmental sustainability. Hence, the companies based in cultures with a high score of individualism, masculinity and power distance possibly have less focus on business role in the environment. In contrast, the firms based at countries with a high score of uncertainty avoidance are more concerned about the impact of their businesses on environmental change. With the control of revenue related variables such as profitability, CSR laws are applicable in few countries on certain limits of business and profits. In the three dimensions (employees, community and environment) of CSR, the logical explanation in the difference of CSR performance is based on geographical region and socially responsible corporate behaviour.

Due to more focus on practical implications in the literature of CSR and corporate reputation, there is an academic need to extend the theoretical framework through the application of institutional theory to foster the understanding of the relationship of these two important variables (Aksak et al., 2016). In the study of European and American government and nongovernment groups, it was found that the standard-setting initiatives in the USA help facilitate in the adoption of visible CSR, and these voluntary forms have a significant impact on reputation-building strategies (Fombrun, 2005). On the other hand, for certain standards and certifications, awards and prizes are given to companies in the UK, Denmark, France, Ire-land, Holland, Germany, Spain, Italy and the USA. There are various forums, national codes and legislation in various countries that bound companies to report how they are carrying out regulatory initiatives (CSR disclosure).

2.2 Formal Institutionalism as Driver of CSR

2.2.1 Leading CSR Policies of Countries

On the basis of emergence of authoritarian capitalism, a study discusses Matten and Moon's concept of CSR development. This concept explains social responsibility in terms of historic institutions related to business and it also evaluates the impacts of this new institutionalism on companies established from societal pressures in their global and national arena. This study found CSR practices in companies of China, reflecting the whole business system w.r.t local reputation and societal expectations on international and national level (Hofman et al., 2017). A study explains three elements are necessary to the firm responses towards social development, including strategic adaptation to external pressures, learning processes associated with CSR and internalisation of sustainable development norms, understood as standards of appropriate behaviour (Dashwood, 2012). After exhaustive literature review of CSR in cross-cultural scenario, we found that year 2005 has been announced as the year of CSR in the European Union (EU) countries by the EU. Our critical cross-cultural analysis tells that in response to this, some member states of the EU have taken imperative decisions. The United Kingdom has employed a minister for social responsibility in the department of trade and industry, France included the social and environmental impact in the annual reports of their companies, financial support schemes for large companies were added by the Netherlands to compliance with the OECD Guidelines for multinational companies and a CSR-focused research institution viz. Copenhagen Centre was setup by the Danish government. At the end this study reviewed recent trends in CSR theory and its practices in small and medium enterprises (SMEs) (Luetkenhorst, 2004). A study has explored the basic character of the Confucian firms, critically analysed its philosophical and cultural foundation w.r.t its moral legitimacy and relevance to today's China. Under China's recent CSR development, Chinese firms have been instructed to emulate and develop good business practice (Taiwan, Hong Kong and Singapore). The finding of this study tells that Confucian familial collectivism has implications for other Chinese communities where Confucian tradition is endorsed and practiced (Ip, 2009). Researchers from other school of thoughts argue that CSR is a North-led agenda with narrow focus. They reviewed that modern CSR trends in India represent that even though the corporate sector in India benefited immensely from liberalisation and privatisation processes, its transition from philanthropic mindsets to CSR indicates an impressive financial growth in the country (Arora & Puranik, 2004).

Establishing an alignment between legal regulations and corporate behaviour for reducing the externalities and promoting a sustainable corporate sector, a model of CSR as a set of mechanisms has been developed in a study. Mechanisms under this model include voluntary action by companies to level down the minimum legal standards, with the aim of enhancing social activities, intrusions of regulators and steps taken by shareholders to put pressure on companies for making the effective utilisation of corporate assets. Our analysis tells that this model has been used to assess the degree to which current British practices in narrowing down the regulations of social responsibility (Deakin & Hobbs, 2007). 'Any form of regulation is the outcome of a political process' in line of this a study analyses the interplay between firms' self-regulation as opposed to the formal regulation of a negative externality. Firms respond to increasing activism in the market by providing more socially responsible goods. Our analysis tells that by determining a softer than optimal regulation, firms can level down the minimum legal standard (Calveras et al., 2007).

As we have discussed earlier, the rules such as laws and regulations are regarded as formal in institutionalism and customs, values, culture and religion in terms of socially shared rules are treated as informal institutions (Farooq et al., 2019). This study has found a gap that in spite of following these two approaches of institutionalism by every country, no research study has discussed CSR in terms of formal and informal institutions being existed in the different countries in detail w.r.t. cross-cultural domain.

3. OBJECTIVES OF THE STUDY

The major objective of this study is to analyse the scenario of CSR of selected countries on the criteria of institutionalism being followed there. So, whole analysis of this study is based on the below mentioned research questions:

RQ1. How positive corporate social responsibility arises with the help of institutionalism?

RQ2. What is the cross-cultural scenario of corporate social responsibility in terms of informal institutions?

RQ3. What is the cross-cultural scenario of corporate social responsibility in terms of formal institutions?

4. METHODOLOGY

The whole study tries to analyse the CSR in cross-cultural scenario with the help of hermeneutics, a qualitative way to analyse the available data extracted through exhaustive review of literature. Hermeneutics is the theory of the operations of understanding in their relation to the interpretation of texts (Ricoeur, 1992). So, relying on phenomenological and constructivist epistemologies hermeneutic is a social research method and is considered as the 'art of interpretation'.

5. DATA COLLECTION

This study of identifying cross-cultural scenario of CSR in terms of institutionalism has been done with the help of exhaustive literature review for which Laplume et al. (2008) strategy was taken into consideration for selecting the articles by using Harzing's (2011) list of journal quality to select journal papers based on monitoring their impact factors (Srivastava et al., 2017). Further for the purpose of retrieving the data with updated facts and figures of CSR in formal institution of different countries, official websites of selected nations like Indonesia, India, the UK, the USA, Japan, China, Nepal, Pakistan, the UAE, Italy and Nigeria were used and then hermeneutics was applied on all the facts to critically analyse the cross-cultural status of CSR.

6. ANALYSIS AND INTERPRETATION

In any society, the norms of institutionalism either it is formal or informal has a major role in creating the social capital. A study argues that an especially important form of social capital is the norm that one should forgo self-interest and act in the interests of the collectivity. Civic norms promote trust and provide commonly shared institutional frameworks that community members use and follow when they communicate and judge observable behaviours of members in the community (Coleman, 1988).

Consequently, social capital encapsulates characteristics of social life networks, norms and trust that enable participants to act together more effectively to pursue shared interests (Putnam, 1995). Researches that focused on community social capital have emphasised its function as a public good (Coleman, 1988; Putnam, 1995). These researchers argued that institutionalism in any community influences not only to those who have social capital but also to people living in regions with a high level of social capital. And it promotes community cohesion and information flow that accruc to community members who do not have high levels of personal social capital themselves (Kwon et al., 2013).

A central theme of these prior studies is that institutionalism in any form facilitates community to create social capital which will further facilitate the well-cultured, socially cooperative actions and confined behaviours that are inconsistent with the prescribed values associated with civic norms.

6.1 Institutionalism Leads to Social Capital and CSR

In response to the first research question, this part of our analysis tells that all the civic norms in any society are the result of both formal and informal institutions existing, there. It is well said by sociologists that society is the mirror to reflect our actions either good or bad. Institutions like formal and informal provide us direction, how we can move towards the goodness by avoiding the deviations of short-term profit and selfishness. In this context (See Fig. 1), positive and negative CSR activities are two distinct forms of corporate actions that fit the analytical framework particularly well (De Jong & Vander Meer, 2017). And both formal

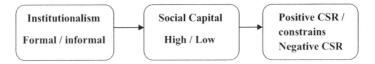

Fig. 1. Leading Role of Institutionalism in Positive CSR. *Source:* Author.

and informal institutions are playing significant role to guide the organisations to follow the positive path in this respect. So, right directions of social institutions lead to positive CSR activities like corporate philanthropy, clean energy, profit sharing programmes, corporate volunteering programmes, diversity-enhancing work rules and business practices that promote human rights (Jamali & Neville, 2011). While in absence of proper guidance by these institutions, negative activities result into environmental pollution, discriminatory human resource practices, failure to recall defective and dangerous products, child labour, unlawful investments that disregard humanity and avoiding behaviour of payment of corporate tax (Jamali & Neville, 2011). These institutions are the way to realise people in communities with high community social capital should view positive CSR activities as conforming to the prescribed values associated with civic norms and perceive negative CSR activities as norm-deviant (Buendía-Martínez & Carrasco Monteagudo, 2020). Consequently, one would expect that followed by ethical behaviour and law and order decided by informal and formal institutions, respectively, community social capital facilitates positive CSR activities and constrains negative CSR activities.

Although business community relationship can be benefited through this endeavour, more research in this context is required for the advancement of endogenous theories (Jamali & Karam, 2018). Our analysis has found, social capital can be built through intuitions like formal and informal and then it leads to positive CSR practices in the society. In addition to the investments in physical capital, human capital and intellectual capital, firms need to extend the span of their priorities on social capital that is based on the quality of relationship built by a firm with various stakeholders (Lins et al., 2017). And this relationship will be possible only when a strong institutional framework will ensure ethical behaviour and robust regulations in cross-cultural domain. With the critical analysis of available literature, we can say that informal institutions usually strengthened with the commonality of religions. Social capital may be available to individuals through social spaces not captured by a geographic neighbourhood, such as membership in a particular community or even ethnic group, and these social spaces religious attitudes, which are based on longstanding social relationships within a context of shared beliefs, represent a social space that may be particularly salient as repositories of social capital (Andrews, 2009). So, with the help of informal institutions, companies are supposed to observe the untouched social needs and want of the community (Hao et al., 2018). Policymakers and government as formal institutions are responsible for giving guidelines and strict regulations to the companies in this regard. It is obvious that with the large social capital, organisations can earn the greater level of trust of stakeholders that help in its valuation. Social capital includes social networks, their reciprocities and the value businesses attained through the social responsibility practices (Sen & Cowley, 2013).

6.2 Cross-Cultural Scenario of CSR in Terms of Informal Institution

In response to the second research question, this fact has been found in the earlier studies that cultural and environmental understanding through social networks significantly strengthened with the usage of social media, may perform a key role in the usage and realisation of CSR (Hao et al., 2018). These social networks indirectly form or we can say are a form of informal institutions because every goodness reflected by these platforms is also encouraging ethical and moral sense in the people either they are from the business or any other profession.

Hence, a change in the way of communication distribution has been observed with the advent of social media. Analysis of CSR blogs of Google, Intel and Hewlett-Packard through social networks shows the trends of an uneven distribution of structural social capital particularly in the corporate dimension among involved stakeholders. Cross-cultural learning interest can also moderate the relationship of social media usage and native to non-native and non-native to non-native communication modes for ultimate impact on the realisation of CSR by the internal customers of organisations (Hao et al., 2018). The difference in beliefs and practices promotes this interest. For example, people who do not know much about Hinduism take interest to learn when they find some Hindus fasting twice in the year during Navratri. It is worth noticing that the mass media audience is greater than the online discussion platforms audiences. Hence, social media attracts the people by actively engaging them in online discussions as compared with mass media predominately passive audience. This is why the impact of social media as informal institution on the larger sphere of public-centric CSR might be limited, if not indirectly reached through opinion leaders (Fieseler & Fleck, 2013).

In justification of approach to CSR, different sets of challenges are faced by SMEs. The motivation for CSR and participation in this type of activities seem consistent when SMEs are viewed with the lens of informal institutions (Sen & Cowley, 2013). The organisational structure of SMEs is simple as it allows flexibility from employees. It has been found in a study that idiosyncrasies of large firms that describe different approaches to CSR. Many studies explain that for large firms, stakeholder theory is tightly related to CSR, whereas social capital led by social institutions is also a significant approach to CSR for SMEs (Russo & Perrini, 2010). This new approach to CSR can be utilised by other organisations for the same purpose.

In contrast to this, if we take the example of another informal institution like religion, then this is the fact that different religions define social well-being differently. In cross-cultural context finding of a study highlights that in terms of subjective well-being, religious differences are cultural differences (Farooq et al., 2019). It has been observed that in countries, religion is an important creed of the way people spend their lives, which marks the difference in cultural representation as well. In cross-cultural scenario, different religions such as Christianity, Islam, Buddhism, Hinduism and Folk have shed light on social responsibilities (Angelidis & Ibrahim, 2004; Brammer et al., 2007; Zinkin, 2007). Justice, love and mercy are almost the common point of understanding among the followers under different informal institutions that echo to bring the goodness and sense of social responsibility. Relationship of religious denomination and CSR has been tried to identify in a study and it found that the people with religious affiliation do not particularly differentiate in prioritising the responsibilities, but this evidence is not true for all religions (Brammer et al., 2007). However, it cannot be generalised for all areas of CSR rather religious individuals generally happen to differentiate between personal and corporate responsibility. Our analysis tells that Brammer, Williams and Zinkin in their study highlighted that institutional norms of Buddhism are very much incline to possess broader conceptions of CSR as compared with nonreligious people. While people following institutional norms of Islam are bored of the opinion that corporations are responsible for handling the poverty and charity issues of society and the same time they think that males and females in the society have the same value but different rights.

6.3 Cross-Cultural Scenario of CSR in Terms of Formal Institution

In response to the third research question as discussed earlier, official websites of selected nations like Indonesia, India, the UK, the USA, Japan, China, Nepal, Pakistan, the UAE, Italy and Nigeria were used and then hermeneutics was applied on all the facts to critically analyse the cross cultural status of CSR (See Table 1).

Table 1. Different Trends of CSR in Cross – Cultural Scenario Country Wise Description.

Sl. No.	Name of Selected Country	Method Used in Analysis	Previous CSR Status	Present CSR Status
1.	Indonesia	Hermeneutics	Voluntary	Mandatory
2.	India	Hermeneutics	Voluntary	Mandatory
3.	UK	Hermeneutics	Self-regulating device	Self-regulating device
4.	USA	Hermeneutics	Soft law	Soft law
5.	Japan	Hermeneutics	Triple satisfaction philosophy	Triple satisfaction philosophy
6.	China	Hermeneutics	Initial stage of regulation	Initial stage of regulation
7.	Nepal	Hermeneutics	Real conceptualisation of CSR is lacking	Real conceptualisation of CSR is lacking
8.	Pakistan	Hermeneutics	CSR general order – 2009	CSR general order – 2009
9.	UAE	Hermeneutics	Voluntary cum mandatory	Voluntary cum mandatory
10.	Italy	Hermeneutics	ESG law	ESG law
11.	Nigeria	Hermeneutics	Bill – integrating CSR into the company culture and operation	Bill – integrating CSR into the company culture and operation

Source: Author.

AMIT KUMAR SRIVASTAVA ET AL.

In the line of analysing the research question, it has been observed that the first nation in the world which has implemented law by mandating businesses to undertake CSR is Indonesia. By leaving the voluntary approach of social responsibility, here CSR law makes social responsibility as a mandate to business. A critical analysis has been done through hermeneutics under this study which had explored the six different laws related to CSR in Indonesia. It has also been analysed that these six laws define the mandate of social responsibility law in order to recognise the form of CSR practiced by companies running in Indonesia. As Indonesia comes in the category of the developing countries, so adequate fund is required here for the development of local community. Our analysis tells that here social responsibility may be seen as a source of fund for the upliftment of local community and hence, CSR law in this country works as an instrument to circulate the companies' resources for prosperity of local communities (Zainal, 2019).

In India, the previous scenario of social responsibility was limited up to the business firms in philanthropic way based on the different informal institutional norms led by the religions, but our analysis found that now it has taken a new mandatory form after enactment of CSR law in different countries. In case of India, New Company Act – 2013 has placed the business responsibility towards society and community under Schedule – VII. Our analysis tells that the main credit of this conversion of philanthropic to mandatory CSR goes to the efforts of Irani Committee because the report of this committee has forced the government and policymakers to include CSR in the law and to make further reforms in it.

In the culture of the United Kingdom, CSR has been found as a self-regulating device where every business holds social responsibility for making a positive social impact of their operations. Our analysis through hermeneutics tells that corporate people at the UK are widely accepting every form of social responsibility initiative as good practice, by their own. It has also been analysed that now country have gradually evolved from a purely voluntary responsibility to a legal requirement. So under new legal framework, some businesses are required to be self-accountable while practicing CSR. This new philosophy encourages the business people to prioritise accountability in all spheres of life, from the way how whole supply chain is working in order to provide the food to each and every individual and the way how humanity is being treated by business in terms of employees and men or women or children in the community and society. It has also been realised in the analysis now people are exhausted here with the traditional usual approaches of business rooted in the culture, this is the reason they are demanding new institutional norms that will take unprivileged community into the lap.

Critical analysis through hermeneutics of an article written by Elizabeth George in 2019 reflects cultural scenario in the United States. Our analysis tells that here social responsibility is considered as a soft law and US government never wishes to impose it as hard regulation. Throughout our analysis of article, we found here social responsibility would be internal policies like minimising the carbon traces to take the edge off environmental variations, enhancing the work policies, ensuring reasonable business practices, doing benevolent deeds, making efforts in uplifting the society and community.

By keenly observing the Japanese philosophy of social responsibility, we have reached to the insights of Sampo yoshi who has defined it in terms of triple satisfaction which tells to the business people that they should be good from the point of view of seller, buyer and society. This triple satisfaction philosophy is a customary Japanese approach for making life of companies long it has also been discussed in the 2012 social responsibility policy of Japan. Our analysis tells that this philosophy provides an insight to business people that at the time of expanding business in cross-cultural scenario, it is important for them to first think about customers and then act accordingly, they should never come in the habit of realising the short-term high profit, always they have to be humble and God fearing, they should be very much caring for the people living in their society, at the time of operationalise their business, they have to have faith in God and try to avoid the malicious mind for maximising the profit. Many companies in Japan like Ricoh and Sony Corp. have been found during the study that in 2003 they institutionalised CSR by establishing CSR departments at their places and this initiative of companies marked the beginning of CSR in Japan.

After analysing the technological advanced nation Japan and its' overall culture regarding social responsibility, our study has moved to analyse the next technologically driven country China and critical examination of Chinese mindset for CSR through hermeneutics has found today, and the Chinese legal system emphasis more on protecting the constitutional rights and concerns of people and has draft a well-defined legal framework under which different regulations had been enacted. The best examples are labour laws, trade union law, law for the protection of rights and interests of women, laws on special protection for child and juvenile workers, laws of production safety law, regulations on occupational disease prevention and cleaner production promotion law of the People's Republic of China, as per their mindset about social responsibility, all these cover CSR elements and requirements. Our analysis tells that China is still in the initial stage of developing a standardised, methodical and extensive dimension of CSR. During analysis we found that here, some organisations like State Grid Corporation and Shanghai Pudong Development Bank in 2006 had published their CSR Reports on public forums first time.

Now our study tried to critically analyse the facts and figure of Nepal regarding positioning of social responsibility in the country. So, through hermeneutics, we have analysed here CSR has been made compulsory for industries, banks and financial institutions and these units are being regulated by the Industrial Enterprise Act (IEA) and Nepal Rastra Bank, respectively. Above and beyond, there is no any compulsory law of social responsibility for insurance and non-industrial sectors. Our analysis also analysed that incursion of social responsibility relatively low in this country even data tells that many companies are still not well-known with the real conceptual background of CSR. In this way, our analysis found a gap between the broader concept of CSR and the notion of Nepalese regarding social responsibility as majority of the CSR activities here have been observed in the form of socially driven projects that help to make marginalised communities more powerful. So, we came to a conclusion that there is a misunderstanding in Nepal that CSR is limited to charity and it is achievable only with heavy expenditure and funding, while in reality, CSR reflects a higher thought than that and can also include activities that did not require heavy investments and grants. Some companies during analysis have been found here which are involved in social responsibility practices from a long time consistently like Chaudhary Group, Nepal Telecom, Ncell, Panchakanya Group and commercial banks. They have gained a consistent place in large-scale CSR practices and have helped their country to come in the forefront of CSR scenario throughout the world. Many SMEs have also found involved in integrated CSR practices with elements like ethical human resource practices, environment-friendly operations and society upliftment programmes like free health check-up, blood donation camps, etc.

It has been found during study that SECP is the main authority in Pakistan which have a right to issue the law and order regarding social responsibility of business and under its' authority it has passed the CSR General Order in 2009. Initially Pakistani companies were not bound to follow this general order passed by SECP. But after the decision on OGRA case in year 2013 in which Supreme Court of Pakistan announced a historical judgement on CSR activities of the corporations. Hermeneutics has analysed this case in which someone claimed and pointed out that a company running in Sanghar area is operating illegitimately and goes against the terms of the trade which had been signed and endorsed with the provincial government. After evaluation of all facts and figures Supreme Court instructed, now companies are supposed to issue an annual report explaining their social welfare obligations and practices under Article 184 (3) of Constitution of Pakistan. With the enforcement of this article, principle of mandatory CSR had been established in the country. Hence, this article has become the first step in the development of CSR in Pakistan and made it clear that the people of the society where the corporations are working can also point out the violations on the part of the companies.

This study of exploring cross-cultural scenario of CSR has analysed the social responsibility law at the UAE. Hermeneutics has critically analysed the facts and figure of CSR law at UAE and states that here social responsibility voluntary cum mandatory because while CSR contributions remain voluntary, but filing a CSR return and listing on the platform is mandatory for all businesses in the UAE which fall within the scope of the social responsibility regulation.

Our analysis has found ESG law regarding social responsibility in Italy which means environmental, social and governance. The difference between CSR and ESG is that CSR refers to sustainability strategies businesses employ to ensure that the company is carried out ethically, while every component of ESG acts as criteria used to measure a company's overall sustainability. Recent constitutional reform amended Articles 9 and 41 of the Italian Constitution, establishing in particular that the Republic safeguards the environment, biodiversity and eco-systems also in the interest of future generations, and that private economic enterprise should be carried out in a manner that does not damage the environment or human health.

At the end our study has analysed the bill under CSR law in Nigeria and analysis of hermeneutics tells that a company's interest should not only be limited to its shareholders, customers and employees but also to the local community and environment in which they operate. Hence objective of the bill is to make companies aware that they have to play fundamental role in social, economic and environmental development. This will become possible by integrating CSR into the company culture and operations means companies can build trust with stakeholders, customers and employees, demonstrate their commitment to corporate citizenship, foster brand loyalty among consumers and develop strong relationships within their communities.

Variations have been observed during the study that CSR policies varied with the nationality of the companies, values of the people and the industrial sector a company belongs (Silberhorn & Warren, 2007). So on the basis of above discussion, we come to a conclusion that legislation from formal institution only follows a trend and sets a minimum standard in the development of CSR because all important legislations of law functions as part of a general set of values of informal institution and these important regulations guide the different actions and functions of CSR. It has also been discussed in the study that different aspects of law are abstract and statutory sense of every legal regulation influence the substance of self-regulation, in the implementation and communication of CSR (Buhmann, 2006). A study on current practice in Southern Africa against the historical development of CSR looks at the impact of new legislation in the country. This study has concluded by reflecting on the contribution that African public relations practice may have on the developmental challenges of Africa (Skinner & Mersham, 2008). A study addresses CSR issues in transnational corporations argue that better relationships between governments' laws and corporations need to be established to reduce low living standards, exploitation, poverty and unemployment, which would contribute to overall sustainable development (Hopkins, 2004).

7. CONCLUSION

On the basis of above analysis of CSR in cross-cultural scenario concludes institutionalisation plays a significant role in positive social responsibility practices in any society. Both informal and formal institutions are creating the goodness in business people to understand the way they can make their society a best place for everyone by guiding or by imposing strict regulation on them. This study also concludes that in cross-cultural domain, most of the country is following institutional framework and direction. But it is very interesting to see that proportions of both institutional directions are different in different countries in shaping the CSR. It is also an observation that countries like Indonesia, India, the UK, Nepal, Pakistan, Italy and Nigeria are framing their CSR policies on the direction of formal institution, that is, their government and its' mandate, while other countries like the USA and Japan are flourishing in CSR which is being governed by the ethical norms of informal institution in a very soft manner without imposing any hard regulation. In contrast to all, the UAE has been observed very strategic in CSR by making soft implementation of social responsibility activities by the companies in their own ways, but all companies are required to strictly follow the mandate regarding the procedure of filing the CSR return and its' listing on the platform.

REFERENCES

Aksak, E. O., Ferguson, M. A., & Duman, S. A. (2016). Corporate social responsibility and CSR fit as predictors of corporate reputation: A global perspective. *Public Relations Review*, *42*(1), 79–81.

Andrews, R. (2009). Civic engagement, ethnic heterogeneity, and social capital in urban areas: Evidence from England. *Urban Affairs Review*, *44*(3), 428–440.

Angelidis, J., & Ibrahim, N. (2004). An exploratory study of the impact of degree of religiousness upon an individual's corporate social responsiveness orientation. *Journal of Business Ethics*, *51*, 119–128.

Arora, B., & Puranik, R. (2004). A review of corporate social responsibility in India. *Development*, *47*(3), 93–100.

Attig, N., Boubakri, N., El Ghoul, S., & Guedhami, O. (2016). Firm internationalization and corporate social responsibility. *Journal of Business Ethics*, *134*, 171–197.

Bochner, S. (1994). Cross-cultural differences in the self concept: A test of Hofstede's individualism/collectivism distinction. *Journal of Cross-Cultural Psychology*, *25*(2), 273–283.

Brammer, S., Williams, G., & Zinkin, J. (2007). Religion and attitudes to corporate social responsibility in a large cross-country sample. *Journal of Business Ethics*, *71*, 229–243.

Buckingham, M., & Coffman, C. (2014). First, break all the rules: What the world's greatest managers do differently. Simon and Schuster.

Buendía-Martínez, I., & Carrasco Monteagudo, I. (2020). The role of CSR on social entrepreneurship: An international analysis. *Sustainability*, *12*(17), 6976.

Buhmann, K. (2006). Corporate social responsibility: What role for law? Some aspects of law and CSR. *Corporate Governance: The International Journal of Business in Society*, *6*(2), 188–202.

Calveras, A., Ganuza, J. J., & Llobet, G. (2007). Regulation, corporate social responsibility and activism. *Journal of Economics and Management Strategy*, *16*(3), 719–740.

Campbell, J. L. (2006). Institutional analysis and the paradox of corporate social responsibility. *American Behavioral Scientist*, *49*(7), 925–938.

Coleman, J. S. (1988). Social capital in the creation of human capital. *American Journal of Sociology*, *94*, S95–S120.

Cui, J., Jo, H., & Velasquez, M. G. (2016). Community religion, employees, and the social license to operate. *Journal of Business Ethics*, *136*, 775–807.

Dashwood, H. S. (2012). CSR norms and organizational learning in the mining sector. *Corporate Governance: The International Journal of Business in Society*, *12*(1), 118–138.

De Jong, M. D., & Vander Meer, M. (2017). How does it fit? Exploring the congruence between organizations and their corporate social responsibility (CSR) activities. *Journal of Business Ethics*, *143*, 71–83.

Deakin, S., & Hobbs, R. (2007). False dawn for CSR? Shifts in regulatory policy and the response of the corporate and financial sectors in Britain. *Corporate Governance: An International Review*, *15*(1), 68–76.

Dobers, P., & Halme, M. (2009). Corporate social responsibility and developing countries. *Corporate Social Responsibility and Environmental Management*, *16*(5), 237–249.

Farooq, Q., Hao, Y., & Liu, X. (2019). Understanding corporate social responsibility with cross-cultural differences: A deeper look at religiosity. *Corporate Social Responsibility and Environmental Management*, *26*(4), 965–971.

Fieseler, C., & Fleck, M. (2013). The pursuit of empowerment through social media: Structural social capital dynamics in CSR-blogging. *Journal of Business Ethics, 118*, 759–775.

Flammer, C., & Luo, J. (2017). Corporate social responsibility as an employee governance tool: Evidence from a quasi-experiment. *Strategic Management Journal, 38*(2), 163–183.

Fombrun, C. J. (2005). A world of reputation research, analysis and thinking—Building corporate reputation through CSR initiatives: Evolving standards. *Corporate Reputation Review, 8*, 7–12.

Gallén, M. L., & Peraita, C. (2018). The effects of national culture on corporate social responsibility disclosure: A cross-country comparison. *Applied Economics, 50*(27), 2967–2979.

Hao, Y., Farooq, Q., & Sun, Y. (2018). Development of theoretical framework and measures for the role of social media in realizing corporate social responsibility through native and non-native communication modes: Moderating effects of cross-cultural management. *Corporate Social Responsibility and Environmental Management, 25*(4), 704–711.

Hao, Y., Farooq, Q., & Zhang, Y. (2018). Unattended social wants and corporate social responsibility of leading firms: Relationship of intrinsic motivation of volunteering in proposed welfare programs and employee attributes. *Corporate Social Responsibility and Environmental Management, 25*(6), 1029–1038.

Hargett, T. R., & Williams, M. F. (2009). Wilh. Wilhelmsen Shipping Company: Moving from CSR tradition to CSR leadership. *Corporate Governance: The International Journal of Business in Society, 9*(1), 73–82.

Harzing. (2011). Journal quality list. https://harzing.com/resources/journal-quality-list

Ho, F. N., Wang, H. M. D., Ho-Dac, N., & Vitell, S. J. (2019). Nature and relationship between corporate social performance and firm size: A cross-national study. *Social Responsibility Journal, 15*(2), 258–274.

Hofman, P. S., Moon, J., & Wu, B. (2017). Corporate social responsibility under authoritarian capitalism: Dynamics and prospects of state-led and society-driven CSR. *Business & Society, 56*(5), 651–671.

Hofstede, G. (1984). *Culture's consequences: International differences in work-related values* (Vol. 5). Sage.

Hofstede, G., & Minkov, M. (2010). Long-versus short-term orientation: New perspectives. *Asia Pacific Business Review, 16*(4), 493–504.

Hopkins, M. (2004). *Corporate social responsibility: An issues paper.* https://ssrn.com/abstract=908181

Ip, P. K. (2009). Is confucianism good for business ethics in China? *Journal of Business Ethics, 88*, 463–476.

Jamali, D., & Karam, C. (2018). Corporate social responsibility in developing countries as an emerging field of study. *International Journal of Management Reviews, 20*(1), 32–61.

Jamali, D., & Neville, B. (2011). Convergence versus divergence of CSR in developing countries: An embedded multi-layered institutional lens. *Journal of Business Ethics, 102*, 599–621.

Kohut, A., Taylor, P., Atkinson, R., Allen, R. A. C. C. D., Mansoor, P., Greentree, V., & Segal, D. R. (2011). Pew Global Attitudes Project. Pew Research Center.

Kwon, S. W., Heflin, C., & Ruef, M. (2013). Community social capital and entrepreneurship. *American Sociological Review, 78*(6), 980–1008.

Laplume, A. O., Sonpar, K., & Litz, R. A. (2008). Stakeholder theory: Reviewing a theory that moves us. Journal of management, *34*(6), 1152–1189.

Lins, K. V., Servaes, H., & Tamayo, A. (2017). Social capital, trust, and firm performance: The value of corporate social responsibility during the financial crisis. *The Journal of Finance, 72*(4), 1785–1824.

Luetkenhorst, W. (2004). Corporate social responsibility and the development agenda: The case for actively involving small and medium enterprises. *Intereconomics, 39*(3), 157–166.

Mihelic, K. K., Lipicnik, B., & Tekavcic, M. (2010). Ethical leadership. *International Journal of Management & Information Systems, 14*(5).

Park, Y. W., & Park, Y. J. (2021). The core challenge of CSR in entrepreneurial ventures. In *Corporate social responsibility and entrepreneurship for sustainability: Leading in the era of digital transformation* (pp. 1–9). Springer.

Perez-Batres, L. A., Miller, V. V., & Pisani, M. J. (2010). CSR, sustainability and the meaning of global reporting for Latin American corporations. *Journal of Business Ethics, 91*, 193–209.

Putnam, R. D. (1995). Tuning in, tuning out: The strange disappearance of social capital in America. *PS: Political Science & Politics, 28*(4), 664–683.

Ramasamy, B., Yeung, M. C., & Au, A. K. (2010). Consumer support for corporate social responsibility (CSR): The role of religion and values. *Journal of Business Ethics, 91*, 61–72.

Ricoeur, P. (1992). *Oneself as another.* University of Chicago Press.

Russo, A., & Perrini, F. (2010). Investigating stakeholder theory and social capital: CSR in large firms and SMEs. *Journal of Business Ethics, 91*, 207–221.

Sauser, W. I. (2005). Ethics in business: Answering the call. *Journal of Business Ethics, 58*, 345–357.

Scott, S. (2007). Corporate social responsibility and the fetter of profitability. *Social Responsibility Journal, 3*(4), 31–39.

Sen, S., & Cowley, J. (2013). The relevance of stakeholder theory and social capital theory in the context of CSR in SMEs: An Australian perspective. *Journal of Business Ethics, 118*, 413–427.

Sharma, S. (2002). Corporate rishi leadership model: An Indian model for corporate development & ethical leadership. In U. Pareek, A. M. Osman-Gani, S. Ramanarayan, & T. V. Rao (Eds.), *Human resource development in Asia: Trends & challenges* (pp. 291–296). Oxford & IBH.

Silberhorn, D., & Warren, R. C. (2007). Defining corporate social responsibility: A view from big companies in Germany and the UK. *European Business Review, 19*(5), 352–372.

Skinner, C., & Mersham, G. (2008). Corporate social responsibility in South Africa: Emerging trends. *Society and Business Review, 3*(3), 239–255.

Srivastava, A. K., Gupta, A., & Dixit, S. (2020). Indian perspective in CSR: Mapping leaders' orientation. In *CSR in an age of isolationism* (Vol. 16, pp. 205–217). Emerald Publishing Limited.

Srivastava, A. K., Gupta, D. A., Singh, D. R., & Srivastava, A. A. (2017). Corporate social responsibility (a literature review). *International Journal of Pure and Applied Researches, 2*(2), 121–131.

Srivastava, A. K., Negi, G., Mishra, V., & Pandey, S. (2012). Corporate social responsibility: A case study of TATA group. *IOSR Journal of Business and Management, 3*(5), 17–27.

Thanetsunthorn, N. (2015). The impact of national culture on corporate social responsibility: Evidence from cross-regional comparison. *Asian Journal of Business Ethics, 4*, 35–56.

Triandis, H. (1988). Collectivism v. individualism: A reconceptualisation of a basic concept in cross-cultural social psychology. In *Cross-cultural studies of personality, attitudes and cognition* (pp. 60–95). Palgrave Macmillan.

Waldman, D. A., & Siegel, D. (2008). Defining the socially responsible leader. *The Leadership Quarterly, 19*(1), 117–131.

Zainal, R. I. (2019). Analysis of CSR legislation in Indonesia: Mandate to business. *Business and Economic Research, 9*(3), 165.

Zinkin, J. (2007). Islam and CSR: A study of the compatibility between the tenets of Islam, the UN global compact and the development of social, human and natural capital. *Corporate Social Responsibility and Environmental Management, 14*(4), 206–218.

THE ROLE OF MISERICÓRDIAS IN THE CONTEXT OF THE IMPORTANCE OF SOCIAL SOLIDARITY INSTITUTIONS FOR THE THIRD SECTOR

Augusto Simões and Humberto Ribeiro

University of Aveiro, Portugal

ABSTRACT

The Third Sector has been receiving increasing attention from society, including academics, due to its importance in the face of the lack of government responses to many of the social problems that affect contemporary societies. Theoretically, the State is supposed to highlight the importance of the services provided by Social Solidarity Institutions, given their proximity to the beneficiaries, the efficiency in the distribution of resources and their innovative attitude towards social problems and needs. As a logical consequence, society is witnessing an increase in the participation of the private sector in social issues and a greater professionalisation of the Third Sector in the search for sustainability. Within the Third Sector, Social Solidarity Institutions play a very important role, acting as social actors. Within the environment of Social Solidarity Institutions, the Misericórdias also play a very important role. 'Misericórdia' is a non-profit institution that takes a form of charity, very popular in some countries, such as Italy and especially in Portugal. However, there are few studies on the governance conditions of this type of institution. In addition, it is possible to discuss whether there is any study that focuses specifically on this type of analysis. This study fills the empirical gap in the existing literature, providing an insight into the ways of adopting governance practices and principles within these institutions, which over five centuries of existence have continuously worked towards a more just, inclusive and supportive society.

Society and Sustainability

Developments in Corporate Governance and Responsibility, Volume 24, 235–253

Copyright © 2025 Augusto Simões and Humberto Ribeiro

Published under exclusive licence by Emerald Publishing Limited

ISSN: 2043-0523/doi:10.1108/S2043-052320240000024010

Keywords: Governance; accountability; transparency; trustworthiness; third sector; charities; Misericórdias

1. INTRODUCTION

The Third Sector has aroused a growing interest throughout society, including academia, given its importance in the absence of state responses to solve many of the social problems that affect contemporary society. The State highlights the importance of the services provided by Social Solidarity Institutions, given their proximity to the citizen, the efficiency in the distribution of resources, innovation, dedication and demonstrated effectiveness (Liou, 2001). Its expansion is due to the increase in the demand for services, the involvement of the private sector in social issues and greater professionalisation, which has been essentially aimed at its sustainability (Mckinsey & Company, 2001).

In Portugal, within the Third Sector, there are institutions with enormous relevance and presence in social areas, with emphasis on the Misericórdias, which are among the oldest charitable institutions, with links to the Church, in supporting the most needy. In Portugal, as in other southern European countries, the genesis of philanthropic and charitable initiatives has links to the Church.

According to the most recent data from the National Institute of Statistics (INE), the institutions of religion and social services are the ones that have the most significant weight in the set of Social Economy entities and the Private Institutions of Social Solidarity, in partnership with the State, represent about two thirds of social action in Portugal.

The Misericórdias are private institutions with public and non-profit purposes that assume a wide range of social services, maintaining the Christian spirit, that is, in the most historical and traditional sense, the Misericórdias are seen as Brotherhoods, with markedly religious objectives (satisfaction of social needs and practice of acts of Catholic worship, in harmony with their traditional spirit, shaped by the principles of Christian doctrine and morals); on the other hand, the Misericórdias are seen as Private Institutions of Social Solidarity, with specific assistance objectives (essentially, social support and health care), recognised as institutions of public utility, collaboration and complementarity, through the signing of cooperation agreements, mainly with the government.

The public nature of Social Solidarity Institutions and the scarce resources with which they operate have aroused interest in the study of governance principles and practices, as a way to protect the interests of stakeholders and optimise performance, contributing to their sustainability. Those who donate or subsidise Social Solidarity Institutions want to be sure that their resources have been and are being used honestly and efficiently, which builds trust. Trust, when affected, can compromise the sustainability and effectiveness of these institutions and the sector (Farwell et al., 2018). There should be public concern as to whether the resources entrusted are being used appropriately, effectively and efficiently; therefore, these institutions should be required to disclose and clarify how they are fulfiling their responsibilities (Vinten, 1997). The success of Social Solidarity Institutions depends not only on the efficiency with which they carry out their activities but also on the quality of disclosure, accountability and transparency, which foster trust (Connolly & Hyndman, 2013a; Cordery & Morgan, 2013). Public trust in charities is essential to the achievement of their missions, while the lack of it potentially affects their sustainability and effectiveness (Hyndman & McConville, 2018).

The adoption of principles and good governance practices aims to increase the value of Social Solidarity Institutions and facilitate access to resources, contributing to their continuity. The adoption of governance principles and practices and the implementation of governance mechanisms are of great importance for a more professional and transparent management, allowing the monitoring of the good use of available resources and a better understanding of how institutions are being managed, mitigating information asymmetries and converging the interests of all stakeholders, maximising value creation (Agency Theory). Good governance practices are seen as a way to improve management. It is necessary to reorient the governance of Social Solidarity Institutions from an amateur to a professional condition (Craft & Benson, 2006). The importance of good governance has been recognised as the basis for effective and efficient performance and for ensuring that charities meet the legitimate aspirations of stakeholders (Connolly et al., 2013). The growing demand for quality in the provision of services and in the allocation of resources leads Social Solidarity Institutions to be essentially good managers and to show this, so the adoption of good governance practices is inevitable, which arouses the interest in exploring governance mechanisms and applying new management models, as a way to become sustainable and fulfil their social mission. Good governance protects stakeholders (Chokkalingam & Ramachandran, 2015).

The social transformations that have taken place in recent decades call for governance practices in the non-profit sector. The importance of Social Solidarity Institutions, in responding to the increasing inability of the State to solve many of the social problems that affect contemporary society, highlights the importance of adopting governance principles and practices, as a way to optimise their performance, protect the interests of stakeholders and contribute to the sustainability of institutions.

It is intended that good governance ensures transparency, defence of *stakeholders'* interests and holds managers accountable for non-compliance with objectives and violation of laws.

As previously discussed by Simões and Ribeiro (2022c), it is very important for nonprofits to adopt appropriate governance practices and principles, as well as to implement appropriate governance mechanisms. This is essential to achieve a more professional and transparent management, while at the same time monitoring the good use of the (scarce) resources made available and better understanding of how non-profit institutions are being managed, facilitating access to financial and non-financial support, mitigating problems of information and agency asymmetry and seeking convergence of the interests of all related parties, maximising value creation and stakeholder satisfaction.

This work aims to evaluate the quality of adherence to governance practices and principles in the Misericórdias, as well as to analyse whether the implementation of governance mechanisms promotes better performance, ensuring a healthier and more sustainable institutional development. At the same time, this study intends, in a particular way, to fill an empirical gap in the literature. Indeed, following previous research by Simões and Ribeiro (2022a, 2022b, 2022c), it can be argued that there is a gap in the assessment of the current state of governance in the Misericórdias and its relationship with the performance of these entities. Thus, this research provides an insight into the adoption of governance practices and principles in these non-profit institutions, with more than five centuries of existence, which continuously work for a more just, inclusive and supportive society.

The main conclusion of the research presented in this article paints a picture that is not rosy. After analysing the Portuguese population of Misericórdias, it was possible to access detailed data from 377 organisations. The analysis of these data, using cluster analysis, allowed us to group this population into two large groups: one cluster that aggregates 357 Misericórdias and another cluster that aggregates only 20 Misericórdias. Regrettably, the smaller cluster is the one with the best levels of governance and transparency. This small group of Misericórdias is composed of organisations with more hierarchical levels in the organisational structure; higher level of education of the current top manager; a greater degree of involvement of associates in the definition of strategic direction; greater degree of availability of information for decision-making, and support for the development of functions, and that have an external audit report.

2. THE IMPORTANCE OF THE THIRD SECTOR FOR SOCIETY

The expression 'Third Sector' was coined by the American John D. Rockefeller, when he published, in 1975, the first detailed study on the importance of private business initiatives with a public character in American society. However, it was in the 80s of the last century that the expression became popular in Europe (Cardoso, 2000), a term that, due to its scope, is the most commonly found in different contexts and the one that has a transnational expression (Ferreira, 2009).

Over the past few decades, most developed market economies in North America, Europe and Asia-Pacific have seen a widespread increase in the economic importance of non-profit institutions as providers of health, social, educational and cultural services of various kinds. On average, the not-for-profit sector accounts for about 6% of total employment in OECD countries, or nearly 10% with voluntary work accounted for (Anheier, 2005).

While in the United States of America, the expression Non-Profit Organizations (NPOs) and voluntary organisations in general are used, in Europe, the expression Third Sector or Social Economy is used, the latter terminology being used in the Portuguese Basic Law that frames these organisations (Law No. 30/2013, of 8 May - Basic Law of the Social Economy).

The Third Sector has been gaining prominence in Europe, filling functions and segments of society that the private sector (maximisation of profit and return on invested capital) and the public sector (which responds to society's problems) cannot satisfy (Chaves & Monzón, 2001). The Social Economy accounts for about 10% of all European enterprises, that is, two million enterprises or 6% of total employment (Lemos, 2010).

The Third Sector in Portugal has gained enormous relevance, due to its social importance and its impact on Portuguese civil society. Within the Third Sector and as already mentioned, there are institutions with growing relevance in social areas, with emphasis on the Misericórdias, as Private Institutions of Social Solidarity that promote actions of a private nature with public purposes.

The European Commission and the European Parliament recognise the importance of the Third Sector and attribute to Social Solidarity Institutions the ability to promote the development and integration of European Union citizens in activities relevant to the societies of the Member States (Travaglini, 2008).

The Third Sector is given a unifying meaning of the non-profit sector and the Social Economy (HE), to designate organisations that are characterised by not having profit as their purpose (they do not distribute profits to stakeholders) and by sharing the same mission (to meet the needs of the community).

Social Solidarity Institutions increasingly play a fundamental economic and social role in responding to local social problems, from a perspective of proximity and solidarity. They play an increasingly essential role in today's society, and new institutions are emerging to respond to the needs of civil society, given the inability of governments to respond. The number of these institutions has increased considerably in recent decades; however, management models and governance practices have not kept pace with this development.

According to the most recent data from the Social Economy Satellite Account (National Institute of Statistics, 2019), Social Economy entities generated 3% of the Gross Value Added (GVA) of the national economy (an increase of 14.6%, in nominal terms, compared to 2013), registering a growth higher than that observed in the national economy as a whole (8.3%), for the same period. The Social Economy accounted for 5.3% of the total remuneration of employees and 6.1% of the total paid employment of the national economy (expressed in FTEs – Full-Time Equivalent Work Units). Compared to 2013, the number of Social Economy entities increased by 17.3%, GVA increased by 14.6%, paid employment by 8.8% and total employment by 8.5%, registering a more favourable performance than that observed in the national economy. Religious and social services entities had a very significant weight in the set of Social Economy entities (respectively, 11.9% and 9.7% of the total units).

3. THE NEED FOR GOOD PRACTICES FOR THIRD SECTOR ORGANISATIONS

Social Solidarity Institutions, in addition to their non-profit nature, have as their main mission to improve the quality of life of the population and contribute to their well-being, especially that of the most disadvantaged, increasingly assuming an essential economic function, as a guarantor of social cohesion. To do so, they need to innovate so that they can continue to respond effectively to the most pressing societal problems by adopting management models that enable them to achieve sustainability and gain society's trust (Hyndman & McConville, 2018).

The continuous updating and discussion of good governance guidelines has the potential to increase public trust in Social Solidarity Institutions. Good governance processes are vital in supporting management decision-making, and proper accountability to key stakeholders is critical for trust, continued health and growth in the sector. When structuring these processes, the spirit of Social Solidarity Institutions must be taken into account, as well as the role played by volunteers. Beneficiary involvement is increasingly accepted as an important aspect of good governance in non-profit institutions (Hyndman & Jones, 2011).

Governance plays a key role in Social Solidarity Institutions, making their donors want to donate more money to the mission they intend to serve. Governance has a positive impact on Charities and common governance practices (such as independent Boards, CEO oversight and transparency) increase the degree to which charitable contributions are allocated to their mission, just as their professionalisation benefits stakeholders more and helps in value creation, reducing agency issues affecting all types of organisations (Blevins et al., 2018). Governance seeks to ensure that the interests of funders, donors, beneficiaries, civil society and government are satisfied by Social Solidarity Institutions and, as such, they have a public function and disinterest in profit. As these institutions have a markedly social role, aimed at helping the most disadvantaged classes, and given the high amount of resources managed, the need to adopt good governance practices is justified. In order to avoid misallocation of resources, governance is related to a number of constraints applied to administrators (Shleifer & Vishny, 1997).

The efficiency with which charities spend the resources entrusted to them has become an increasingly important aspect of their action, as well as transparency in efficiency, including the reporting of relevant measures and information to understand, contextualise and evaluate them, is considered important for stakeholders (Hyndman & McConville, 2016).

The accountability and prudence of charities are necessary components to maintain their support (Grey Matter Research, 2008). Despite the philanthropic and charitable nature with which Social Solidarity Institutions operate, at the basis of their proper functioning are integrity (ethical issue and basis of trust), transparency and accountability.

In Social Solidarity Institutions there, is a strong relationship between accountability, transparency and trust in Social Solidarity Institutions (Farwell et al., 2018).

Given the public interest in effective and well-run Social Solidarity Institutions, society has an interest in adequate disclosure that allows the public to make informed decisions and control the use of its resources. The scarcity of publicly available information on Social Solidarity Institutions, their management and the way in which donated resources are used, makes it difficult for donors, as well as for the general public, to select the Social Solidarity Institutions to support. The exercise of transparency is therefore a modern-day imperative necessary for its survival. The success of the nonprofit sector depends not only on its economic and social activities but also on its ability to demonstrate accountability and transparency, which in turn can improve trust (Connolly & Hyndman, 2013b; Cordery & Morgan, 2013). The prevailing opinion is that Social Solidarity Institutions seeking resources from stakeholders must demonstrate transparency and accountability in the use of the resources received (Abraham, 2007).

Disclosure is the first step towards accountability and can be a useful tool for greater and better accountability, if the logic of disclosure is clear, if the data disclosed are accurate and comparable, and if there is a receptive public with the necessary resources to react to the information disclosed. Disclosure is not an end in itself and, in the absence of related control procedures, disclosure may not provide effective oversight of charities (Breen, 2013). There will be a greater motivation to support the development of Social Solidarity Institutions if their activities are known and the competence with which they are developed, and if those who allocate resources are concerned with their use and with maximising the satisfaction of the needs that these institutions aim to satisfy.

Accountability is particularly important in these institutions, as the donated funds must be used to fulfil missions that provide well-being to society (Yasmin et al., 2014). For accountability to be useful, it must be targeted at different stakeholders, and it is also important to prepare and publish quality reports that meet the information needs of many external stakeholders, who rely on formal and informal information channels (Connolly & Hyndman, 2017). The Social Solidarity Institutions that raise more than half of their income are the ones that revealed the most and best information (Dhanani, 2009). Good accounting and reporting (an important aspect of accountability) to key stakeholders is essential (Hyndman & Jones, 2011). Poor accounting and poor reporting (and, as a consequence, the possibility of scandals) can severely undermine trust in the non-profit sector and reduce both donations and its activities, so more robust and reliable accounting reporting and treatment is desirable (Hyndman & McMahon, 2010). Governance mechanisms (supervision, monitoring) improve the accuracy of Charities' reporting, as well as audits of large companies are associated with more accurate expenditure reporting, as well as non-profit institutions with more donor-imposed restrictions on the use of resources report more accurate expenditures. Charities involved in activities subject to government oversight, with stricter regulation and oversight, also report more accurate spending (Yetman & Yetman, 2012).

Craft and Benson (2006) consider that it is rare to find efficient management in Social Solidarity Institutions. Liou (2001) also argues that Social Solidarity Institutions face problems in terms of management competences, present failures or even lack of coordination and forget standards of transparency and accountability. For Hyndman and McKiloop (2018), these institutions are decidedly focused on achieving societal goals and have traditional management (and governance) norms that are more committed to partnership than control or direction, so levels of trust in these institutions are generally high, reflecting the enormous value and appreciation expressed by the general public. Governance structures in the non-profit sector are often neglected, resulting in weak accountability and governance, weak financial management and internal controls and a lack of adequate transparency (Newton, 2015). The implementation of the code of good governance significantly changes the governance structure of Social Solidarity Institutions (Perego & Verbeeten, 2015). Good governance is vital to support proper decision-making and accountability, which is desirable, if not necessary, for the health and continued growth of the sector (Hyndman & Jones, 2011).

External governance mechanisms (reporting and monitoring required in government funding contracts) and internal governance mechanisms (governance codes and traditional governance mechanisms) are related to the efficiency of Social Solidarity Institutions. State funding is positively associated with an increased capacity of Social Solidarity Institutions to redistribute funds to beneficiaries (probably the reason why external governance mechanisms accompany such funding) and the restriction on the use of funds that such government funding usually imposes on these institutions, as well as the restriction on the use of funds imposed by private donors (a traditional governance mechanism), they can increase their efficiency, so that the requirements of state funding and control and the traditional structures of Social Solidarity Institutions are positively related to efficiency (Jobome, 2006). The importance of good governance has been recognised as the basis for effective and efficient performance and for ensuring that charities meet the legitimate aspirations of key stakeholders (Connolly et al., 2013). According to several authors, there is a relationship between performance and governance (Bellante et al., 2018; Gregg, 2001; Hilmer, 1998; Kiel & Nicholson, 2002; Zainon et al., 2012), as well as studies linking best governance practices to economic growth and development (Claessens, 2006; Clarke, 2004; Reed, 2002). Governance aims to ensure that the interests of funders, donors, beneficiaries, civil society and government are met. Social Solidarity Institutions have a markedly social role in helping the most disadvantaged classes and the high amount of resources managed justifies the need for good governance practices.

It is recognised that good governance practices will not eliminate all failures of Social Charities, but if implemented, monitored and updated regularly, they will reduce fraud and help entities maximise the use of scarce resources, just as best governance practices in non-profit institutions would also lead to lower risks and maximise the use of scarce resources (Reddy et al., 2013). Strong governance reduces the likelihood of misappropriation of funds, and follow-up by debt holders and the government, audits, and internal maintenance of management functions are strongly associated with a lower incidence of fraud (Harris et al., 2017). The solution to many of the management problems faced by non-profit institutions may be the adoption of good governance practices (Carvalho & Blanco, 2007). For Claessens et al. (2002), good governance practices allow nonprofit institutions to have easier access to resources, reduce capital costs, improve stakeholder reputation and improve institutional performance.

AUGUSTO SIMÕES AND HUMBERTO RIBEIRO

Governance creates conditions to optimise the performance of Social Solidarity Institutions, protecting the interests of all stakeholders, so it is necessary to improve the practices that indicate the way in which these institutions are managed and controlled, with a special focus on the Misericórdias, due to their importance in Portuguese society.

4. MISERICÓRDIAS AS THE MAIN INSTITUTIONS OF SOCIAL SOLIDARITY IN THE DEVELOPMENT OF SOCIAL ACTIVITIES

Portugal is considered one of the first countries in Europe to have specific legislation for the Social Economy Sector (Law No. 30/2013, of 8 May – Basic Law of the Social Economy), defining it as a set of economic and social activities, which aim to pursue the general interest of society, as well as the interests of its users and beneficiaries.

The European Parliament has recommended that Member States support and protect entities in this sector, as they are not only sustainable, but also have a high potential for wealth generation and development and for creating lasting jobs. This sector accompanies hundreds of thousands of people in situations of fragility in Portugal on a daily basis, in addition to ensuring the largest social support network for Portuguese families and generating thousands of jobs.

The entities in this sector are autonomous and act within the scope of their activities in accordance with the following principles: the principle of the primacy of people and social objectives; principle of free and voluntary membership and participation; the principle of democratic control of their bodies by their members; the principle of reconciling the interests of members, users or beneficiaries with the general interest; the principle of respect for the values of solidarity, equality and non-discrimination, social cohesion, justice and equity, transparency, shared individual and social responsibility and subsidiarity; the principle of autonomous and independent management of public authorities and any other entities outside the social economy and the principle of allocating surpluses to the pursuit of the objectives of social economy entities, in accordance with the general interest, without prejudice to respect for the specificity of the distribution of surpluses, which is specific to the nature and substrate of each social economy entity, as enshrined in the Constitution of the Portuguese Republic.

The Misericórdias are among the oldest non-profit institutions in Portugal (Andrade & Franco, 2007), some of them have more than 500 years of activity in supporting the most needy and are present in practically all municipalities in the country (Lemos, 2010). The districts of Castelo Branco (26 Misericórdias), Évora (25 Misericórdias) and Portalegre and Viseu (both 24 Misericórdias) have the highest number of Misericórdias.

According to the União das Misericórdias Portuguesas, the Misericórdias are present in four continents in the world: America, Europe, Africa and Asia. In Brazil, the Misericórdias are present in 14 of the 27 Brazilian states, the Santa

244 *The Role of Misericórdias*

Casas and Philanthropic Hospitals in Brazil total about 2,100 entities and are responsible for a large part of hospital beds and hospitalisations carried out through the Unified Health System; in Spain and although there have been more than a 100 Misericordies, at the moment the Misericordia of Pamplona, Barcelona, Bilbao, Azpeitia, Olivenza, Avila, Alcuéscar (Cáceres) and Tudela are active, the one in Barcelona being the oldest, founded in 1,583; in France, it is the Misericórdia de Paris, founded on 13 June 1994, the first branch to be created in the Portuguese diaspora of modern times, whose activity, essentially of a social nature, aimed to support the Portuguese community in France; in Italy, the Misericórdia of Florence, founded in 1,244, was one of the first of all the Misericórdias, and it is worth highlighting the work carried out by about 700 Italian Holy Houses, with civil protection, transport of the sick, reception of immigrants in situations of need or risk, among others; in Luxembourg, there is a Santa Casa da Misericórdia, created in 1996, with the aim of supporting the Portuguese of that country through initiatives such as literacy courses, visits to the sick and elderly, distribution of food to needy families, among others; in Ukraine, there is a Misericórdia in Kiev with a home for the terminally ill and a home support service that provides care for people in need, which was forbidden in Soviet rule to provide any social support or humanitarian aid; in Angola, there are two Misericórdias: one in Luanda that provides support to the most needy by assuming the expenses of funerals of people without possessions and also through partnerships with religious congregations, and another in Huambo, a Brotherhood of Mercy, established since 2007; in Mozambique, there is a Misericórdia in Maputo, which develops projects in the area of education and is currently working in the parish of Polana Caniço, an institution that accompanies children and young people through teaching support; in São Tomé and Príncipe, there is a Santa Casa da Misericórdia whose activity is vast, since, in addition to caring for the elderly, the institution also supports children and young people, and also has a project for the training and promotion of local artisans; in Macau, there is one of the oldest Misericórdias in the world, having celebrated 450 years of existence in 2019, whose beneficiaries of its action are children, the elderly and people with disabilities; and in Palestine, there is in Bethlehem the first Brotherhood of Mercy, which was officially inaugurated on 21 November 2013 and inspired by the Italian brotherhoods, which develops its activity by providing medical and social assistance to its population.

Misericórdia is a type of charity with greater relevance and presence in Portugal, with links to the Catholic Church. Founded in Florence, Italy, in 1244, it is a very common type of institution in Portugal, with the Santa Casa da Misericórdia de Lisboa being the first to be founded in 1948, with royal patronage. The expansion of the Misericordies throughout the kingdom was part of the Crown's effort to organise assistance.

According to Sá and Lopes (2008), the Misericórdias emerged at a time of great national economic prosperity, during the reign of Manuel I (1495–1521) and became comprehensive and multifaceted institutions that absorbed a varied spectrum of charitable practices. Although they were protected by the royal power, on which they depended directly, they acted with a great margin of freedom in relation to the monarchical power, and distinguished themselves from other institutions by their juridical nature, which was civil, and by their activities, which were of a social nature and directed outside themselves. Both Liberalism (1834–1910), the first Republic (1910–1926), as well as the Estado Novo (1926–1974), saw in the Misericórdias the central organs of Portuguese assistance and it was after the Revolution of 1974 that the State ceased to consider them central to social protection. However, the Misericórdias have adapted and survived to this day, continuing to be thriving institutions, assuming a wide range of services and maintaining the Christian spirit, responding in practice to the current formulations of protection and social support that arise from the appeal to the dignity of the human person.

The Brotherhoods of Mercy or Holy Houses of Mercy are institutions established in the canonical juridical order with the aim of carrying out acts of Catholic worship and satisfying social needs, according to their traditional spirit, informed by the principles of Christian doctrine and morals. Without prejudice to their canonical obligations, they have a specific regime, provided for in the statute of Private Institution of Social Solidarity (Santana et al., 2014), with two aspects and without prejudice to their canonical obligations: on the one hand, in the most historical and traditional sense, they are seen as Brotherhoods, with markedly religious objectives (satisfaction of social needs and the practice of acts of Catholic worship, in harmony with their traditional spirit, shaped by the principles of Christian doctrine and morals), having a canonical statute, the approval of which, when revised and updated, will be entrusted to the protection of the Church as a guarantor of fidelity to doctrine and canonical discipline; on the other hand, they are seen as Social Solidarity Institutions, with specific assistance objectives (essentially, social support and health care), recognised as institutions of public utility, collaboration and complementarity, materialised in the signing of cooperation agreements, namely, with the State. The Commitment is the fundamental and statutory text of the Misericórdias and its governing bodies are the General Assembly, the Board of Directors (Administrative Board) and the Fiscal Council, also called the Definitory.

According to the most recent data from the Social Economy Satellite Account (National Institute of Statistics, 2019), religious and social services entities are those that have a very significant weight in the set of Social Economy entities (respectively, 11.9% and 9.7% of the total units). The Misericórdias accounted for 12.4% of the total GVA of the Social Economy, 12.8% of the total remuneration of employees and 16.8% of the paid employment. Compared to 2013, the GVA of Misericórdias increased by 10.2% and wages increased by 16.3%, in line with the increase in paid employment.

The National Institute of Statistics (2020), in collaboration with the António Sérgio Cooperative for the Social Economy (CASES), carried out, between June and September 2019, a survey on the Social Economy Sector, which sought to characterise this Sector, namely, the Misericórdias (377 institutions). It was concluded that the Misericórdias are local and municipal entities (main municipalities: Porto, Lisbon and Coimbra), whose main users, beneficiaries or users are the elderly population, followed by children. The main guiding principles of its activity (provided for in the Basic Law on the Social Economy) are respect for the values of solidarity, equality and non-discrimination, social cohesion, justice and fairness, transparency, shared individual and social responsibility and subsidiarity, as well as the principle of the primacy of people and social objectives. The main partner of the Misericórdias is the government, which must support these entities and ensure the transparency of their relations with their stakeholders through supervision and control mechanisms.

According to the 16th Edition of 'Quem Somos nas Misericórdias', which translates to 'Who We Are in the Misericordies', by the União das Misericórdias Portuguesas, in 2021 there were a total of 387 active Misericórdias (and 75 inactive Misericórdias), which supported 167,632 users daily and had about 45,978 direct collaborators. The 17th Edition of 'Who We Are in the Misericórdias', of the União das Misericórdias Portuguesas, already reports the existence of a total of 388 Misericórdias (and 106 inactive Misericórdias) in 2022. Their number and regional distribution can be seen in Fig. 1 below.

Regarding 2021 (since for 2022 the number of users and direct employees was not reported), on average, each Misericórdia provides services to 433 users and has about 119 direct employees (an average of approximately four users per employee), registering a growth in its activities, with emphasis on responding to social problems that affect society.

Also according to a survey carried out in 2000, within the scope of the Social Economy Project of ISEG (Higher Institute of Economics and Management of the University of Lisbon), Pereira (2002) characterised the Misericórdias in the following general way: there is a Misericórdia for each municipality and

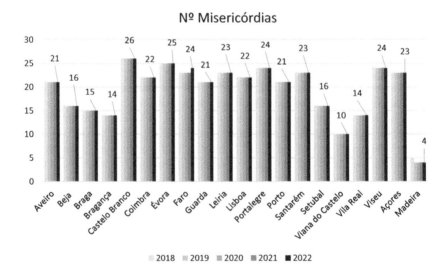

Fig. 1. Number and Regional Distribution of Misericórdias in Portugal.
Source: União das Misericórdias Portuguesas (2019, 2020, 2021, 2022, 2023).

autonomous region and it was the districts of Évora and Castelo Branco that had the largest number of Misericórdias (which is still the case today); the Misericórdias are organisations of a private nature, most of which are defined as religious organisations, whose scope of action is predominantly local, privileging the rural area of operation and with main action in the urban and rural areas; the Misericórdias have as their preferred objectives the support of the elderly and children (more than half of the Misericórdias have these valences), followed by the support of poverty and allocate, above all, their budget and financing to these activities; in the Misericórdias are the protocols with the government (which represent almost half of its revenues) and the provision of services, followed by donations, which, on average, have the greatest weight in its revenues; and their involvement in society is essentially guided by participation in civic actions aimed at defending social and humanitarian causes, as well as considering it a priority, in the future, not only to restore moral and ethical values but also to maintain concern for the elderly and include in their projects the training of young people and support for socially disadvantaged groups.

5. THE ORGANISATIONAL MODEL OF THE MISERICÓRDIAS IN PORTUGAL

There are approximately 200 distinct codes of good governance and best governance practices in 64 countries (Aguilera & Cuervo-Cazurra, 2009), whose growth, in the opinion of Hermes et al. (2007), has been accompanied by an increase in the publication of scholarly papers on good governance and its best practices.

The social transformations that have occurred in recent decades call for governance practices in the non-profit sector, which is why the Portuguese Institute for Corporate Governance (IPCC) published, in 2014, the Code of Governance of Third Sector Entities (internal mechanism for good governance). The adoption of this Code can bring benefits by proposing a set of guidelines, principles and recommendations that serve the reform of the current governance models of Social Solidarity Institutions, promoting principles such as equity, transparency, accountability and responsibility, generating greater trust in most stakeholders and improving their performance and sustainable development. Just as *Corporate Governance*, which is applied to for-profit entities, is based on the publication and dissemination of a Code of Good Practices with the character of recommendations, in a logic of *comply or explain*, governance in relation to the Third Sector should also follow the same path (Santana et al., 2014). Not least because there is already a Code of Good Governance Practices for Third Sector Entities, which proposes a set of guidelines, principles and recommendations that take into account the specificities of these entities, and they should include in an autonomous chapter of the activity report, the 'Governance Report', in which complete information must be provided, clear and objective, on the degree to which the Code's recommendations are accepted (or not, duly justified and reasoned).

Pereira (2002) considers that the historical character of the Misericórdias is the main characteristic of the governance model, in which the governing bodies and their relationship remain unchanged (in some cases, for more than 500 years), that is, the mission of the Misericórdias was fixed in the Commitment, whose norms guide the activities of the Governing Bodies and the Confraternity and inspire the functioning of the Misericórdias. The governing bodies common to the Misericórdias, usually elected for periods of 3 years, are the Brotherhood (General Assembly) that elects the Administration, the Board of Directors (Administrative Board, whose President is the Ombudsman, who generally assumes executive functions) and the Ruler (Definitory – supervisory council). Also according to this author, from the literature review, the Misericórdias do not provide a standard governance model, and the following aspects should be highlighted: they have a mission and act to publicise it; the members of the Board of Directors are volunteers, work part-time and tend to be elderly, with a low level of education (which is seen as an important constraint to the development of these institutions); they do not have a structured internal communication system; the decision-making process is formal in character and relatively centralised and hierarchical; the Agency Model is the one that best describes governance in the Misericórdias (weak active participation of agents other than the Board of Directors in governance decisions – Stakeholder Model); and in addition to the Board of Directors, the role of the State (by imposing conditions for financing contracts), the role of employees (still tenuous, given that the decision-making process and the decisions of the Board of Directors are not shared with qualified employees), the role of 'global organizations' (the role played by the União das Misericórdias Portuguesas in governance decisions and its influence and relationship with the Misericórdias), the role of the markets: donors and clients (it is denied that competition is a conditioning factor for the activity of the Misericórdias; in fact, the main revenues for the activity of the Misericórdias are State funding and the provision of services, so it makes no sense to talk about competition in the donor market and much less, in 'regulatory' force).

Based on the aforementioned survey carried out by INE, in collaboration with CASES, we can conclude that the Misericórdias have an organisational structure divided or hierarchical into three or four levels and are, essentially, senior institutions (20 years old or older), in which a large percentage of their top management members (function/highest position) exercise executive functions and are elected by the governing bodies (with limits on the number of mandates). C-suite members think that 'taking responsibility' is one of the characteristics that best describes them, just as they think that the statement that best describes their leadership style is 'the top manager presents the problem, collects suggestions, and makes decisions'. Regarding the management and accountability practices in the Misericórdias, it is concluded that: most Misericórdias use key indicators to monitor and evaluate the performance of their activity, where the most used key indicator is the evolution of own revenues; almost all of the Misericórdias have a website or electronic page and use social networks (Facebook, LinkedIn, Twitter, among others); a small percentage of the Misericórdias hire external consultants to improve some areas of management and have a document management system;

almost half of the Misericórdias carry out questionnaires to assess the satisfaction of their users, beneficiaries or users; and a small percentage of the Misericórdias use at least one method of measuring social impact or hold some type of certification (quality, environmental, social responsibility or family-responsible entity). In general, most Social Economy institutions (including Misericórdias) prepare only four management documents (Activity Plan, Budget, Activity Report and Annual Report) and among the entities that prepare management documents, most do not disclose them on their website or website. A very small percentage of Social Economy institutions (including Misericórdias) report having prepared a Social Impact Report, an Internal Audit Report and have an External Audit Report. It should also be added that a small percentage of Social Economy institutions (including Misericórdias) have: Code of Ethics, Code of Conduct, Training Plan, Manual of Procedures, Diagnosis of Training Needs and Strategic Plan.

In order to establish some typologies that characterise the Misericórdias studied, we used the multivariate statistical procedure of cluster analysis, a method used to detect homogeneous groups in the data, based on variables or cases, and 'in this analysis the elements of the groups are unknown and often it is not even known how many clusters there are' (Pestana & Gageiro, 2003). This type of analysis aims to separate the elements of the population into groups, so that the elements belonging to the same group are similar to each other and the elements of different groups are heterogeneous (Mingoti, 2005). The hierarchical method was used, in which the homogeneity within the group decreases and the heterogeneity between groups increases as new groups are formed, in a continuous process (Mingoti, 2005). Cluster analysis groups the Misericórdias according to their governance characteristics and the groups are suggested by the data and a priori (Hair et al., 2009). The governance characteristics were based on the guiding principles established in the Code of Governance of Third Sector Entities, which seek to serve the modernisation and professionalisation of the current governance models in the sector's institutions, generating greater confidence in all stakeholders.

From the analysis of the final cluster centres, it was possible to identify two groups of Misericórdias (one group consisting of 357 Misericórdias and another group consisting of 20 Misericórdias), whose main characteristics that most influenced these groupings were: (i) the hierarchical levels existing in the organic structure of the Misericórdias; (ii) the level of education of the senior manager in office; (iii) the degree of involvement of the associates in the definition of the strategic orientation; (iv) the degree of availability of information for decision-making and support for the development of functions in the Misericórdias; (v) the preparation of the external audit report and (vi) the number of registered members.

It is concluded that, although the Misericórdias have not adopted the IPCC's Code of Governance of Third Sector Entities, they have been adopting some of the principles and recommendations proposed by it, such as: having clear and transparent decision-making structures and a manual of procedures; greater involvement of members in its governance; the development, by top management, of the strategic plan and sustainability policies and the establishment, by top management, of an adequate system for the preparation and disclosure of financial information, which serves the purposes of internal control, monitoring and sustainability.

It is also concluded that it is the group with the lowest number of Misericórdias, the one with the best governance: more hierarchical levels in the organic structure; higher level of education of the incumbent senior manager; a greater degree of involvement of associates in the definition of strategic direction; and, finally, a greater degree of availability of information for decision-making and support for the development of functions in the Misericordies.

6. CONCLUSIONS

Although there is a large amount of theoretical and empirical studies related to the governance of for-profit entities, less is known about the governance practices of the Third Sector (Dyl et al., 2000).

The theme gains even more importance when considering the Third Sector, a segment that has been growing and diversifying, linked to the use of good governance practices and principles aimed at valuing society, as well as the long-term vision of activities with social aspects, performance improvement and access to donations and contributions.

It is important that the Misericórdias, unique within the scope of the national institutions of the Social Economy, awaken to the interest in exploring governance mechanisms and applying new management models, as a way to become sustainable and fulfil their social mission. Its mission and the high amount of resources managed, as well as the lack of specific models for managing and disseminating information to stakeholders, justify the need for good governance practices.

The bibliographic research carried out allows us to conclude that there are practically no studies that have analysed the practices and principles of governance used by the Misericórdias in Portugal, so it is suggested to carry out studies on their use in non-profit institutions, given their importance in the search for conditions that optimise performance and protect the interests of all their stakeholders. The contributions not only provide evidence to assess and guide the introduction of new practices and processes within the sector but also seek to inform policy-making, not just at the government level. This type of work supports decision-makers in strengthening these institutions so that they can be legitimised in the public interest and become more trustworthy and accountable (Hyndman & McKiloop, 2018).

This study focuses on the adoption of governance practices and principles in the Misericórdias, taking into account that these entities have more than five centuries of national existence, working for a more just, inclusive and supportive society, and that, from the literature review, it is concluded that the theme is little explored, nationally and internationally. Although the IPCC Governance Code for Third Sector Entities is not being adopted by the Misericórdias, they have been adopting some of the guidelines, principles and recommendations proposed therein, as a way to minimise risks and maximise the use of resources, improving their performance and ensuring their sustainability.

ACKNOWLEDGEMENTS

This work was financially supported by the research unit on Governance, Competitiveness and Public Policy (UIDB/04058/2020) + (UIDP/04058/2020), funded by national funds through FCT – Fundação para a Ciência e a Tecnologia.

REFERENCES

Abraham, A. (2007). Tsunami swamps aid agency accountability: Government waives requirements. *Australian Accounting Review, 17,* 4–12.
Aguilera, R., & Cuervo-Cazurra, A. (2009). Codes of good governance. *Corporate Governance: An International Review, 17*(3), 376–387.
Andrade, A., & Franco, R. C. (2007). *Economia do Conhecimento E Organizações Sem Fins Lucrativos.* http://www.spi.pt/coleccao_economiadoconhecimento/documentos/manuais_PDF/Manual_VIII.pdf. Accessed on July 25, 2018.
Anheier, H. K. (2005). *Nonprofit organizations. Theory, management, policy.* Routledge.
Bellante, G., Berardi, L., Machold, S., Nissi, E., & Rea, M. A. (2018). Accountability, governance and performance in UK charities. *International Journal of Business Performance Management, 19*(1), 55–74.
Blevins, D. P., Eckardt, R., & Ragozzino, R. (2018). Understanding the link between governance and performance in charities. In Paper presented at the 78th Annual Meeting of the Academy of Management, Chicago, USA.
Breen, O. B. (2013). The disclosure panacea: A comparative perspective on charity financial reporting. *International Society for Third-Sector Research, 24,* 852–880.
Cardoso, R. (2000). Cidadania empresarial: o desafio da responsabilidade. Update Br/EUA. *Amcam, 363,* 115–120.
Carvalho, A., & Blanco, I. (2007). Accountability nas entidades não lucrativas: estudo de casos nas Fundações Culturais Portuguesas. In II Jornada de ASEPUC de Contabilidade de Entidades não Lucrativas, Zaragoza – Espanha.
Chaves, R., & Monzón, J. (2001). Economía social y setor no lucrativo: Actualidad científica y perspectivas. *Revista de Economía Pública, Social y Cooperativa, CIRIEC-España, 37,* 7–33.
Chokkalingam, T. S. V., & Ramachandran, T. (2015). The perception of donors on existing regulations and code of governance in Singapore on charities and non-profit organizations – A conceptual study. *Asian Social Science, 11*(9), 89–95.
Claessens, S. (2006). *Corporate governance and development.* Oxford University Press.
Claessens, S., Djankov, S., Fan, J. P., & Lang, L. H. (2002). Disentangling the incentive and entrenchment effects of large shareholders. *The Journal of Finance, 57*(6), 741–2771.
Clarke, T. (2004). Introduction: Theories of governance-reconceptualizing corporate governance theory after the Enron experience. In T. Clarke (Ed.), *Theories of corporate governance: The philosophical foundations of corporate governance.* Routledge.

252 *The Role of Misericórdias*

Connolly, C., & Hyndman, N. (2013a). Towards charity accountability: Narrowing the gap between provision and needs? *Public Management Review, 15*(7), 945–968.

Connolly, C., & Hyndman, N. (2013b). Charity accountability in the UK: Through the eyes of the donor. *Qualitative Research in Accounting & Management Journal, 10*(3/4), 259–278.

Connolly, C., & Hyndman, N. (2017). The donor–beneficiary charity accountability paradox: A tale of two stakeholders. *Public Money & Management, 37*(3), 157–164.

Connolly, C., Hyndman, N., & McConville, D. (2013). UK charity accounting: An exercise in widening stakeholder engagement. *The British Accounting Review, 45*, 58–69.

Cordery, C., & Morgan, G. (2013). Special issue on charity accounting, reporting and regulation. *International Society for Third-Sector Research, 24*, 757–759.

Craft, R., & Benson, R. (2006). How to assess and improve your board's performance. *Nonprofit World, 24*(1), 13–15.

Dhanani, A. (2009). Accountability of UK charities. *Public Money & Management, 29*(3), 183–190.

Dyl, E. A., Frant, H. L., & Stephenson, C. A. (2000). Governance and funds allocations in United States medical research charities. *Financial Accountability and Management, 16*(4), 335–352.

Farwell, M. M., Shier, M. L., & Handy, F. (2018). Explaining trust in Canadian charities: The influence of public perceptions of accountability, transparency, familiarity and institutional trust. *International Society for Third Sector Research, 30*, 768–782.

Ferreira, S. (2009). A invenção estratégica do terceiro sector como estrutura de observação mútua: Uma abordagem histórico-conceptual. *Revista Crítica de Ciências Sociais, 84*, 169–192.

Gregg, S. (2001). *The art of corporate governance: A return to first principles.* Centre for Independent Studies.

Grey Matter Research. (2008). *Where'd my money go? Americans' perceptions of the financial efficiency of non-profit organizations.* http://greymatterresearch.com/. Accessed on May 25, 2019.

Hair, J., Black, W., Babin, B., Anderson, R., & Tatham, R. (2009). *Análise multivariada de dados* (6a Edição). Bookman.

Harris, E., Petrovits, C., & Yietman, M. H. (2017). Why bad things happen to good organizations: The link between governance and asset diversions in public charities. *Journal of Business Ethics, 146*, 149–166.

Hermes, N., Postma, T. J., & Zivkov, O. (2007). Corporate governance codes and their contents: An analysis of Eastern European codes. *Journal for East European Management Studies, 12*, 53–74.

Hilmer, F. (1998). *Strictly boardroom: Improving governance to enhance company performance* (2a Edição). Melbourne. https://www.ump.pt/Home/uniao/noticias-ump/ump-quem-somos-nas-misericordias-2022/. Accessed on April 20, 2022.

Hyndman, N., & Jones, R. (2011). Editorial: Good governance in charities—Some key issues. *Public Money & Management, 31*(3), 151–155.

Hyndman, N., & McConville, D. (2016). Transparency in reporting on charities' efficiency: A framework for analysis. *Nonprofit and Voluntary Sector Quarterly, 45*(4), 844–865.

Hyndman, N., & McConville, D. (2018). Trust and accountability in UK charities: Exploring the virtuous circle. *The British Accounting Review, 50*, 227–237.

Hyndman, N., & McKiloop, D. (2018). Public services and charities: Accounting, accountability and governance at a time of change. *The British Accounting Review, 50*, 143–148.

Hyndman, N., & McMahon, D. (2010). The evolution of the UK charity statement of recommended practice: The influence of key stakeholders. *European Management Journal, 28*, 455–466.

Instituto Nacional de Estatística. (2019). *Conta Satélite de Economia Social.* https://www.ine.pt/xportal/xmain?xpid=INE&xpgid=ine_destaques&DESTAQUESdest_boui=379958840&DESTAQUESmodo=2&xlang=pt. Accessed on August 6, 2021.

Instituto Nacional de Estatística. (2020). *Inquérito ao Setor da Economia Social 2018.* https://www.cases.pt/inquerito-ao-setor-da-economia-social-ises/. Accessed on August 6, 2021.

Jobome, G. O. (2006). Public funding, governance and passthrought efficiency in large UK charities. *Corporate Governance, 14*(1), 43–59.

Kiel, G., & Nicholson, G. (2002). Real world governance: Driving business success through effective corporate governance. *Mt Eliza Business Review, 5*(1), 17–28.

Lemos, M. (2010). História e Cultura: 500 anos de soluções para os desafios de cada tempo. *Revista Dirigir (IEFP) – Economia Social, 109*, 23–27.

Liou, K. (2001). Governance and economic development: Changes and challenges. *International Journal of Public Administration, 24*(10), 1005–1022.

Mckinsey and Company, Inc. (2001). *Empreendimentos Sociais Sustentáveis: como elaborar planos de negócio para organizações sociais* (3a Edição). Fundação Peirópolis.

Mingoti, S. A. (2005). *Análise de Dados Através de Métodos de Estatística Multivariada: Uma abordagem Aplicada.* Editora UFMG.

Misericórdias no mundo. (2023). Portal da União das Misericórdias Portuguesas. https://www.ump.pt/Home/misericordias/misericordias-no-mundo/. Accessed on August 20, 2023.

Newton, A. N. (2015). Executive compensation, organizational performance, and governance quality in the absence of owners. *Journal of Corporate Finance, 30*, 195–222.

Perego, P., & Verbeeten, F. (2015). Do 'good governance' codes enhance financial accountability? Evidence from managerial pay in Dutch charities. *Financial Accountability and Management, 31*(3), 316–344.

Pereira, G. (2002). The Portuguese Misericórdias: General characterisation and some insights into nonprofit governance. In Paper presented at the Fifth International Conference of the International Society for Third-Sector Research (ISTR), Cape Town – South Africa.

Pestana, M., & Gageiro, J. (2003). *Análise de dados para ciências sociais: a complementaridade do SPSS* (3 Edição). Edições Silabo.

Reddy, K., Locke, S., & Fauzi, F. (2013). Relevance of corporate governance practices in charitable organisations: A case study of registered charities in New Zealand. *International Journal of Managerial Finance, 9*(2), 110–132.

Reed, D. (2002). Corporate governance in developing countries. *Journal of Business Ethics, 37*(3), 223–247.

Sá, I., & Lopes, M. (2008). *História breve das Misericórdias portuguesas.* Imprensa da Universidade de Coimbra.

Santana, M., Campos, N., & Castro, I. (2014). Terceiro Sector. In J. Pinto (Ed.), *A Emergência e o Futuro do Corporate Governance em Portugal* (pp. 227–246). Edições Almedina.

Shleifer, A., & Vishny, R. (1997). A survey of corporate governance. *The Journal of Finance, 52*(2).

Simões, A., & Ribeiro, H. (2022a). Governança em Instituições de Solidariedade Social: O Caso das Misericórdias Portuguesas. In E. N. Corrent (Ed.), *Ciências Sociais Aplicadas: Estado, Organizações e Desenvolvimento Regional* (pp. 200–217). Ponta Grossa, Atena Editora.

Simões, A., & Ribeiro, H. (2022b). The importance of the charities in the scope of the social economy in Portugal. In Economic and Social Development Book of Proceedings – 90th International Scientific Conference in Zagreb, Croatia (Vol. 90, pp. 29–30).

Simoes, A., & Ribeiro, H. (2022c). Governança nas Instituições de Solidariedade Social: O Caso das Misericórdias Portuguesas. In Livro de Atas do Desenvolvimento Económico e Social – 78a Conferência Científica Internacional em Aveiro, Portugal (Vol. 78, pp. 39–51).

Travaglini, C. (2008). Improving NPOs accountability in the enlarged EU: Towards a common framework for financial reporting in European NPOs. *Social Science Research Network*, 1–12.

União das Misericórdias. (2019). *Quem Somos nas Misericórdias 2019.* Lisbon, União das Misericórdias.

União das Misericórdias. (2020). *Quem Somos nas Misericórdias 2020.* Lisbon, União das Misericórdias.

União das Misericórdias. (2021). *Quem Somos nas Misericórdias 2021.* Lisbon, União das Misericórdias.

União das Misericórdias. (2022). *Quem Somos nas Misericórdias 2022.* Lisbon, União das Misericórdias.

União das Misericórdias. (2023). *Quem Somos nas Misericórdias 2023.* Lisbon, União das Misericórdias.

Vinten, G. (1997). Corporate governance in a charity. *Corporate Governance, 5*(1), 24–28.

Yasmin, S., Haniffa, R., & Hudaib, M. (2014). Communicated accountability by faith-based charity organisations. *Journal of Business Ethics, 122*, 103–123.

Yetman, M. H., & Yetman, R. J. (2012). The effects of governance on the accuracy of charitable expenses reported by nonprofit organizations. *Contemporary Accounting Research, 29*(3), 738–767.

Zainon, S., Atan, R., Ahmad, R. A. R., & Wah, Y. B. (2012). Associations between organizational specific-attributes and the extent of disclosure in charity annual returns. *International Journal of Mathematical Models and Methods in Applied Sciences, 6*, 482–489.

Printed and bound by CPI Group (UK) Ltd, Croydon, CR0 4YY

30/10/2024

14583849-0005